THE DEFEAT OF BLACK POWER

THE DEFEAT OF BLACK POWER

CIVIL RIGHTS AND THE NATIONAL BLACK POLITICAL CONVENTION OF 1972

LEONARD N. MOORE

LOUISIANA STATE UNIVERSITY PRESS   BATON ROUGE

Published by Louisiana State University Press
Copyright © 2018 by Louisiana State University Press
All rights reserved
Manufactured in the United States of America
First printing

Designer: Barbara Neely Bourgoyne
Typeface: Chaparral Pro
Printer and binder: Sheridan Books

Library of Congress Cataloging-in-Publication Data
Names: Moore, Leonard N., 1971– author.
Title: The defeat of black power : civil rights and the National Black Political
    Convention of 1972 / Leonard N. Moore.
Description: Baton Rouge : Louisiana State University Press, 2018. | Includes
    bibliographical references and index.
Identifiers: LCCN 2017037431 | ISBN 978-0-8071-6903-2 (cloth : alk. paper) |
    ISBN 978-0-8071-6904-9 (pdf) | ISBN 978-0-8071-6905-6 (epub)
Subjects: LCSH: Black power—United States—History—20th century. | National
    Black Political Convention (1972 : Gary, Ind.) | African Americans—Politics and
    government—20th century. | Civil rights movements—United States—History—
    20th century. | United States—Race relations.
Classification: LCC E185.615 .M625 2018 | DDC 323.1196/073—dc23
LC record available at https://lccn.loc.gov/2017037431

For Leonard R. Moore and Peggy S. Moore

CONTENTS

ACKNOWLEDGMENTS

This book is dedicated to the more than 20,000 undergraduate students I have taught since earning my PhD at The Ohio State University in 1998. There is no greater professional joy than walking into a classroom and seeing five to six hundred eager students ready to engage and learn about the African American experience. I cherish seeing the different groups in my class: black football players sitting in the first few rows; other black students congregating in the middle center; Nigerians in the front left; East Africans in the front right; Latinos in the middle center; white liberals in the back left; white conservatives in the back right; and Asian students sprinkled throughout. The class discussions, debates, and arguments we have in my Race in the Age of Obama class or my class on the Black Power Movement serve as constant reminders of why I became a professor. I also want to thank the special group of students who have gone abroad with me to Beijing or Cape Town. Knowing how impactful these trips have been in the lives of students, many of whom are first-generation university students, is another joy of mine. Every day I spend in the classroom is a learning experience for me. As a believer in reverse mentoring, I want to thank all of you for making me a better husband, father, and friend, someone who tries his best to live out the teachings of the young country brother from Nazareth.

I also want to thank the brothers from the African American Male Research Initiative and the sisters from the Fearless Leadership Institute at the University of Texas at Austin. Over the past few years we have tried our best to create an HBCU culture of care at UT, and when I see the success of so many of our AAMRI/FLI students I am encouraged that we are doing just that.

I am especially grateful to Rand Dotson, my editor at LSU Press, and the rest of the team that guided this project to publication.

I want to thank my family: Mom, Beverly, Kevin, Kevin N., Shayanna, Tre, Reggie, Geoffrey, Gabrielle, Sandra, Michael, Alexis, Uncle Ralph, and Nedra. Also, Aunt Synolve and Iris, who went home to be with the Lord while I was working on this project. Being in Texas, I miss the hours-long political discussions at the dinner table in Cleveland that can stretch into the early hours of the morning. Additionally, Doris and Barbara Bass, my in-laws, have always been a great source of encouragement.

My children, Jaaucklyn, Lauryn, and Len, are a blessing from God. Whether playing family basketball in the driveway, volleyball in the back-yard, monopoly, or spades, or exploring the world together, we always have a good time. I am proud to be their father.

Most importantly I want to dedicate this book to my wife Thaïs. Proverbs 18:22 says that "He who findeth a wife findeth a good thing and receives favor from the Lord." She is my "good thing."

ABBREVIATIONS

BARTS	Black Arts Theater School
BEO	black elected official
CAP	Congress of African People
CBC	Congressional Black Caucus
CORE	Congress of Racial Equality
DSC	Democratic Select Committee
FCC	Federal Communications Commission
FEC	Federal Election Commission
HBCUs	Historically Black Colleges and Universities
IBW	Institute of the Black World
NAACP	National Association for the Advancement of Colored People
NBPC	National Black Political Convention
NCNW	National Council of Negro Women
PUSH	People United to Save Humanity
SCLC	Southern Christian Leadership Conference
SEC	Securities and Exchange Commission
UAW	United Auto Workers

THE DEFEAT OF BLACK POWER

INTRODUCTION

In March of 1972 black elected officials, civil rights activists, black integrationists, black nationalists, and Black Power apostles met for three days in Gary, Indiana, looking to end the intense four-year feud that had effectively divided black activists into two broadly defined camps: integrationists and black nationalists. While these tensions always existed within the black freedom struggle, things escalated in the aftermath of Martin Luther King's assassination on April 4, 1968. As the titular head of the movement, King commanded the respect of Black Power advocates, although they bitterly disagreed with his integrationist approach. King's death created a leadership void within black America, and civil rights movement veterans, along with black elected officials, fought for this space against those who called themselves black nationalists. Initially called by Amiri Baraka, but later co-opted by members of the newly formed Congressional Black Caucus, the National Black Political Convention (NBPC) would bring together approximately 8,000 people, who included 4,327 official delegates, hundreds of black elected officials, civil rights movement stalwarts, and black nationalists, as they attempted to chart a political strategy to mobilize black political power at the local, county, and state levels, as well as guide themselves through the 1972 election season. One observer noted that the crowd at Gary was evenly split between those who favored working within the system to bring about change (integrationists), and those who preferred to work outside the system, or better yet, dismantle the system (black nationalists).

The Convention was an attempt to develop a national black agenda that would merge these competing ideologies under the theme "unity without uniformity." While there was a great deal of ideological disagreement between the two philosophies, both black nationalists and black moderates did find common ground on the issue of black political power. Prominent nationalists such as Stokely Carmichael, Maulana Karenga, and Amiri Baraka had no desire to integrate or assimilate, but they did agree that black political power was an important step along the road to black self-determination. Similarly, black moderates and black elected officials such as Whitney Young, Roy Wilkins, Charles Diggs, Carl Stokes, and members of the Congressional Black Caucus believed strongly in integration and assimilation, and they saw the nascent potential in mobilizing black voters. The Convention dealt principally with four major ideas: (1) should black people pull out of the major political parties and form an all-black party; (2) should the black community embrace the concept of black nationalism and reject integration and assimilation; (3) to what extent should politically active black people work with the broader white system; and (4) that black people be encouraged to run for office at the local, state, regional, and federal levels. The significance of the Convention cannot be overstated. Historian Manning Marable calls the National Black Political Convention the "zenith" of the postwar black freedom struggle, and Peniel Joseph argues that the Gary Convention was arguably "the most important political, cultural, and intellectual gathering of the Black Power era."[1]

This attempt at black political unification was the largest political gathering in the history of black America. It was the first time that, in one place and under one roof, almost every representation of the movement was present: integrationists, separatists, nationalists, black elected officials (BEOs), Democrats, Republicans, students, hustlers, capitalists, feminists, Marxists, pastors, NAACP'ers, Urban Leaguers, entertainers, athletes, negro women's councils, old-line politicians, gangsters, labor leaders, Black Panthers, community activists, professors, intellectuals, and members of the Congress of African People, the Republic of New Afrika, the Nation of Islam, and countless other organizational representatives. Prior to Gary, integrationists and separatists did not hesitate to criticize each other. Nationalists often referred to integrationists as "sellouts," "Uncle Toms," "handkerchief heads," and the ubiquitous "white man's nigger." Conversely, integrationists often considered their more radical counterparts to be "shit talkers" who were long on rhetoric, posturing, and fiery speeches, who had fanciful dreams of black liberation, yet who did not know how to bring pragmatic, material benefits to the black masses. Wearing natural hair and African clothing, and learning to love one's blackness, were indeed admirable, integrationists would say, but how did this help black folk meet their day-to-day needs? Black Power apostles would counter that even with the civil rights legislative victories of the 1950s and 1960s, black people still suffered from high unemployment, poor housing, limited educational opportunities, lack of access to health care, and other social ills. So, they argued, integration was not the solution. Why, they asked, would you want to integrate with your oppressor? The NBPC represented the first time that both sides would have an opportunity to put forward their case where it could be challenged, critiqued, or agreed upon.

The year 1972 was the perfect time to hold a political convention. First, it was a presidential election year and black people were eager to develop a strategy to get Nixon out of office. Second, it also represented the first presidential election year when black southerners could exercise the leverage of the black vote and take full advantage of the 1965 Voting Rights Act. Third, many of those in the movement realized that black activism needed to make the transition from protest to politics since mass demonstrations as a protest tool could no longer be relied upon to bring about change. Last, the split between black nationalists and integrationists had the potential to effectively stifle black political activism at the national level and stop black political progress at the local and state levels just when the black voting age population was rapidly expanding and black people were moving into elective office. For example, between 1964 and 1972, the number of eligible black voters increased from 10.3 million to 13.5 million, and the number of black elected officials nationally increased from approximately 100 in 1964 to 1,400 by the end of the decade. By 1974, the number of black elected officials would rise to 3,499, with much of this massive growth taking place in the South. Thus the National Black Political Convention was an opportunity for black activists to plot a political strategy for the 1970s and to give the community a compass for the 1972 election season.[2]

Historians generally agree that the term "Black Power" came into popular political discourse during James Meredith's 1966 March Against Fear. Julius Lester argues that the term "Black Power" did more to generate black consciousness than anything else during the entire black freedom struggle. In an effort to capitalize on this rising consciousness, on September 3, 1966, Congressman Adam Clayton Powell Jr. hosted the Black Power Planning Conference in the Rayburn House Office Building in Washington, DC. Organized by Powell's longtime aide and assistant Chuck Stone, the one-day affair attracted 169 delegates from 37 cities and 18 states, representing 64 organizations. In an effort to be inclusive, Powell invited the leaders of the nation's most prominent civil rights organizations: Roy Wilkins of the National Association for the Advancement of Colored People (NAACP), Martin Luther King Jr. of the Southern Christian Leadership Conference (SCLC), and James Farmer of the Congress of Racial Equality (CORE). All three declined the invitation, although Roy Wilkins did send Powell a letter suggesting ten points for discussions during the event. They all publicly cited prior commitments that kept them from attending, but privately they did not want to associate themselves with the unpredictable, mercurial, egotistical, and controversial pastor and congressman. But Powell did not mind their absence because this was not a gathering of racial moderates or integrationists. This event was for the "Young Turks" of the Black Power movement who eschewed integration in favor of black unity and empowerment. The meeting was held in strict secrecy, as Capitol Police officers not only guarded the doors to the meeting rooms but also blocked off adjacent corridors as well. In Powell's words, the purpose of the planning session was "to set up guidelines which can operate within the framework of the concept of Black Power."[3]

At a news conference held several days after the session, Powell told the press that Black Power was for young people, and specifically for young black people in the nation's urban areas who felt excluded from mainstream America. This gathering, according to Powell, was a way to get them "channeled in the right direction." Powell then spoke to the historic nature of the meeting: "Integrationists, political separatists and cultural nationalists, all were represented. The entire thrust of the conference was its emphasis on positive accomplishments. Thus, the conference was not anti-white but pro-black. It did not advocate violence but simply rejected unconditional nonviolence and strongly endorsed self-defense to achieve the full dignity of black people." When one journalist asked Powell where this new emphasis on Black Power left people like Wilkins, King, and Farmer, Powell responded simply, "In the process of praying. Praying for God to give them guidance." Due to the ambiguous nature of the term "Black Power," Powell was asked what the term meant to him. "Black people must develop power—political, economic, and cultural power in black communities before they seek any coalition with white people," he stated. Powell then told the press that he assembled a committee to plan a much larger and more robust Black Power conference the following year. On that committee was Maulana Karenga, Omar Ahmad, Jewell Mazique, and Dr. Nathan Wright.[4]

Armed with a mandate from Congressman Powell, Dr. Nathan Wright of Newark, New Jersey, took the lead in planning the second Black Power conference in his hometown. Although Wright was a staunch Republican, he had radical credentials based upon his being an activist minister and scholar. That reputation grew when he refused to postpone the conference in the aftermath of the Newark riots, which occurred just four days before the scheduled start of the proceedings. The conference opened on July 26, 1967, and for four days over 1,000 delegates, from 26 states and 126 cities, representing 248 black organizations, debated the movement's most pressing question, reform vs. revolution. The secondary question for attendees was how to take the energy of the civil rights movement and mobilize it into "an actionable unity involving the black masses and then translate it into constructive programs of black empowerment." Engaging the black masses was critical because organizers realized that the typical black person "has never joined a civil rights organization, never walked a picket line, and has failed to involve himself in the black man's freedom struggle."[5]

The conference was principally organized around fourteen workshops with topics such as "The City and Black People," "Black Power Through Politics," "Black Power Through Economic Development," "Black Power in World Perspective," and "Black Professionals and Black Power." These sessions were facilitated by folks who became Black Power celebrities such as Maulana Karenga, Robert S. Browne, Nathan Hare, Ossie Davis, Hoyt Fuller, H. Rap Brown, and Floyd McKissick. The pattern of male leadership would continue throughout the period as women were all but excluded from positions of movement leadership. Although organizers and attendees did not expect immediate action items, at the end of the conference they were excited that the conference passed a number of resolutions in the arenas of economics, politics, education, international affairs, and foreign policy. There was also an air of optimism around the idea that virtually every ideology within the movement was represented and that attendees got a chance to hear "a broad spectrum of political thought." In what is perhaps the best eyewitness account of the conference, Chuck Stone called it the most "diversified ingathering of black people ever assembled. It was a black people's conference, conceived and organized by black people for black people to talk to black people on what black people must do to empower black communities." But not everyone shared Stone's sentiments. Author Robert Allen called the Newark conference a "bourgeois affair" since it was held at a downtown white-owned hotel, required a $25.00 registration fee to attend, and was financed by approximately fifty white-owned corporations.[6]

The third and final Black Power Conference of any significance was held the following year in Philadelphia, Pennsylvania, with over 4,000 black attendees representing 600 organizations. The gathering was very similar to the Newark conference as the weekend centered around workshops and speeches by Black Power celebrities such as Karenga, Stokely Carmichael, H. Rap Brown, Max Stanford, and black moderates such as Jesse Jackson, Congressman John Conyers, and Whitney Young of the National Urban League. Although the conference was still under the leadership of Dr. Nathan Wright, Karenga was the event's "chief organizer and foremost theoretician." As a cultural nationalist, Karenga was often criticized for not having a practical program for black empowerment. However, as Komozi Woodard writes, the "public rhetoric" often offered by radicals such as Karenga differed from the "practical advice" they gave for organizing black communities. Thus, while Karenga emphasized the development of a distinct black culture, art, and aesthetic as the key to black liberation, he also understood the necessity of black political mobilization. It is precisely within this context that the delegates in Philadelphia voted unanimously in favor of black people forming an independent black political party.[7]

Toward the end of 1968 the term "Black Power" became "all things to all people." Historian Manning Marable notes that the popularity of the term was partly rooted "in its ambiguity." Thus "Black Power" could mean whatever you wanted it to mean, and this ambiguity would divide the movement into two camps: "new-guard nationalists" and "old-guard integrationists" or "ideologically dogmatic nationalists" and "compromise-oriented pragmatists." Stokely Carmichael believed that Black Power meant "a call for black people in this country to unite, to recognize their heritage, to build a sense of community. It is a call for black people to begin to define their own goals, to lead their own organizations, and to support those organizations. It is a call to reject the racist institutions and values of society." The foundational underpinning of this power was group solidarity. "Black people must come together and do things themselves. Only they can help create in the community an aroused and continuing black consciousness." This call for black self-determination explicitly rejected integration in all forms since the concept of integration "is based on the assumption that there is nothing of value in the black community and that little of value could be created among black people." For Carmichael, integration was based on the faulty premise that in order for black folks to have a good life they must "move into a white neighborhood or send their children to a white school." This idea reinforced the popular thinking that "white is automatically better and black by definition is inferior."[8]

The rejection of integration in favor of group solidarity was warmly embraced by the ideological descendants of Malcolm X, those who called themselves black nationalists. Nationalists looked at black America as a nation, separate and distinct from white America. Black nationalists during this period typically fell into three categories: (1) territorial black nationalists; (2) revolutionary black nationalists; and (3) cultural black nationalists. The territorial nationalists were best represented by the Nation of Islam and the Republic of New Afrika, both of whom believed that black people needed a geographical home to themselves within the existing United States. They demanded reparations in the form of the US government handing over the Black Belt states of the US South and placing them under black control. The Black Panther Party and the Revolutionary Action Movement espoused the tenets of revolutionary black nationalism by calling for a violent overthrow of the US capitalistic government and replacing it with a socialist state. Cultural nationalists like Maulana Karenga, however, saw the reclaiming of African values and culture as the key to black liberation. Karenga developed a black value system called the Nguza Saba, which stressed seven core ideas that if adopted would lead to a liberation of self: black unity, self-determination, collective work and responsibility, cooperative economics, creativity, faith, and purpose. These principles were to be celebrated during the African American holiday that Karenga established, Kwanzaa. On a more day-to-day level cultural nationalists embraced African-inspired clothing, hairstyles, language, jewelry, and trinkets. Despite the ideological differences among black nationalists they all rejected integration and assimilation. They were not seeking nor did they want access to the white man's system.[9]

Integrationists defined Black Power differently. They did want access to the white man's system, and for them the term "Black Power" served as a rallying point for black people to control or get their fair share of political positions, jobs, housing, educational opportunities, and economic opportunities. Floyd McKissick of CORE argued that there were six components of Black Power: (1) the growth of black political power; (2) the building of black economic power; (3) the importance of black self-image; (4) the development of black leadership; (5) the attainment of federal law enforcement; and (6) the mobilization of black consumer power. For integrationists the most important of these was the mobilization of black political power. With the full implementation of the Voting Rights Act and continued white flight to the nation's suburban areas, racial moderates saw a unique opportunity to develop black political power at the local level and then to leverage that power in regional, state, and federal elections. In their eyes this was the easiest way to translate the energy of the Black Power movement into something practical, because the rules of the game were clear. But this was not easy work, they cautioned. Mobilizing the black political community required more than just slogans and rhetoric. It involved the tireless work of ringing doorbells, telephoning, caucusing, speechmaking, and fund-raising, all with no guaranteed victory. As evidence of something practical, moderates pointed to the mayoral elections of Carl Stokes in Cleveland and Richard Hatcher in Gary as proof of what was possible throughout urban America. Advocates of black political power talked about how black elected officials, particularly mayors, controlled the cities and city governments; held the power of appointive office such as "the taxing power, the power to disburse money"; had the power to control law enforcement, education, housing, and employment; could implement affirmative action mandates; and could articulate black interests and concerns.[10]

Racial moderates and integrationists agreed that Black Power generated racial pride and group unity, but they were skeptical about its ability to do anything practical in terms of improving the quality of life for black America. Calling for an armed revolution, a geographical separation from white folks, or repeatedly for reparations were typical black nationalist examples of "talkin' loud and sayin' nothing," since these proposals were neither practical nor probable. But black nationalists did not take these critiques lightly. They countered by suggesting that electoral politics was nothing more than reformist politics and that it did not deal with the "fundamental issue of power." Further, once elected, black elected officials would be nothing more than "partners in an oppressive status-quo power structure." Black nationalists during this period had four main critiques of black elected officials: (1) they were pawns hand-picked by white folks; (2) they had not worked hard on behalf of racial legislation; (3) they were not responsive to the black community; and (4) black office-holding did not automatically translate into Black Power. These "competing strains of black politics," radicals vs. moderates, black nationalists vs. integrationists, reform vs. revolution, electoral politics vs. protest politics, working within the system vs. co-optation, insider vs. outsider, black Marxists vs. black capitalists, coalition politics vs. independent black politics, and the practical vs. the theoretical, had effectively divided the movement by 1968. Indeed there were Black Power spokespersons and ideologies that were much more complex and that overlapped the above-mentioned dichotomies, but in each case the black political community was largely split into one of the two camps. In a 1968 essay Nathan Hare suggested that Black Power advocates of all ideologies needed to realize that "unity involves a bringing together of diverse factions." He then gave an explicit charge to the black community that was long overdue. "There is a need for a kind of interdependence between honest moderates and radical factions. Rather than fighting one another, diverting our agency from the attack on the true or foremost enemy, black activists might well establish a grassroots or underground system of functional interdependence. Moderates could then present one face to the white world and another privately to blacks." Hare's admonition was all the more timely in the aftermath of the assassination of Martin Luther King Jr. and the presidential election of Richard M. Nixon later that year. The black community was indeed at a political and ideological fork in the road.[11]

The NBPC was birthed in an effort to bridge this divide, and the official conveners of the Gary Convention were poet Amiri Baraka, who was by 1972 the most popular black nationalist in the country; Congressman Charles Diggs from Detroit; and Richard Hatcher, the youthful black mayor of Gary, Indiana, who along with Carl Stokes in 1967 became one of the first two black mayors of a major American city. This leadership represented the broader ideological divide. Baraka represented the black nationalists; Diggs represented civil rights activists and black elected officials (BEOs); and Hatcher represented a bridge between the two camps as a Black Power politician. As an elected official, Hatcher governed a majority-black city, and he used the power of his office to address black frustration. Black Power advocates were excited about the possibilities in Gary because they realized that their own strategy rendered them useless in improving the quality of black lives. They needed the infrastructure, credibility, and power of elective office to bring about real change, so they desperately needed to work in a coalition with those who preferred to work within the system. Conversely, civil rights activists and BEOs were not really comfortable with the event. In many ways they believed they had nothing to gain by partnering with their black nationalist counterparts. Both Baraka and Hatcher believed that black elected officials were drawn into the NBPC, and that there were several attempts to keep black nationalists completely away from an event that was their idea in the first place. So co-opting the event served as a way to control the goings-on at the Convention.

As the planning for the NBPC took place, it became clear that the most important people within black America would be involved in some way with the black strategy meetings leading up to the Convention. Some of those involved were: Jesse Jackson, Coretta Scott King, Julian Bond, Shirley Chisholm, Carl Stokes, Barbara Jordan, Percy Sutton, Carl Holman, Mervyn Dymally, C. Delores Tucker, Dick Gregory, Vernon Jordan, Dorothy Height, Coleman Young, Harry Belafonte, Queen Mother

Moore, Louis Farrakhan, Isaac Hayes, Bobby Seale, Roy Wilkins, Yvonne Brathwaite, Howard Fuller, Roy Innis, Frank Reeves, and John Cashin. Those in attendance at the NBPC came looking for answers, and they hoped to leave with a unified black political strategy that would guide black folks through 1972 and beyond. Many black politicos were tired of the integrationist/nationalist divide, and they wanted a unified black electorate as the election season approached. Over the course of three intense days, the Convention produced a 12-page tabloid-like document called "The National Black Political Agenda," which covered seven areas critical to black life: (1) political empowerment; (2) economic empowerment; (3) human development; (4) rural development; (5) foreign policy and black people; (6) environmental protection; and (7) communications. Researched and written by some of the leading scholars within black America, the Agenda represents one of the most comprehensive political documents of its kind. While attendees and delegates agreed with nearly everything within the document, integrationists had fundamental issues with certain planks in the Agenda, such as the calling of a constitutional convention along with the nationalist demand for reparations. Many observers saw the Agenda as a black nationalist document, and as a result civil rights activists and black elected officials withdrew their support for the NBPC and the Agenda less than ten weeks after the Convention. Since nationalists did not hold elective office, have a broad constituency, or have access to levers of real power in pragmatic ways, their popularity within black communities rapidly declined, leaving civil rights activists and black elected officials holding the mantle of black political leadership in 1972 and beyond. This is the untold story of the 1972 National Black Political Convention.

1

THE SOONER WE GET ORGANIZED FOR GROUP ACTION, THE MORE EFFECTIVE WE CAN BECOME

The Creation of the Congressional Black Caucus in Richard Nixon's America

The Congressional Black Caucus was birthed in obscurity in 1969 during the heyday of the Black Power movement. Energized by the movement's emphasis on race pride, cultural unity, and black institution–building, Congressman Charles Diggs capitalized on the increasing black presence in the United States Congress to form an organization. Initially called the Democratic Select Committee, the group changed its name officially to the Congressional Black Caucus (CBC) in 1971. Born in 1922, Diggs grew up in a family that, by virtue of its lucrative funeral business, was part of black Detroit's upper middle class. After short stints at the University of Michigan and Fisk University, Diggs returned home to get his bachelor's degree from Wayne State University. He followed his father into politics by gaining election to the Michigan State Senate in 1951, and in 1954 he was elected to Congress as Michigan's first African American congressperson. He was present at the Emmett Till trial, and in 1957 he becomes the first black congressperson to visit Africa when he was chosen to join the US delegation at Ghana's independence celebration. His increased interest in African independence movements took him to the All-African Peoples' Conference in 1958, and in 1959 he joined the House Foreign Affairs Committee, where he served as chair of the African Affairs subcommittee.[1]

The structural catalyst for the creation of the Congressional Black Caucus lay in three separate yet overlapping developments: the implementation of the 1965 Voting Rights Act; white flight; and congressional redistricting. The Voting Rights Act brought thousands of previously disenfranchised black voters into the electoral process, who were committed to making the system work for them and their communities. Secondly, with rapid white flight to neighboring suburbs, large urban communities started to become predominantly African American. This demographic shift created majority-black congressional districts, which made it easier for black voters to elect their own to the US Congress. Further, many large urban communities underwent congressional redistricting during the late 1960s such that by 1969 there were nine black representatives in the US Congress: William Dawson (Chicago), Charles Diggs (Detroit), Robert Nix (Philadelphia), Adam Clayton Powell (Harlem), Augustus Hawkins (Los Angeles), John Conyers (Detroit), William Clay (St. Louis), Louis Stokes (Cleveland), and Shirley Chisholm (Brooklyn).[2]

This growth in the black congressional delegation was one of five major developments that led to the CBC's founding. The second major development was the political trends that the new members participated in. Since most of them came from majority-black districts, they were free to be racially assertive with their political ideologies. Further, many of them were veterans of the civil rights movement who looked at their election as an extension of or the next step in the black freedom struggle. Third, the black delegation realized that Martin Luther King's death left a significant leadership void in the black community. The movement had now splintered, and as Bayard Rustin wrote in 1965, it was now time to make the transition from protest to politics. Fourth, the African American contingent in Congress was deeply influenced by the Black Power era, a period when African Americans placed a tremendous emphasis on racial pride, group unity, and self-reliance. Indeed, many of them used the rhetoric of Black Power, and thus they owed their election to the energy of the Black Power movement, which inspired thousands of black grassroots activists to get involved in both local and national politics.[3]

Fifth, President Richard Nixon's election in 1968 was arguably the most important development that led Diggs to establish what would become known as the Congressional Black Caucus. While black voters did not mistakenly assume that Nixon would be an ally, they were deeply shocked at some of his rhetoric during the campaign season. In an effort to undercut support for George Wallace, the infamous segregationist governor from Alabama who was running as a third-party candidate, Nixon made overt racial appeals to white voters. Code words such as "law and order," "states' rights," "federal interference," and "welfare cheats" signaled to white voters that a Nixon presidency would suppress black radicalism, forestall school integration, and potentially roll back some of the gains of the civil rights movement. By arousing racist white southerners and their northern counterparts, Nixon was able to ride this backlash into the White House. Once he was in office, his official approach to black concerns was "benign neglect," a strategy proposed by Nixon staffer Daniel Patrick Moynihan. Moynihan suggested that the administration quietly ignore black issues: "The time may have come when the issue of race would benefit from a benign neglect. We may need a period in which Negro progress continues and racial rhetoric fades." Once this memo became public it just confirmed what many black voters assumed privately about how Nixon would approach issues of civil rights. To be sure, Nixon owed absolutely nothing to the black community, since he only received approximately 10 percent of the African American vote. Consequently, Nixon was not obligated to address black concerns and black politicos did not expect him to.[4]

In an effort to quiet his black critics in the aftermath of the Moynihan memo, Nixon co-opted the rhetoric of the Black Power movement by promoting the idea of black capitalism, which was warmly received by many "bootstrap" black nationalists, those who believed that black folks needed to "do for themselves" instead of relying upon government handouts and welfare. Black capitalism from the Nixon perspective meant that the newly created Office of Minority Business Enterprise, in conjunction with the Small Business Administration, would launch initiatives to spur black entrepreneurship through generous tax breaks, guaranteed loans, contract set-asides, affirmative-action mandates, and racial quotas. This pro-business ideology was acceptable to CORE's Floyd McKissick and Roy Innis as well as many Republican Party operatives. But the entire concept was loudly denounced by black radicals and mainstream black moderates. Author and activist Earl Ofari devoted an entire volume to why black capitalism was problematic. In his aptly titled book *The Myth of Black Capitalism,* he suggested that black capitalism "in theory and in hope" needed to be destroyed. "Black folks have been little attracted to trade, shopkeeping, buying and selling, or employing labor for the purpose of exploitation," he wrote. Ofari was not alone in his criticism.[5]

With the opening of the 91st legislative session, black congressional representatives met often at the urging of Diggs and Clay under the banner of the Democratic Select Committee. But Diggs insisted that they institutionalize their efforts in a more formal way. "The sooner we get organized for group action the more effective we can become." Clay echoed Diggs by suggesting that "without adequate programming and planning, we the DSC, a loose knit group might well degenerate into the Congressional Koffee Klatch Klub."[6]

While they were still in the process of institutionalizing, the DSC requested a meeting with President Nixon in February of 1970. Nixon rebuffed the request via a rejection letter signed by a low-level White House staffer. Nixon's chief of staff told *Newsweek* that they would not meet with the black group because "we try not to permit opportunities to use the President as a grandstand." Throughout the remainder of the year the black delegation was unsuccessful at getting a meeting with him, but they did see their numbers increase with the 1970 elections of Harlem's Charlie Rangel (Powell's successor), Ron Dellums of Oakland, and Parren Mitchell of Maryland.[7]

In January 1971, the CBC boycotted Nixon's State of the Union speech. The only black congressperson who attended was Republican senator Edward Brooke from Massachusetts, who represented a majority-white district. Although he was invited to join the CBC he repeatedly declined. The boycott was virtually ignored in the media, sending a message to the group that they still lacked national influence. Although the CBC was growing in membership it did not have the leverage or credibility to put pressure on Nixon. In the aftermath of the boycott the group decided to officially institutionalize their efforts, but first they needed a name. The "Congressional Committee on Minority Rights" and the "Congressional Committee" were among the names that were discussed. Congressman Charlie Rangel introduced the name "Congressional Black Caucus," and it was unanimously agreed upon. The CBC was established on the principle of racial cohesion, race consciousness, and the idea that the delegation would look after black interests. Congressman John Conyers recalled that the Caucus was launched because of Nixon's refusal to sit down with CBC members and address black concerns.[8]

The creation of the CBC is an important development in this story. For the first time in history, African Americans had visible representation in Congress, and by institutionalizing they had a bigger voice. All thirteen members of the CBC, unlike Congressman Adam Clayton Powell and Congressman William Dawson in the previous generation with their personality disputes and power struggles, were similar in outlook, orientation, and the belief that political power was the next step in the black freedom struggle. They were united, in sync, and excited about representing the people. Further, the CBC's actions toward Nixon grew out of the criticism that many members of the CBC were feeling from their black nationalist critics. Nationalists felt that although the rhetoric and energy of the movement sent black people to Congress, they soon grew distant from the communities that they were elected to represent. Further, black nationalists were growing frustrated that the CBC appeared to be acting as spokespersons for the race. This criticism was in many ways the catalyst for the CBC's demands to meet with the president.[9]

The Congressional Black Caucus and President Richard Nixon

In the aftermath of the State of the Union boycott, Senator Brooke arranged a meeting between the newly formed CBC and President Nixon in the Oval Office for March 25, 1971. In preparation for the meeting, the Caucus understood that they needed to talk policy with Nixon and not chitchat. In the days and weeks leading up to the meeting, the CBC put together a research team to draft a list of policy recommendations that they would present to Nixon. A team of nine people worked day and night at the headquarters of Delta Sigma Theta, an African American sorority, in Washington, DC, to assemble a document. A screening committee was established to look at approximately four hundred policy proposals and ideas that the CBC should consider, and they prioritized them. A team of academics, economists, and lawyers compiled the documents, with approval and consultation provided by civil rights leaders such as Whitney Young, Roy Wilkins, and Bayard Rustin, who all gave their blessing to the document. The fledgling organization made a brilliant move by consulting Young, Wilkins, and Rustin. CBC members knew that all three were not really relevant to the black masses anymore, but were astute enough to respect their historic contributions to the movement. Plus, by their bringing all three of them to the table, their white critics would not be able to use Young, Wilkins, and Rustin against them.[10]

The CBC presented their set of goals to President Nixon in a thirty-two-page booklet. In attendance were the full CBC delegation and many of Nixon's cabinet members and undersecretaries. Diggs began the meeting by stating that the CBC sought the meeting with Nixon "out of a deep sense of conviction that large numbers of citizens are being subjected to intense hardship, are denied their basic rights, and are suffering irreparable harm as a result of current policies." He went on to mention the obvious, that "most of the districts that we represent are predominantly Black," but that their concerns "and obligations as Members of Congress do not stop at the boundaries of our districts." Diggs wanted Nixon to understand that their concerns were national and international in scope. "We are petitioned daily by citizens living hundreds of miles from our districts who look on us as Congressman-at-large for Black people and poor people in the United States." Reports from the Nixon meeting make it clear that the CBC was not hesitant to voice their concerns to the president. They were not scared, they did not cower, and they were aggressive in raising the issues that most affected the black community. They were functioning in their role as representatives, and Nixon was unsure how to respond.[11]

Diggs and the Caucus were hopeful that the meeting with Nixon would not be a one-time event but rather the beginning of a regular conversation and dialogue with the president. Prior to laying out their concerns and issues to Nixon, Diggs talked about how the United States spent $2 billion a year on Vietnam, while since the president took office 2 million more people had become unemployed and the country's welfare rolls had increased by 2.5 million. They then talked about the need for a redistribution of the wealth. "The racist policies of public and private U.S. institutions insure that Blacks and other oppressed peoples suffer much more than others, whether in good times or bad." In the eyes of the Congressional Black Caucus what was needed was a radical redistribution of wealth and income.

Before laying out their specific demands to Nixon, the Caucus listed nine principal goals:

1. The eradication of racism within the United States and its dealings with other nations.

2. The earning of a decent and living wage, or the means to survive in dignity when work is not available.
3. Decent housing for our families and equal access to the total housing market.
4. Fair and impartial justice and adequate protection against drug abuse and crime.
5. The enforcement of civil rights and other constitutional guarantees through various affirmative actions by the government.
6. A fair share of public funds used to support business and community development and full participation in determining how tax dollars are spent in our communities.
7. The guarantee by the federal government of ample health care for all citizens.
8. The protection of federal standards and guarantees in programs financed by federal funds.
9. The full participation by the members of our communities in executive, judicial, and legislative branches of government at every level.[12]

In making their requests to the president, the CBC members were also making a stinging critique of American society.

The CBC's Sixty Recommendations

The CBC presented Nixon with a document that listed sixty recommendations over four main subjects. The first area was Economic Security and Development. The twenty-four recommendations in this section were broken into the following:

1. Manpower and Employment Rights (7 recommendations)
2. Welfare Reform (3 recommendations)
3. Federal Assistance to the State/Local Governments (6 recommendations)
4. Minority Economic Development (6 recommendations)
5. Poverty Programming (2 recommendations)

This section of the document wanted a guaranteed adequate income system; incentives for a progressive income tax; and an independent agency, led by black folks, to assist minority businesses to the tune of $1 billion annually.[13]

The next section of the document was Community and Health Development. The twenty-one recommendations in this section were broken into the following:

1. Education (9 recommendations)
2. Housing and Urban Development (6 recommendations)
3. The Drug Crisis (6 recommendations)

This section called for increased funding for day care and pre-K programs; a universal literacy program; increased funding for inner-city schools; an increase in the Federal Pell Grant program; increased funding for Historically Black Colleges and Universities (HBCUs); more money for public housing; an end to illegal drugs coming into the United States; and federally funded rehabilitation centers for drug users.

The next section of the document was "Justice and Civil Rights." Here, there were ten recommendations across the following areas:

1. Criminal Justice (3 recommendations)
2. Civil Rights (4 recommendations)
3. Veterans' Affairs (2 recommendations)
4. The District of Columbia (1 recommendation)

Some of the specific demands were for help for inner-city communities to develop fair and effective criminal justice systems; the appointment of black federal judges, US attorneys, US marshals, and especially black judges in the South; the implementation of the 1970 Report of the U.S. Commission on Civil Rights; corrective action against efforts to disenfranchise black voters in the South; the creation of a division on civil rights; and congressional representation and increased funding for the District of Columbia.[14]

The last section of the document was "Foreign Policy," where there were six major recommendations. The CBC wanted sanctions against South Africa and other colonial governments; a Marshall Plan for Africa; the reduction of military expenditures, with that money being redirected to urban and economic development; and the immediate removal of troops from Vietnam.[15]

In all, these recommendations were aggressive, radical, and revolutionary. Although militants such as Amiri Baraka and others were often critical of black elected officials, these recommendations show that they were honest about serving their communities, challenging Nixon, and not selling out. These recommendations were also easy to implement, represented participatory democracy, and were an example of what black elected officials should do. However, nationalists would argue that these were reformist proposals, and what was needed was a complete overthrow of the system.

The meeting with Nixon lasted for a full hour, and Nixon accepted the recommendations in front of both national and international camera crews. At the conclusion of the meeting the president asked Arthur Fletcher, undersecretary of labor, who was one of Nixon's highest-ranking African Americans, if he had anything to say. He did. "No, Mr. President. I have been telling you for fifteen months the same things as these congressmen and nobody's been paying any attention to me." White House staffer Robert Brown, another African American, told the press that he didn't understand why the CBC complained about not getting a meeting with the president. "When the CBC came up on the list, they got it, like everyone else. Some wait three years. The President can't see everybody."[16]

Before adjourning, Nixon appointed a committee of White House staff members to study the list of recommendations and seek ways to implement them. Clark MacGregor, counsel to the president, would chair the group along with other Nixon staffers including a young Donald Rumsfeld. Diggs told reporters after the meeting that the tone of the meeting was productive but that "of course, implementation will be the important factor in our judgment." The day after the meeting, however, the CBC was much more critical of Nixon. "He listened, but we don't know if he heard. If he did not hear, he and the country will suffer."[17]

Diggs asked Nixon to respond to the recommendations by May 17, 1971, the anniversary of the *Brown* decision. If Nixon did not respond by that day, then the Caucus would present their demands to leaders in Congress. Nixon responded on May 18, 1971, with a 115-page paper that basically reaffirmed "current administration policies and programs." The CBC was livid. They felt that Nixon had basically ignored their recommendations. Later that week Congressmen Diggs, Hawkins, and Clay went on *Meet The Press* to talk about the 61 recommendations, and they expressed their deep disappointment with Nixon. In an effort to counter the criticism from *Meet the Press,* Nixon assembled 36 black Republicans at the White House and encouraged them to counter whatever was said about the Nixon administration in the media. In hopes of sharing their frustration with the president with a wider audience, the Congressional Black Caucus released a "Report to the Nation," which outlined their dissatisfaction with President Nixon for not considering their proposals.[18]

If Nixon expected these newly elected Congress members to play it safe and assume a rather conservative posture, he quickly learned otherwise. Since many of them came from all-black districts they did not worry about any kind of political backlash. They were free, they were in power, and they wanted to bring pragmatic results to their constituents. In fact, their aggressiveness, combined with the rise of black elected officials nationally, began to diminish the role of black nationalists at both the national and local levels. But on a more personal level, literally every member of the Congressional Black Caucus ended up on Nixon's "enemies list" and would encounter some sort of federal surveillance during their time in the nation's capital. So although black nationalists and black moderates divided themselves along ideological lines, the FBI targeted both groups closely.[19]

The CBC as the Voice of Black America

Emboldened by their meeting with Nixon, their increasing numbers, and the political mood of black America, the CBC realized that they had an obligation to be the collective voice of black America. Because of the leadership void with the death of MLK and then most recently Whitney Young, the Caucus wanted to move away from the messiah tradition of black leadership and instead move to leadership by committee. This is why they decided to set up the CBC as a permanent organization with a budget and an adequate staff. Congressman Clay stated, "We want to set up a national system of communications with the Black community to allow us to touch base with Black businesses, the Black press and all other Black organizations. We've already got commitments from a number of individuals, both Black and white, from across the country to assist us in developing projects and to come up with specific proposals." He then quoted one of the CBC's founding principles: "We have no permanent friends, no permanent enemies, just permanent interests." Speaking on a local news program in New York City, Charlie Rangel said that "Black people throughout the country, whether they have a Black Congressman or not, now have a body to deal with. Not a Black, a Puerto Rican, a brown or yellow man can now say he doesn't have a friend in the Congress." Caucus members were riding a wave of momentum after boycotting Nixon's State of the Union speech and by presenting him with a list of demands. This was Black Power Politics 101, and the CBC was stronger now, although still in its infancy. One observer cautioned not to give the CBC too much credit for their embrace of Black Power politics. "They suddenly found themselves together and found they were much better off because of it. They were a few years late, but they were influenced by the national mood of Blacks regarding Black power, Black Nationalism, and pan-Africanism."[20]

The CBC held its first annual Congressional Black Caucus Dinner on June 18, 1971, in an attempt to raise money for the fledgling organization. They were hopeful that they could raise at least $100,000 at the dinner. They raised more than $250,000! This event also gave them another opportunity to bring black America together and work on a strategy for 1972. The main speaker for the dinner was actor Ossie Davis, who gave the crowd his infamous quote, "It's not the rap, but the map, not the man, but the plan," making an effort to remind the crowd that they needed to start doing more acting than talking, and also encouraging them not to get caught up in personality politics. "Give us a plan of action a Black ten commandments simple and strong that we can carry in our hearts and in our memories no matter where we are, and reach out and touch and feel the reassurance that there is behind everything we do a simple, moral, intelligent plan that must be fulfilled in the course of time. Even if all of our leaders, one by one, fall in battle, somebody will rise and say, 'Our leader died while we were on page three of a plan: now that the funeral is over, let us proceed to page four.'" Davis envisioned a broad-based political agenda that was exclusive of personalities. He then appealed to the Caucus: "From our noble thirteen, we need that they think the problems out; that they investigate the possible solution; that they codify the results; and they present their program to us, the people, so that we may ratify what they have thought and organized and left to us as a program of action."[21]

Davis felt that in 1971 black America was at a crucial crossroads. "We have become hip to the meaning of political power, and that's why we're here. This is an exercise in political power tonight. We've eaten a good meal, we've paid money for it, we've had good fellowship. We've heard good music and entertainment. But brothers and sisters, the name of the game is power and if you ain't playing power you're in the wrong place." While Ossie Davis was the main speaker comedian, Bill Cosby reminded the audience that they (black folks) had not yet arrived. "I think that all you Niggers need to check yourselves out. So I say 'Good Evening Niggers' because that's what a lot of you gonna be when you leave this room. You gotta tighten up your ship. Tighten up your game. Because it just doesn't end here. You don't need speakers to tell you every day who you are, and where you have to go, and who's cheating you. And you have to stop blaming people." The crowd roared in laughter, not realizing that he was actually insulting them and other middle-class African Americans. He then went on to state that "I'm going to support the Caucus as long as I live. I'll support 'em because . . . the Black establishment has for too long been the entertainers. And Black entertainers very seldom get a chance to enjoy what the white entertainers have—that is to be able to go out on the Riviera with sunglasses and float around on a raft. No, 'cause, you know, if you saw a picture of me out there on a raft with my sunglasses on you'd say, 'Look at that nigger and we up here struggling.'" Cosby spoke of the need for the Caucus to continue this type of gathering.[22]

In an op-ed titled "After the Sequins, What," Carlos Russell of the *New York Amsterdam News* expressed his disappointment after the event because he felt that in light of Davis's speech, the Caucus should have announced plans for a black national political convention. "Rather than offering suggestions or making some attempt to reap the benefit from this momentous occasion—Blacks from almost all political persuasions and importance were present—instead, they fed into the ritual of sensuous escapism." Perhaps, he felt, this escapism "was the only thing that could be done since aside from the rhetoric there was no content." Russell's words were harsh. "Imagine what would have happened if rather than solely extolling Blacks for being apathetic, which we have been, if one call would have been made for the creation of a National Black Coalition with representation by all of the political entities that were present, leaving the way open for those who were not present. And another call for the cessation of internal hostilities and a move for tangible Black solidarity."[23]

Russell then made the call. "What we need, in my view, is the calling of a National Black Political Convention today, not tomorrow. The function of this conference would be to plan and map, and develop strategy, and leading toward true Black liberation. The National Black Congressional Caucus in Washington provided the war chest, now let us get to the map, the plan, so we can stop being niggers twenty-four hours a day." In spite of Russell's harsh critique of the fund-raising dinner, in many ways the lavish affair was the CBC's coming-out party. They raised a ton of money, brought the black middle class together, and were given the mandate by Davis that it was their turn to lead.[24]

The Carlos Russell op-ed about the CBC dinner was the theoretical foundation for a special issue of the *New York Amsterdam News* on July 24, 1971, under the subject, "Politics, Power, and the Black Community." In that issue several guest columnists were asked to write on the aforementioned project. The writers were: Congresswoman Shirley Chisholm; George Wiley, executive director of the National Welfare Organization; and an unnamed staff writer from the Institute of the Black World. Chisholm made a strong appeal for voter registration campaigns and an end to talk: "We don't care what you say. Rhetoric is easy; talk is cheap. What have you done? What are you doing? What do you intend to do?" She also took a shot at black nationalists such as Baraka who did understand electoral politics. "The time is past for Black Power charades, and the time has come to reject leaders who deceive the people." George Wiley suggested that jobs and income be the focus of any broader political strategy. "So in '72 the issues of jobs and income must be foremost. Candidates must be tested on the basis of economic aid programs to Black communities that put direct cash into the pockets of our people." He continued: "With this kind of economic base, we can build viable Black enterprise, Black organizations, Black institutions, a Black nation. Without it talk of economic development, community control, and Black power is meaningless rhetoric." The staff writer from the IBW stressed the need for black politicos to challenge gerrymandering and other tactics used to "prevent the accumulation of political strength in numbers."[25]

For readers who did not want to read all of the pieces, the paper suggested the following in terms of concrete actions as the black community moved from rhetoric to action. First, the editorial board felt that the $250,000 raised by the CBC weeks earlier "must be used wisely toward concrete ends. But, we must go beyond Congressional lobbying that has been the focus of discussion to date. Some of that money must be used for political organizing." Second, they felt that Russell's call for a National Black Political Convention was not "only feasible, but absolutely necessary." They suggested that the convention be held in New York City "under the general coordination of the Black Congressional Caucus but with extensive involvement of community people, non-politician professionals, etc." Third, the writers were adamant about the convention being a grassroots-based community effort and not a top-down effort of the nation's leading black elected officials. It read: "It is crucial that they participate only as 'members' of such a Coordinating Committee, not as 'leaders.' The proposed convention must not be seen as theirs, even though they may initiate it. It must belong to the Black communities in a collective sense. All people must feel a sense of ownership. If it is to succeed it cannot be the property of any vested interest except the interests of Black people generally." The necessity of a community-based leadership instead of the messiah complex style of leadership was one that was mentioned throughout the 1971–1972 strategy sessions. Some of the organizers of the various events were certainly jockeying to be the spokesperson of black America, and while they may have talked in terms of a broader base of leadership, they knew that the opportunity to be the nation's top black spokesperson was simply an opportunity they could not afford to waste.[26]

While some CBC members were seen as elitist and "not of the people," black nationalists considered themselves the ghetto spokespersons, despite the relatively small membership size of their organizations. They themselves could be elitist, cultish, and overly sectarian. In their eyes black nationalism was not *a* way to black liberation; it was *the only* way. Thus, while they appreciated the attempts by the CBC to put together an agenda for black people, they wanted to have a voice in the process. However, what the black nationalist community failed to realize was that the CBC had in fact become the voice of black America not merely through their positions but through their actions. Manning Marable writes that in the midst of these strategy sessions, members of the CBC were quietly supporting black candidates at the local level; lobbying for major reforms in the areas of job training, health care, and social service programs; and attempting to put an informal structure in place to increase black political power from the local to the national level.[27]

The influence of the Black Power movement on the Congressional Black Caucus cannot be overestimated. With the black community in a state of disillusionment in the immediate post–civil rights era, black nationalists like Baraka, Stokely Carmichael, and others were gaining increased acceptance, even from mainstream black folks. As Richard Hatcher mentioned, "the Nationalists were talking and people were listening." This broader political environment allowed the CBC to be much more aggressive politically as they prepared for the all-important 1972 elections.[28]

While the CBC continued to develop as the voice of black America, Amiri Baraka was emerging as the movement's foremost black nationalist after he hosted over 4,000 of his black nationalist counterparts at the Atlanta Pan-African Congress meeting in Atlanta over the 1970 Labor Day weekend. While Baraka appreciated the energy and excitement of the Black Power conferences, he grew frustrated at their inability to materialize into anything organizationally or pragmatically. Political scientist Cedric Johnson argues that although the summits were significant since they created space for public dialogue, networking, and exchange, there was very little meaningful follow-up after the close of the gathering. Thus, Baraka convened the Atlanta meeting with the goal of producing "workable agendas."[29]

Born in 1934 in Newark, New Jersey, Everett Leroy Jones went to Rutgers before attending the all-black Howard University in Washington, DC, where he changed his name to Leroi Jones. Upon leaving Howard he then served in the Air Force before settling in as a writer, poet, and play-wright in New York's Greenwich Village. While living within this hippie community, he married Hettie Cohen, a white woman. The hippie-like Jones had his racial awakening during a trip to Cuba in the aftermath of the Cuban revolution. While there, he and other black activists such as Harold Cruse felt a sense of belonging with the rebels, and once he arrived back in New York he got involved in a broader community of activists who were working in global liberation efforts, particular after the assassination of Patrice Lumumba.[30]

The death of Malcolm X on February 21, 1965, was Baraka's racial awakening as he rediscovered his blackness and slowly reinvented him-self. He quickly divorced his wife Hettie, leaving two daughters behind. Baraka's biographer argues that his white wife was a "liability" since he now wanted to be seen as a black man, and no racially conscious black man would be taken seriously by the community with a white wife by his side. He then moved to Harlem where he could "be black," "be seen as black," and "lead blacks." Shortly thereafter he founded the Black Arts Theater School (BARTS) in Harlem. As Baraka became more involved with the emerging cultural black nationalist community, author and activist Harold Cruse cautioned him to stay relevant and to meet the needs of the people instead of getting immersed in the trappings of black conscious-ness. This, Cruse suggested, could prevent him from solving problems in the ghetto. Ironically, BARTS failed because many of its members were so narrow in their black consciousness that they excluded anyone who did not subscribe to their same ideology. Disappointed that he was unable to sustain BARTS, Baraka retreated to Newark and created Spirit House, a black repertory group. As Spirit House became immersed in the ideology of black cultural nationalism, Baraka found a mentor in Maulana Karenga, founder of US and arguably the leading black cultural nationalist in the country. Karenga believed that the key to black liber-ation was for black people to reclaim the old African ways. It was under Karenga's influence that Leroi Jones changed his name first to Ameer Barakat and then to Amiri Baraka.[31]

Prior to the death of Malcolm X, Baraka had very little interest in black political life. He became increasingly political after attending the annual Black Power conferences organized by Dr. Nathan Wright. These

conferences dealt broadly with the debate concerning reform or revolution. It was at these conferences that Baraka moved from a theoretical
black nationalism to a practical black nationalism, because he wanted
to meet the needs of Newark's black citizens. Komozi Woodard writes
that this is when Baraka moved away "from narrow sectarian politics
toward the power of mass mobilization." With this newfound awakening,
Baraka and his supporters got involved in the successful 1970 effort to
elect Kenneth Gibson as the first black mayor of Newark. This grassroots
effort taught Baraka much about the political mobilization of local black
communities and the power that came with it, and now he wanted to
take the model of Newark throughout black America. "My view was that
Newark should be a model for the country, for the black movement of
how to gain practical Black Power. It was also my idea and some other
people's that the Black Power Conference, with its informal structure,
had to give way to an organization, a national, even Pan-African organization, whose function would be to struggle for Black Power wherever
black people were in the world."[32]

After the successful election of Gibson, Baraka was convinced that
black nationalists along with black elected officials needed to create a
black united front and put an end to the sectarian divisions that separated them. This was his rationale for creating the Congress of African
People (CAP) and hosting the 1970 Atlanta meeting, which became one
of the most ideologically diverse meetings of the mid-twentieth century.
Actively participating in the Atlanta proceedings were moderates such
as Juilan Bond, Richard Hatcher, Kenneth Gibson, Jesse Jackson, Ralph
Abernathy, and Whitney Young. Their participation convinced Baraka
that a working coalition of black nationalists, black moderates, black
elected officials, and civil rights organizations was not only possible,
but highly probable. While in Atlanta Baraka convinced his fellow black
nationalists that the philosophy of Mao, Castro, Marx, or Ho Chi Minh
could not be reproduced in the United States, and that black folk had
no desire to go to Africa or to move somewhere else. Baraka was slowly
starting to understand that the most revolutionary Africans were those
who could deliver goods and services. The Atlanta meeting was important
for several reasons. One, Baraka now became the most visible and vocal
black nationalist in the country because of his stewardship of the Atlanta

congress. The media and other interested observers saw that Baraka had the ability to galvanize participation from different ideologies within black America. This was important because many people just saw him as someone who spouted a ton of rhetoric without a ton of action to back it up. Second, the full range of black opinions regarding black liberation were expressed in Atlanta. Baraka didn't try to muffle or limit the views of those he disagreed with; rather, he encouraged the tension within the broader debates of black advancement. Third, the Atlanta meeting of the Congress of African People signaled that black nationalists were now part of the larger black political community, no longer relegated to the margins. Fourth, it illustrated that black nationalists and black moderates could agree upon the broad notion of black political power. However, the contradictions expressed at Atlanta between Baraka and racial moderates like the National Urban League's Whitney Young, who castigated the idea of racial separatism, were not addressed in Atlanta, and this foreshadowed what would happen throughout the 1971–1972 black strategy sessions.[33]

Baraka had a profound sense of optimism after the Atlanta meeting: "The Conference was a historic meeting much like the conventions held during the early part of the 19th Century. . . . All of the Black Power Conferences must be compared to those 19th Century conventions. They had the same objective: Black Liberation!" The success of the Atlanta meeting along with Gibson's election as the first black mayor of Newark taught Baraka that black control of central cities was possible and that it was also a necessary first step to creating an eventual black nation. During the Political Action Workshop of the Atlanta CAP meeting, the call was made for a 1972 National Black Political Convention to give black people a unified voice for the upcoming presidential election, and black nationalists were nearly unanimous in calling for an independent black political party. Although black nationalists and black moderates found common ground on the issue of black political power, the vehicle for attaining this power would be the source of tension throughout the 1971–1972 strategy sessions.[34]

2

WE CAN NO LONGER AVOID THE CHALLENGE OF CREATING AND DISSEMINATING A COMMON BLACK AGENDA

The 1971–1972 Black Strategy Sessions

While it was clear that black elected officials were excited about the political possibilities of 1972, it seemed that very few liked the idea of black people leaving the Democratic Party and forming their own political party, as some had suggested. Some of them owed their status to the Democratic Party, and they were not going to jeopardize that in hopes of launching an all-black political party. Others genuinely felt that the Democratic Party would begin to take black concerns seriously, so that is why they stayed. Last, very few black elected officials were going to be led by Amiri Baraka and the ideology of black nationalism. This simply was not going to happen. The strategy sessions held during the 1971–1972 election cycle explored the full range of these possibilities.[1]

The impetus for the strategy sessions was the lack of black influence within Democratic Party circles. Although black folks had given the party 70–90 percent of their vote since the 1940s, they were seldom rewarded with influence and positions in the broader party structure. Since the New Deal, black voters had been solidly democratic. FDR received 70 percent of the black vote, as did John F. Kennedy, but predictably, LBJ got a whopping 94 percent of black support, and the senator from Minnesota, Hubert H. Humphrey, got 85 percent of the black vote without even working for it. This overwhelming support for the Democratic Party was also evident in state and local elections, as black voters provided "the margin of victory in thousands of campaigns across the nation." It was clear that the Democratic Party took black people's support for granted because they never had influence within the party commensurate with their loyalty. At the 1964 DNC Convention only 2 percent of the delegation was black, and demands for more black representation in delegations from Mississippi, Georgia, Texas, and North Carolina were defeated "in divisive floor fights." Four years later in Chicago, only 211, or 5.5 percent, of the 3,049 delegates were black. Thus, black voters had little say in picking the presidential candidates, the party platform, or the overall strategy of the party.[2]

In an effort to address this imbalance, the CBC, led by Hatcher, met with DNC committee chairman Lawrence O'Brien. At the meeting, Hatcher made the following demands based upon the data that revealed that black voters represented 20 percent of the party:

1. A minimum of 20 percent black representation on all staff and convention committees
2. 20 percent of the DNC's annual budget so that its allocation for the Minorities Division could be boosted from $130,000 to $300,000
3. 20 percent black representation on the delegate slates supporting presidential aspirants
4. Financial support from the DNC for black candidates in the 1972 congressional and local elections
5. DNC help to elect blacks to the US Senate in states such as Michigan and Ohio
6. DNC pressure on state parties to redistrict with reapportion, with an eye toward broadening rather than limiting black participation

O'Brien agreed to all of the demands out of practicality. He knew black voters were often the swing voters in races across the country, and he could not afford to alienate the DNC's loyal black base. The question is, why didn't Hatcher and the CBC ask for more? In the aftermath of the meeting Hatcher felt victorious: "We wanted to impress the national party and particularly its chairman that we are prepared to seriously consider boycotting the national convention or the possibility of [taking] either fourth-party action or simply sitting out the national campaign." Hatcher was simply saber-rattling at this point; he knew that there was no way black folks would not vote in the upcoming elections.[3]

As a way of addressing black discontent within the Democratic Party, a writer for the *New York Times Magazine* suggested that the party nominate a "moderate militant" black as the party's vice-presidential candidate. This would (1) symbolize the possibility of achieving racial justice and harmony in America; (2) show the rest of the world the possibilities of cultural pluralism; (3) reinforce flagging black loyalty to the Democratic Party; and (4) guarantee Democrats the support of liberals, young activists, and under-25 voters who were not activists. Apparently, presidential candidate Edmund Muskie did not take this advice to heart because he categorically excluded any black as his running mate.[4]

O'Brien knew that black voters had leverage, and he wanted to exhaust any and all possibilities of black people pulling out of the Democratic Party. If you consider that the Democrats had conceded white southern voters during the LBJ presidency, to lose the black vote would effectively spell the end of the party. Despite O'Brien's efforts at appeasing the CBC, Amiri Baraka was not impressed. He still had no desire to negotiate with Democrats; he wanted an all-black political party. "Side by side with our Black rhetoric must be our Black candidates, and at the same time our Black institutions, all as alternatives to what the white boy has captured our people's mind with. We must run candidates from district leaders to president. For President because it is the only way to qualify for an entire line of statewide tickets and also because we might be able to make alliance with more mainstream American Negro political figures."[5]

Black Leadership Unity Conference

The all-black political party that Baraka advocated would set goals for blacks and demonstrate how to achieve them; increase black voting power; teach blacks political sophistication; run first-rate candidates for office; seek community control of institutions; only support candidates that embraced black nationalism; and establish alliances with third world movements. He expressed this desire during the Atlanta meeting and later in Newark, as well as at a meeting he hosted at Howard University in June 1971 under the name "Black Leadership Unity Conference." While some activists were pursuing strategies at the national level, Baraka's focus was on blacks' control of the nation's urban areas, which was a direct outgrowth of the Gibson election in Newark. The theme of the conference was "Strategy for Unity: 72 and Beyond." In calling the meeting Baraka invited a wide spectrum of black leaders. "What was talked about was a 'Black Leadership Conference,' bringing together the heads of Black organizations to begin to chart some path, just some commonalty of ideology, that somehow would be agreed upon, thereby strengthening the entire race. I remember talking to Jesse Jackson about such a conference, how we should pull it together." While waiting to hear from Jesse, Baraka noticed that it was taking a long time for Jesse and others to get back to him about the meeting. Just two days before the meeting at Howard, Baraka got some disturbing news. "We had been told two days before that another meeting was being called: this one in Cleveland, at the home of Carl Stokes, ex-mayor of Cleveland. This meeting was around the same theme, with much the same people who had been in Chicago the few weeks before." To make matters worse for Baraka, that meeting was limited to black elected officials and their middle-class establishment-oriented peers, and not the broad spectrum of black community leadership that was evident in Atlanta at the Congress of African Peoples. Because of these competing agendas, no elected officials or "media-famous activists other than nationalists had even bothered to show up (in Washington, D.C.) . . . they did not think it important enough." Baraka summed up the actions by Jackson and Stokes as "in-crowd elitism and cooptation. Why would Jesse Jackson or Carl Stokes and the rest not come to a meeting of Black Leaders in D.C.!"[6]

By the end of the summer it was clear that there were two distinct camps: one led by Baraka and other black nationalists; and the other led by the Congressional Black Caucus and other black elected officials. Both groups had large constituencies, but each also needed the other for legitimacy. The black nationalists needed the funding, credibility, and publicity of the CBC and other black elected officials, while the CBC needed the street credibility of Baraka and his peers. These were two distinct groups with different ideologies, philosophies, and strategies for achieving liberation, and bringing these two camps together would not be easy. In meetings throughout the summer and fall of 1971, their debates would continue in New Orleans, Mobile, Newark, Chicago, Los Angeles, and Washington, DC.

Southern Christian Leadership Conference Meeting

During the four-day annual convention of the Southern Christian Leadership Conference (SCLC) held August 10–13, 1971, the focus was also on black political empowerment. Still looking for an identity since the death of MLK, its founder, the 1,200 delegates in attendance at New Orleans placed a heavy emphasis on black political power. This was a drastic change from their previous agenda, which consisted of agitation and protest, largely through the black church. Ralph Abernathy, King's former lieutenant, did not see this as a problem. "We've seen that politics is one of the avenues to power. We are not changing our goals. We are still after the same things—a place of dignity and opportunity for Black people—and we're going to simply use politics to help us get that." The SCLC wanted specifically to focus their energies on the 1972 elections at the local, state, and congressional levels, and they had a strong desire to elect a congressperson from the Deep South.[7]

Southern Black Political Caucus

After leaving New Orleans, many of the SCLC delegates took a quick trip on Interstate 10, heading east to Mobile for the inaugural meeting of the Southern Black Caucus. Created by Julian Bond and Alabama's John Cashin, founder of the Alabama Democratic Party, the Southern Black Caucus was designed to give black southerners a voice. With so much emphasis being placed on black political power in the Northeast and Midwest, Bond realized that there was untapped potential for a black political revolution in Dixie. According to the *New York Times,* the delegates were "mayors, sheriffs, town clerks, county councilmen, county commissioners, and aldermen."[8]

The meeting was timely considering the newfound black political strength in the South. Since 1966, the number of black elected officials had risen from approximately one hundred to more than eight hundred, with more to come. In fact, Louisiana and Mississippi were on the verge of discrimination-free elections, and the numbers of black elected officials would certainly rise after those elections. The gathering was attended by many of the black politicos across the country such as Congressman Mitchell, Maynard Jackson, and comedian Dick Gregory. Others such as Carl Stokes, Hatcher, Chisholm, and Dellums were supposed to attend but were "unable to do so." Throughout the weekend "there were polemics against both national parties, protests against the Nixon administration, and criticisms of Governor George Wallace." Maynard Jackson told the assembly that political power gave black folks the opportunity to bring about substantial changes in the system. That mood was reflected throughout the gathering. "We're going back home now to organize and vote and win like we've never done before," said Thomas Gilmore, the sheriff of Greene County, Alabama. A. J. Cooper, a Mobile lawyer, was inspired as well. "I'm running over with confidence—in fact I've decided to run for Mayor of Pritchard next year. And I'm going to win." (Pritchard is a suburb of Mobile that at the time was known for its virulent racism.) The primary focus of the meeting was the importance of local politics, and the participants understood that black unity was critical to black political power. They discussed the basics of building a campaign, precinct organization, candidate qualification, voter registration, voter education, voter participation, and campaign strategy. Zelma Wyche, the town marshal of Tallulah, Louisiana, spoke to the importance of the meeting. "There was a lot of strength in this meeting. It can mean a whole lot in little places like mine to have this kind of unity going for us." The delegates institutionalized this gathering under the name of the Southern Election Fund.[9]

With regards to the national elections and the broader discussions, the group decided not to endorse a political strategy for the 1972 national elections. The gathering in Mobile was critical because it was a grassroots effort at taking power at the local level. In many counties, parishes, and jurisdictions in the South, the full implementation of the Voting Rights Act gave black folks an instant numerical majority. While they took a vigorous interest in the national debates, they were more focused on what was going on at home. They believed that all politics was local. On the other hand, in the aftermath of the Mobile gathering, the CBC made an attempt to create an umbrella organization for the newly emerging black caucuses across the country. They wanted to bring in the Southern Election Fund; the Black Legislative Clearinghouse (a caucus of state legislators across the country) under the leadership of State Senator Dick Newhouse from Chicago; and the Conference of Black Elected Officials, which was headed by Dymally, Bond, Hatcher, and Sutton. The goal was "to establish a common agenda and move as a unit toward the organizing of an independent power bloc—a third force."[10]

In an August 21, 1971, op-ed in the *New York Amsterdam News*, Ivanhoe

Donaldson made a strong appeal on the need for black political unity. He cautioned his readers not to celebrate the alleged civil rights victories of the 1960s. "Although thousands of articles and books are published constantly reminding us that there has been much won at the many bargaining tables, the tragic and simple truth is that for the majority of Black people, very little change has occurred in the economic conditions of their lives." He was now calling for the community to transition from protest to politics: "This leadership must now move the Black community from the platform of a social movement, raising questions into the political arena where it can provide and act on answers." Despite an increase in the number of black elected officials in recent years, Donaldson wanted to be sure that black politicians were held accountable. "The community will also be faced with the serious task of keeping these officials honest. There is little doubt that many Black elected officials are not only on an ego trip, but are crooks, using the rhetoric of Blackness and social justice to rob their communities blind." Donaldson's critique of some black elected officials was a familiar refrain from the nationalist camp. Floyd McKissick of CORE referred to them as "Jive-Ass" Niggers. In his opinion the J.A.N. was a black person who made a fetish of blackness for his or her own personal gain. The J.A.N. was not a new phenomenon. "The butler who sang Spirituals with his Soul brothers and sisters in the quarters after supper and kept massa informed of what was happening down there might have been among the first of the 'jive-ass' niggers." Surely, he felt that many members of the traditional black leadership class fit this classification as well. "There are even some jive-ass niggers in the front ranks of fighting organizations who use their Blackness for their personal gain."[11]

Observers were hopeful that elected black officials across the country would create a practical black political agenda that met the needs of people and was easy to understand. While some understood that the electoral process was not the final step towards liberation, it was the necessary next step. But in order for this to happen, a reawakening about the benefits of black political power was needed. "The utilization of politics as a tool for liberation depends, then, on an informed, educated, increased, involved and active electorate. It is incumbent upon those directly involved in politics to begin to inform residents as to the Who, What, When, Where, and How of the electoral process," Donaldson added. Hilton Clark, a candidate for a local position in Harlem, was frustrated at the political apathy in Harlem and in particular the high percentage of nonregistered voters. This he put at the feet of "the incompetence of some of Harlem's elected officials, who have failed to create and practice a principled political program." Instead, he believed that black politicians in Harlem spent the majority of their time "jockeying within the party, manipulating, compromising and making deals that primarily serve their own individual status." Clark made it plain that the overriding concern of black elected officials "must be to serve the needs of the community while implementing on the local, state, and federal level, a concrete program to improve the conditions of the Black community." If they didn't, he suggested, then an informed electorate "must learn to remove from office those Black representatives who have ceased to function on behalf of the community."[12]

Congress of African People's Meeting

One of the most interesting strategy sessions during 1971 took place in September at the Congress of African People's Regional Conference in Newark, which was attended by over 1,000 people. The conference was for all intents and purposes a black nationalist gathering with moderates sprinkled in. Leading the Congress were Baraka and Hayward Henry, a Harvard professor and executive director of the Congress. With more than 1,000 delegates in attendance, the gathering was a "fusion of nationalist and moderate alliances to advance the ideological concept of Black nationalism and Pan-Africanism." The conference was held at West Kinney High School in Newark; the Congress had held other regional meetings in California and Kansas, and leadership conferences in Philadelphia and Boston, with participants from Maine, Vermont, New Hampshire, Massachusetts, Connecticut, Rhode Island, New York, New Jersey, Maryland, Pennsylvania, Washington, DC, Delaware, West Virginia, Ohio, and Michigan. In all a total of eleven workshops were held on the following subjects: economic autonomy, education, law and justice, communications and systems analysis, religion, black technology, history, creativity, community organization, social organization, and political liberation. During the political liberation session and in a press conference, the Congress resolved to create a National Pan-Africanist

Political Party. This party would hold political conventions in the region with the goal that "by 1972 we should be able to run candidates in city, county, as well as statewide candidates," stated Henry. Baraka added that they would hold black political conventions in the states of New York, New Jersey, Pennsylvania, Connecticut, Massachusetts, and Ohio. Baraka believed that a political party would give the people an "identity, purpose, and direction."[13]

Baraka's desire to create an all-black "national-international African political party" was rooted in the electoral success he had had with Newark mayor Kenneth Gibson's campaign, and also the examples of Gary and Cleveland. Baraka believed that these local successes could be reproduced nationally if black voters were adequately educated. This would take a serious investment of time and energy to get adequate numbers of black voters registered and then to get them to the polls on election day. "If we fail" to register black voters, Baraka warned, "thieves, stooges, and toms will become local power figures." To counteract the "toms," Baraka stated, everyone had to be committed to black nationalism. Baraka clearly looked at the Congress as the potential voice for black people across the globe. In attendance at the conference were community activists, black elected officials, representatives from national civil rights organizations, and people across the African Diaspora such as Sharfudine Khan of the Mozambique Liberation Front; E. W. Mwasakafyuka from the Republic of Tanzania; Bruce McGuinness from Australia, who was there representing aboriginals; and Cyril Karg, president of the Black Power Movement of Surinam. McGuinness summed up his experience at the conference: "Even if our ideologies do not agree on other subjects, unity is foremost. I think that's developing here."[14]

The idea of unity was a central one for people like Baraka and those who agreed with him politically. For CAP to embrace an electoral agenda proves that the nationalists had realized that talk of revolution was not practical. Black people had no desire to overthrow the government; no desire to return to Africa; and no desire to turn a portion of the United States into a new black country. Although Baraka was a Black Power celebrity, he understood the limits of black nationalism, and CAP's entry into the political mainstream was indicative of that reality and a huge step for the movement. Many black nationalists had heretofore stayed out of politics, considering it either a waste of time, or a futile endeavor since the system was rotten at its core. Further, many nationalists spent a great deal of their time segregating themselves from the mainstream, critiquing black elected officials and the black middle class for buying into the system, attempting to build bridges between Africans and African Americans, and putting on the trappings of an African-centered life.

The concept of unity was in a sense an "operational unity." Baraka realized that the nationalists and the black elected officials would never see eye-to-eye on everything, but he was hopeful that there were some points of agreement that could move the black community forward. In Maulana Karenga's teaching on Kawaida, the first point in the Nguzo Saba value system is Umoja, or Unity. Baraka wrote about this concept and why he included non-nationalists at the CAP events in 1971 and 1972: "What was intended here was a beginning of widespread unity movement. An attempt to minimize ideological difference for the sake of Umoja Mweusi, black unity. Before we can have any further movement, we must have unity. Before we can have self-determination, we must have a self, a unified body, which itself demands independence. Splintered and disunified, we are millions of separate, often warring egos, straining to outdo each other, while our actual enemy sits somewhere 'above,' jiggling the strings." This embrace of Karenga's teaching is what propelled Baraka throughout the strategy sessions.[15]

Northlake

In all, six such strategy meetings were held in the fall of 1971. Arguably the most important one took place in September 1971 in the Chicago suburb of Northlake. It was convened by Mayor Richard Hatcher of Gary, Georgia state representative Julian Bond, Manhattan borough president Percy Sutton, and California state representative and future San Francisco mayor Willie Brown. Sixty black leaders "meeting here in extraordinary secrecy" made plans to call a national black political convention in 1972. Those in attendance at Northlake featured key members of the black leadership class, including Congressman Diggs, Coretta Scott King, Jesse Jackson, Julian Bond, Amiri Baraka, Vernon Jordan, Walter Fauntroy, John Conyers, Augustus Hawkins, Barbara Jordan, Maynard Jackson, Roy Innis, and others. Because the meeting was held in the strictest of confidence and without interference from white media, security was tight. In fact Roy Innis of CORE and Baraka's bodyguards "kept outsiders from a spiral staircase leading to the meeting room." But despite his bodyguards posted around the hotel, Baraka noticed that some of the attendees had tipped off the press about the gathering: "The meeting was supposedly confidential, yet when we arrived, there were newsmen and television cameras in the lobby trying to get statements. There was even a white woman reporter who demanded entrance into the meeting saying it was a free country and no one could bar her from anything. She didn't make it." He continued: "For all the swearing to secrecy by the brothers and sisters who attended the meeting, specific word of what had been talked about reached the white press before any of us were back in our homes. A couple of dudes were seen standing in the lobby giving interviews, whose appearance in well-circulated journals was predictable." Shirley Chisholm had a major problem with the masculinist presence of bodyguards: "I might remark that no elected black officials I know have bodyguards, only the self-appointed and media-anointed ones, and they must know better than I why it is they need them."[16]

With virtually every major ideology and institution in black America represented, those in attendance settled in for intense debate and strategic thinking. The attendees kept the press out of the loop, and in fact the two floors upon which the meeting was being held were off limits to the press. Attendees were given notebooks with "National Assembly for a Black Political Strategy in 72" printed on them.[17]

Over the course of the weekend there were several strategies presented. First was a proposal by Julian Bond, whose decision it was to hold a strategy meeting in Northlake. In a precirculated proposal he put forth the idea that each locale with a good-sized population run a popular local black person as a favorite-son candidate in the primaries. This would achieve several goals. "It would free Black politicians from dependence on any of the presidential candidates; invigorate Black voters through a campaign by a local, well-known local-based Black politician; and give Black delegates to the 1972 conventions bargaining power they have not possessed before." The state senator from Georgia felt that this strategy would help black folks win a presidential primary, win important blocs of delegates, and help turn out enough black voters to elect more independent black delegates. Bond understood that a black candidate had no chance of being elected to the White House in 1972, and that blacks were not about to leave the Democratic Party in favor of an all-black political party. His proposal was practical, thoughtful, and realistic. "In an era of decreasing party loyalty, but in an era where Black voters are steadfastly Democratic; in a period where there are more Black elected officials than ever, but fewer Blacks voting in proportion to the number of registered and eligible Blacks, the strategy should help solidify the Black vote, enable Black politicians involved in this strategy to barter at the convention from a position of greater strength and should decrease the possibility of putting all our eggs in one basket before the convention, thus denying us the opportunity for independence during platform debate as well as Presidential selection," Bond stated. Examples of favorite-son candidates were attorney Al Hastings from Florida, Mayor Richard Hatcher of Gary, and State Senator Barbara Jordan of Houston. Bond concluded by stating that with several candidates in a primary, there was a strong possibility of a black candidate winning a district in Florida.[18]

Congressman John Conyers made a strong argument at Northlake concerning why they should run an African American for president: because the Democratic Party had neglected black interests, supported racist state parties, and limited meaningful participation at the national level to the African American community. Conyers felt that black people had no choice but to draft a candidate to run as the Democratic nominee. For Conyers, this would stimulate voter registration, education, and participation. Like Bond's proposal, this strategy would give black folks maximum leverage. This proposal was based upon two overlapping pieces of political evidence: First, the vast majority of registered black voters in the United States were Democratic. "To attempt to sway that many people to support a third-party effort in 1972 is a herculean task that would waste time, effort, and other human resources." Second, any attempt at a national strategy had to be based on coalition politics. "By coalescing Blacks within the party we can solidify and enhance our power base and thus increase our bargaining position."[19]

For Conyers, what made the mayoral campaigns of Hatcher, Gibson, and Stokes successful was not "whether they won or lost or even whether they ran a pro-Black platform. What each of them did was to accept the idea that to win political office a candidate must build an effective political organization. Any emerging Black strategy on a national level is going to have to face the same reality." Thus, the black candidates could not limit themselves just to states with a large black population. Indeed the candidate would need to "hike through the snowy mountains of New Hampshire, to cover the lush dairy land of Wisconsin, to track the arid expanses of New Mexico and to bask in the golden sunshine of California."[20]

Conyers believed that running a black presidential candidate would achieve several goals. One, it would put the entire country "on notice that we are no longer satisfied being Black leaders, but have resolved to take our rightful place as national leaders." Two, it would force other presidential candidates seeking the Democratic nomination to broaden their appeal, to recruit blacks to work as key members of their staffs, and to name blacks as delegates to the convention. Last, it would force the DNC "to endorse a platform that is at least more fair to Blacks." In Conyers's eyes, Stokes was the most logical black presidential candidate. "The Democratic party needs a candidate who will speak to the critical reform needed in this country and who will go beyond just replacing Richard Nixon. Mayor Stokes's ability is recognized across the country and would attract across-the-board support."[21]

In a similar vein, Manhattan borough president Percy Sutton suggested that Congresswoman Shirley Chisholm from Brooklyn should be the black presidential nominee. This ignited a controversy that would plague black political talks until the 1972 election. Although Chisholm was a well-respected member of Congress, Sutton's promotion of her was purely symbolic. Nonetheless, her supporters thought her candidacy was legitimate for several reasons: she was the first black woman ever to serve in the House of Representatives; she had access to funds for a national campaign; and she had strong support from women's groups. But her potential candidacy would be a persistent thorn in the side of the political strategy meetings, and it would highlight the gender constraints within the black political community.

Born in 1924 in Brooklyn, New York, Chisholm moved with her grandmother to Barbados at the age of three. She was raised on a farm where she fed cows, took sheep to pasture, and collected firewood. In a 1972 interview she recalled that her grandmother gave her "strength, dignity, and love. I learned from an early age that I was somebody. I didn't need the Black revolution to tell me that." She returned to the United States at the age of eleven when her parents brought her back. Enrolling in school in Brooklyn was a bit different from farming in Barbados. "It's the first time I recall being completely in a world of whites. I kept making spitballs in class and propelled them with rubber bands. I was quite the discipline problem. They finally gave me an I.Q. test and found I had a near-genius I.Q. of 170. So they skipped me to the fifth grade." Shirley was not one to downplay her talents; in fact, she often boasted. For instance, "Even as a child I couldn't understand why most people couldn't think like I do."[22]

At the age of 13 they moved to Bedford-Stuyvesant as the community was in the midst of a Jewish-to-black transition. This is where she had her first racial encounters. "The Jewish children would tell me their mothers had forbidden them to play with me." After attending Brooklyn College, she married Conrad Chisholm, a private investigator who would later invest himself in his wife's political career. In 1958 she entered local politics by running for a position in the 17th Assembly District Democratic Club. She remembered how the local bosses humiliated residents. "I'll never forget the clubhouse, Blacks and whites sat separately, the Blacks on one side of the room and the whites on the other. Carney (the boss) and his henchmen sat up on a raised dais puffing on stogies and wearing big diamond rings. And I can still see the people sitting on those benches for as long as three hours waiting for a tap on the shoulder to go walk up to the platform as if they were going to see God Almighty. It just got to me." Because of this anger she challenged for the leadership of this organization, but she lost. She recalls that the ward bosses attempted to give her perks and positions to quiet her down, but she would not stop. "They thought that if they gave me some status, I'd quit challenging all their decisions. But they were constantly plotting to curb people and I wouldn't go along and they thought I'd be too embarrassed to show my face again. But the very next week I came to the clubhouse and sat out on the floor with the slobs. When they saw me out there, I saw them nudging each other. . . . I walked up and shook their hands and they got rattled. I kept on asking questions, kept on needling. It began to crystallize in me that I had something that could be used for people who had no input into things."[23]

In 1964 Chisholm was elected to a newly created state assembly seat without significant opposition, where she battled for student financial aid, unemployment insurance, and tenure rights for public school teachers. But her campaign was not without controversy. "Everyone had agreed that I would run for the State Assembly. When I thought it was settled, a special meeting was called. I was moved to tears when I realized that all of this was a ploy to prevent me, as a woman, from being elected to the Assembly. Even today, my Black male colleagues would not be so put out with me if I had been a man." But she also became a political maverick while in Albany by refusing to support local bosses for statewide positions. She did this to establish her independence. Her time in Albany made her the perfect candidate for the new congressional district created in 1968. She won election to Congress with little opposition.[24]

Although she was the first African American female to serve in the House after being elected in 1968 from the Bedford Stuyvesant area, she was from a small, politically apathetic district, without a national following. But she had supporters at Northlake who felt that her "candidacy would give Black people a basis that they would not otherwise have for measuring the other candidates." Although Chisholm was considered the most likely black presidential candidate, the idea of her running for president did not sit well with nationalists and some black elected officials. Yet Congressman Ron Dellums was ready to throw his support behind her. "She could help in the development of a new kind of power base. And if Black elected officials would buy into her campaign then the Black community would buy in." He also mentioned that for those thinking of creating a separate political party, she was the perfect candidate because "she could bring together the elements necessary to create a third force in American politics. By 1976 we should be able to put together a ticket to win." But her campaign manager was not concerned about symbolic campaigns. He was optimistic about something greater. "Our goal right now is 1600 Pennsylvania Avenue, and nothing less." He believed that if they entered the primaries they would have early success. "It's our vote—the Black, the Spanish-speaking and the women—which will be solid. Besides, we expect the field to reduce very quickly after New

Hampshire." Part of black folks' concerns about Chisholm was her ties to white feminist groups. They were not about to let black political power be usurped by white women. "Will she be the candidate of Blacks or the candidate of women? When the deal goes down and she has to negotiate away something, is it going to be the interests of Blacks or the interests of women that are hurt?" one Northlake attendee asked. Her twenty-five-year-old campaign manager, Thad Garrett, believed that this concern was baseless. "She is a Black woman, of the Black experience and from one of the Blackest districts in the country. She can do nothing but be Black in all her dealings." Those in attendance thought otherwise.[25]

Chisholm could have perhaps addressed some of these concerns had she been at Northlake. Despite being invited to the gathering, she did not attend. Instead, she sent a young staffer. Writing several years after the Northlake summit, Chisholm wrote that she didn't attend "because nothing would come of it," because there "was no plan, no unity, and nothing agreed upon except to hold more meetings." Plus, she added, "If I attended I would be the focus of much dissension." Those in attendance were infuriated that she was not there. In their eyes she did not want to be accountable. She was avoiding the strategy talks so that she would not be put in a position to be rejected by her own people. It was a shrewd move. However, Thad Garrett told the crowd that Chisholm was going to run for president whether they liked it or not. When asked why Chisholm did not attend, he responded, "I can tell you what she would say if she were here. I write every word she says anyway." Those at Northlake were offended at Chisholm's snubbing of the meeting.[26]

Many of those involved in the black strategy sessions were suspicious of Chisholm, with much of the suspicion based upon her close relationship with white feminists. It was assumed that she would not be a black candidate but a candidate whose ultimate allegiance lay with white feminists. This conundrum was not unique to black women in the freedom struggle. Historically, black women activists had had a very complicated relationship with the nascent feminist movement because they typically made a conscious decision to prioritize race over gender, feeling that they would be "hard-pressed" to confront the sexist attitudes of black men while they were fighting the white man. In fact, throughout the 1971–1972 election season, Chisholm received very little support from her fellow black female activists. Author Kimberly Springer argues that black women did not participate in the women's movement because it would increase tensions between black men and women; it would divert energies from the black freedom movement; black women simply did not trust white feminists; and black women had been stereotyped historically. And for those who did forge ahead and build alliances with white feminists and raise gender concerns within the movement, they would face the likelihood of being labeled "manhaters," "lesbians," "sellouts," "inauthentically black," "domineering," and "emasculating." Chisholm would confront gender stereotypes and expectations throughout the strategy sessions.[27]

Members of the Congressional Black Caucus at Northlake made a strong appeal for their "Sixty Recommendations" to be the basis of any black political strategy. They wanted those recommendations to become the official platform of black America and make candidates seeking the presidency have to state their position on each of the recommendations. When Senator George McGovern endorsed the Caucus recommendations shortly after announcing his candidacy, it gave them hope.

While much of the discussion at Northlake centered on the idea of leveraging the black vote within the Democratic Party, both Jesse Jackson and Amiri Baraka were in favor of the idea of forming an all-black political party. Historian Komozi Woodard argues that although the Baraka-led gatherings prior to Northlake were centrally focused on an all-black political party, Baraka soon realized that the idea of such a party was premature if activists wanted the support of black elected officials in 1972. Yet CAP had developed a number of options that might lead to a black political party, and the political convention was at the top of that agenda. With that in mind, Baraka no longer made the idea of a black political party a priority at the strategy meetings, but rather, the idea of a black national political convention. He then made a push for a meeting "somewhat like the Atlanta conference, but bigger, and particularly oriented toward Black political development."[28]

Baraka recalled: "The convention would try to bring all the tribes of Black people in America together to talk about our political priorities. Certainly about 1972, and what an American presidential year meant to the national Black Community; but also what kind of continuing priorities should be sounded for Black people. And, as always, we hoped that there would be some talk of a continuing mechanism, some structure upon which to build what we still feel is the absolute sine qua non of Black political movement, i.e., a permanent structure, or party."[29]

Nothing was decided at Northlake, but there was general agreement that the group should continue to meet, and Andrew Young of SCLC was charged with raising $14,000. While the idea of more meetings could be a sign of progress, Baraka was skeptical. "Concrete follow-up on the meeting seems to have generally spun away like concrete follow-up on most of the other meetings. The same questions had been asked. Some new ones. Some new answers. A new continuous structure was put together on paper. New responsibilities given out, on paper. And so, to whirl away, having talked, to the next conference."[30]

While nothing was decided at Northlake, author Robert Smith said that it produced three important developments: it provided an opportunity for frank discussion among all parties; each ideology was given a fair hearing so that everyone's position would be clear; and last, Baraka made a strong case for a convention that sounded increasingly appealing to black elected officials, although some had reservations about such an idea.[31]

Black Expo 71

The strategy meetings continued days later at an event called Black Expo 71. Under the direction of a young "country preacher" by the name of Rev. Jesse L. Jackson and through the institutional arm of Operation Breadbasket, Black Expo 71 was a haven for businesses seeking to connect with black consumers. According to Jackson, "The 500 companies we expect to rent space employ 20,000 people (mostly Blacks), have a combined payroll of nearly $90 million, and have annual sales between $300 million and $500 million." He was hopeful that the business generated by the Expo "will strive to see the dream of the late Dr. Martin L. King Jr. come true." But Jesse was not just about economic empowerment or the business of Black Power; he was also about political power, and with the movement at a critical juncture, he used Black Expo as a way to promote his candidacy to be the black leader. Thus, during the Expo there were several political sessions that featured Stokes, Hatcher, Sutton, and Congressman John Conyers. All gave keynote addresses.[32]

"Harambee Black Expo 71" was held September 25–October 3 and featured a "Who's Who" of black America. There were "Exhibits, Entertainment, Workshops, Seminars, Shows, and Conferences." The first two days consisted of the National Labor Leaders Conference, while the second two days were titled "African/Afro-American Conference," which was not open to the public. The official opening night of Black Expo featured entertainment by Aretha Franklin, Ossie Davis and Ruby Dee, Stevie Wonder, the Jackson Five, Donnie Hathaway, Bill Cosby, the Four Tops, Billy Eckstine, and Albertina Walker and the Caravans. The Expo got down to business when Carl Stokes, mayor of Cleveland, delivered a talk titled "The Politics of 1972."[33]

Stokes opened his speech by making it clear that he was not speaking for any organization either "closely or loosely, official or unofficial group or organization, not of the Black elected officials, not by the Congressional Black Caucus, not by the Panthers nor the Baptists." This disclaimer was a clear indication that black nationalists and black elected officials across the country had been and were currently meeting to discuss a strategy for the 1972 presidential election. Stokes went on to mention that he could not understand why "white Americans can support, with widely varying degrees of order, intelligence and justification, such widely disparate individuals as Richard M. Nixon, George Wallace, Hubert H. Humphrey, George McGovern, and John Lindsay," and yet believe that black folk "are some kind of completely homogenous, monolithic, one-opinion group."[34]

While this seemed to be a shot at white America, it appears that it was an indictment of black politicians who were attempting to come up with a black strategy that all black folk could agree upon. Stokes was adamant that he was not interested in running for president. "The views to be expressed are those of Carl Stokes only, they do not represent, in any sense, a beginning of a campaign on my part for the presidential nomination next year." He was only at the Expo to speak for effective black political action in 1972. This was necessary because his name had been whispered in many camps as the most logical candidate for president who had the respect of black America. Stokes opined that he would spend his time trying to get effective representation at the major political party conventions of 1972.[35]

Stokes was clearly advocating that black folks work within the existing two-party system and ignore some of the talk coming from the nationalist camp that black folks should form an all-black separate third party. As a staunch believer in coalition politics, the Cleveland mayor suggested that was the wisest course of action. "If we develop and examine that power, not to satisfy the ambitions of any individual among us, but rather to meet the needs of people, of Black, brown, and other minority groups, of poor people, of young people and the elderly then we will accomplish something worthy, something valuable, something useful and meaningful for this country."[36]

Because of the conditions of the nation's urban areas Stokes declared that a political revolution led by the most affected was absolutely necessary. Because of the urgency, Stokes felt that "Black leadership must now become real or retreat to the old islands of petition and protest." This was the real reason for the call for a black political strategy for 1972. Stokes understood the range of black political strategies: "This may mean the actual running of a Black person for president of the United States, a number of different Black persons for favorite sons and other varieties of committing presidential delegates, or a combination of them all. The specific rationale for the strategies will be spelled out at our (forthcoming) political workshops by our distinguished Black political leaders." But Stokes warned the audience and workshop leaders, "we cannot do it alone! We have to affect the coalition of interest with other similarly oppressed and denied people."[37]

Stokes was passionate about using the coalition approach because of his success as mayor of Cleveland and as leader of the Twenty-First District Congressional Caucus, the only effective black political machine in American political history. "The 21st District Caucus in Cuyahoga County, I submit to you, shows how we are to proceed. It shows the kind of independence, the kind of unity, the absolute refusal to be ignored and the implementation of basic political mechanics, that are necessary on a national level, if Black people, if just plain folks are to participate meaningfully in the political process." Putting together the basics of a political structure and agenda were critical issues for Stokes. "We worked hard on the basics. We elected precinct committeemen, organized our campaigns house by house, block by block; we raised our own money, we developed campaigns and literature on the issues; we rang doorbells, telephones and put everything done on paper in a systemized and planned order of approach. We registered our people and then went back and got them to vote and to vote right!!!"[38]

The mayor's paternalistic tone was an overt message to black nationalists who were long on rhetoric about Black Power, revolution, and power to the people. Lashing out in great detail about how to put together a political campaign, Stokes knew his audience had little experience with actual black political power. But he wasn't done. "In other words, we put it together by the numbers, not press releases, and that's what has to be done by Black people nationally for the 1972 elections." While many black power advocates were gifted orators who without question could move the crowd through their spoken words, Stokes knew that wasn't enough. "Rhetoric will never substitute for work in professional politics. It would be so easy to stand on this platform and prattle unity, love, militancy, etc., or togetherness, on behalf of this candidate or that candidate or potential candidate and then sit down. But those kinds of speeches are among the things that have held America back, and held Black people within America back even further. This is a business with me. The pros at the convention count votes not rhetoric."[39]

Despite the success African Americans had experienced politically with the passage of the Voting Rights Act, Stokes did not want those in attendance to underestimate the difficult job that lay ahead in trying to exercise black political power at the national level. The first step was to work within the system and ignore calls for overturning the government. The second thrust was to move away from the civil rights movement's protest and demonstrations to a stance of self-determination through the acquisition of political power. The third thrust was to coalesce the Mexicans, Puerto Ricans, poor whites, liberal whites, and other minorities. Last, to reject political labels. "There is nothing inherently responsive about the label Democrat, nor the label Republican. Black people can ill afford 'belonging' if the only thing they get out of belonging is to be able to say 'I belong.'"[40]

As Stokes neared the end of his speech, he reiterated that electoral politics was not for the politically ambitious. "Politics is tough. Good rhetoric, good looks, don't mean you can get elected dogcatcher. And don't round up a bunch of entertainers, football players and performing artists—God-love-em—and permit them to make political decisions. They can help you raise funds by giving a concert, but unless you have the folks registered to vote, unless you know how to get the vote out on election day and know the ones you get out will vote right, unless you know how to count precincts and wards and counties and delegates and electoral votes, you may end up with pleasant memories of a campaign, but you won't end up in office." In closing, Stokes laid out a five-point strategy for the 1972 election:

- That black elected officials and black voters make no commitment to any of the announced and easily draftable candidates for president
- That black voters concern themselves with issues, not personalities
- That black voters in their respective states start now in the process of deciding upon delegates to next year's political party conventions
- That communication be developed with other political minority groups as the issues are formed and common interests identified for coalition purposes
- That black delegates go to the conventions with a full understanding of why they are there

As the keynote speaker in what was the first of the large black political gatherings in search of a 1972 strategy, Stokes clearly spoke for the other black elected officials and the other establishment-oriented activists and community leaders. He was the perfect person for the role. He was arguably the most powerful black politician and the most popular urban politician in the country, and he was just ending his two-term tenure as mayor of Cleveland, the country's eighth largest city. His distinction as the first black mayor of a major city gave him the credibility and authority needed to deliver what would be the opening salvo in the 1972 black political strategy sessions. As mayor of Cleveland Stokes embodied the transition from protest to black political power. He leveraged his office to address black concerns, and he created a template for all future black politicians to follow. He addressed black concerns over housing, education, employment, and police brutality. Also, he institutionalized his power by creating the Twenty-First District Democratic Caucus, which was arguably the most powerful black urban political machine in the history of the United States. At the time of his keynote address at Black Expo, the Twenty-First District Caucus was involved in a heated election season with the goal of maintaining black control of city hall and city services.

That afternoon attendees at the Black Expo headed to "closed session" workshops led by Stokes, Congressman John Conyers, Manhattan borough president Percy Sutton, Gary mayor Richard Hatcher, and California assemblyman Mervyn Dymally. During Sutton's workshop, which was held at Kennedy-King College, he came out squarely in favor of a black presidential candidate. "The running of a Black presidential candidate creates a strategy and sense of internal unity which carries far beyond the convention floor and elections of 1972. It carries with it a political awareness that will flow into the elections in every city, town, and village in America where Black people live." Sutton went on to mention that the black community would be a force to be reckoned with after supporting a black candidate, even if that candidate failed to receive the democratic nomination.[41]

Sutton was the unofficial cheerleader for Chisholm's presidential ambitions, and her presence at Expo was interesting considering that she was not at Northlake. At the Women's Day event, Chisholm spoke to a crowd of over 1,000 people. Her participation was not without controversy. As Chisholm entered the meeting hall where she was speaking, she was confronted by three or four well-dressed men: "I took them for politicians. They saw me, and one of them said to the others, loud enough for me to hear, 'there she is, that little Black matriarch who goes around messing things up.'" Upset, and rightly so at the obvious sexual intimidation by the unknown group of men, Chisholm let loose at the podium. "Black women have got to realize what they are in for when they venture into politics. They must be sure they have the stamina to endure the endless obstructions that are out in their way. They must have enough confidence so they will not be worn down by the sexist attacks they will encounter on top of racial slurs.[42]

But Chisholm did not stop there. She then made a long directed attack upon the black male political establishment. "Well I am about ready to make my decision to run and I just want to say a few things to my Black brothers, who I know are not going to endorse me. I don't expect their support, nor will I bother them about it. I know their feelings. I have learned too much for too long in my dealings with politicians, Black and white. There are people who believe I should go to these men and discuss my intentions with them, but this kind of thinking is folly. Anyone in his right mind knows that this group of men, for the most part, would only laugh at the idea. They would never endorse me. They are prisoners of their traditional attitudes, and some of them are just plain jealous, because they have been wounded in their male egos."[43]

She continued: "Brothers, Black women are not here to compete or fight with you. If we have hang-ups about being male or female, we're not going to waste the talent that should be put to use to liberate our people. Black women must be able to give what they have in the struggle." Chisholm recalled that her "outburst" at Black Expo made her "feel better and put me fairly on record as to what my relationship to the self-appointed leaders of the problematic Black coalition would be." Chisholm was unwilling to be a part of the coalition because she realized that she did not have the support of the masses of black people. For her to participate in the coalition and then get rejected by the coalition would have killed any nascent white support.[44]

Chisholm provided other reasons why she didn't participate. One, she believed "that if a Black coalition were to be formed, it would not be done by some of the gentlemen who were organizing the meetings." This is absurd. If the most popular black elected officials could not establish a coalition, then who really had the capacity to do it? Second, in a moment of clarity, she realized "that if the coalition did somehow take shape, there was no realistic possibility that it would endorse me." Third, she was not convinced that a black coalition would work in the first place because of the ideological differences. "The more they tried to arrive at a strategy for 1972, the more alienated they became from each other, because of the philosophical and ideological differences among them." She then basically stated that the entire idea was absurd. "They seemed to think that their common skin pigmentation would somehow produce a magic sympathy and agreement, and that if they met enough and talked enough, the rhetoric would eventually culminate in a plan that, even if not totally acceptable, would unite them for action. But there was no chance of this unless there could be found a way to submerge the under-lying differences among the various Black leaders, elected, appointed or self appointed."[45]

Chisholm's repeated use of the word "self-appointed" came from a place of envy. Why wouldn't the leaders of the Congressional Black Cau-cus been seen as leaders? How could she dismiss Baraka's leadership and stature among black nationalists? Because she did not have the same following as her peers, she continually took shots at their credibility and their desire to chart an agenda for the black community. While there had been lukewarm support for a Chisholm candidacy, any political novice re-alized that she was incapable of a strong showing at the polls. Her public attack upon black male politicians was misplaced. Did they probably hold traditional sexist attitudes toward the idea of black female leadership? Certainly. But her broad indictment about her black male counterparts and their sexism doesn't add up to the historical record for several rea-sons. One, other female leaders such as Coretta Stott King and Dorothy Height participated in the strategy sessions, and they came out publicly against the idea of endorsing Chisholm or any other candidate. Second, although Chisholm was invited to the strategy sessions, she often chose not to participate. Third, because of her alignment with feminists and white women her candidacy was not considered "black."

Nonetheless, some of Chisholm's public criticisms of black male lead-ers and their sexism were spot-on. The 1971–1972 strategy sessions were an all-male affair with only token and symbolic participation by black women. Ironically, black women had much larger roles within the civil rights movement because of their community work, although they were still marginalized. However, the Black Power movement did not create much space for women to step up and be visible, let alone lead. Much of the rhetoric coming from the black nationalist community during the Black Power movement was centered around the idea of black men reclaiming their masculinity. Further, many of the more popular black nationalist organizations such as the Nation of Islam, US, the Black Pan-ther Party, and the Congress of African People assigned black women to traditional gender roles such as taking care of "the black warrior" (their husbands) and childbearing or "nation building." This, according to Kimberly Springer, was the role of the "Truly Revolutionary Black Women." Ironically, some of the most sexist attitudes towards black women in the movement came from their black male counterparts who were fighting for black liberation. In an effort to maintain racial unity, some black female activists often willingly took a back seat to black men by neglecting to take leadership roles, refraining from challenging black men in public, and operating in the gendered space that was carved out for them. But Shirley Chisholm, like many other black female radicals, chose to deny convention by being visible and outspoken, and in the process she would make headlines for challenging members of the Congressional Black Caucus for their sexist views.[46]

Western Conference of Black Elected Officials

Another important strategy session was held in October in Los Angeles. It was hosted by California state senator Mervyn Dymally, who was also cochair of the National Conference on Black Elected Officials. At the gathering, attendees heard reports from the previous strategy sessions held across the United States. They then spent a considerable amount of time covering state election laws in the Southwest and West, before having an open discussion titled "Black Strategy for the Presidency in '72." The meeting ended with a "closed caucus" that was only open to black elected officials. Noticeably absent from the caucus agenda were any black nationalists. Despite Los Angeles and the Bay Area being a hotbed of black nationalist activity, it appears that this session was exclusively limited to black elected officials and their invited guests.[47]

Conference of Black Elected Officials

The last major strategy session of 1971 occurred in November at the Conference of Black Elected Officials held in Washington, DC, at the Sheraton Park Hotel, November 18–20. Congressman Louis Stokes laid out the purpose of the event: "We see this conference as a means of Black elected officials coming together for the purpose of effectively linking together a united program of legislative and political action for the benefit of their constituents." While this sounded good, this meeting was to find a way for the CBC to control the black political agenda for the 1972 elections. More than three hundred elected officials, delegates, and panelists attended the event, and much of the discussion was held in one of the fourteen workshops, each chaired by a CBC member. The workshops were the following:

- Development of Black Political Power in the Seventies
- Congressional Redistricting and Legislative Reapportionment
- Convention Delegate Selection Process
- Report on National Political Strategy Sessions for 1972
- Utilization of News Media for Black Political Development
- Money Resources—Federal and Foundations
- Voter Education and Registration—New Trends, New Problems, and New Strategies
- Employment, Income Maintenance, and Economic Opportunities
- Vietnam Veterans—War Cost to the Black Community
- Education and Early Childhood Development
- Problems of Aging
- Health
- Housing and Economic Development
- Drugs, Law Enforcement, and Corrections[48]

The layout of the conference workshops was very similar to that of the Congress of African People's meetings. The idea to discuss literally every facet of black life and offer solutions was a testament to Baraka's leadership of CAP. The CBC realized that they needed to be relevant to the masses of black people, and this gathering was a step in that direction. When the conference opened, the CBC did not intend to call for a black convention. Instead they had planned to hold a series of hearings that would lead to the creation of a black agenda for the 1970s, "which presidential candidates would be forced to adopt if they wanted the Caucus members' support."[49]

However, before any serious discussion about the agenda could begin, Congresswoman Shirley Chisholm continued her attacks upon her male colleagues. During a session led by Congressman Clay on the Development of Black Political Power in the Seventies, he opened by stressing the need for black political unity. "Blacks are the only people in the United States who place others' interests before their own. We must play by the rules of the game, which also say that you take whatever you can, from whomever you can and however you can." On the panel with Clay was Coretta Scott King, Gary mayor Richard Hatcher, Congressman Diggs, Percy Sutton, and Amiri Baraka. But they didn't get much further without controversy. Clay tells it best. "At that point, Florida State Representative Gwendolyn Cherry, a supporter of Congresswoman Shirley Chisholm's presidential aspirations, stood up and accused male members of the Congressional Black Caucus of attempting to undermine the Chisholm campaign and all hell broke loose. Cherry declared that I, as moderator of the workshop ought to relinquish the microphone, in her words, 'to our illustrious presidential candidate on the Democratic ticket, Shirley Chisholm.'" Embarrassed, Clay gave her the microphone, and months of frustration from Chisholm came out in a ten-minute attack on black males and the CBC for their unwillingness to support her. When she got the microphone she mentioned that some of the black males in attendance had "insecure egos" that prevented them from supporting her candidacy. She could not understand why they were "always plotting and planning" against her, and that throughout her lifetime she had dealt with discrimination both as a woman and as a black person. "There is a hang-up about this maleness and femaleness," she said. She felt slighted. "I am the highest elected woman official today and for those who don't know, the Democratic National Committeewoman from the State of New York." She then looked at the Stokes brothers, Carl and Louis, and said, "You'd better wake up."[50]

What triggered Chisholm's remarks was the realization that she was not a panelist at the session chaired by Clay. Instead, she had agreed to chair a session on childhood education that was being held at the same time. But in her defense, Chisholm had not known about the political panel. She felt that she had been misled into chairing the session on education as a way to minimize her candidacy for president. "I am a childhood education person and I will chair my panel, but in God's name I just can't understand how you can bring Black elected officials from all over this nation today, talking about the political strategies for 1972 and about the new kinds of emerging powers," and leave her off the panel. Here is how Chisholm recalled the event in her autobiography, *The Good Fight*: "Representative Louis Stokes was chairman of the arrangements, and the way the meeting was organized left me convinced that he, Representative William Clay of Missouri and other Caucus members were out to do what they could to play down my candidacy. The point of the meeting was to bring the growing number of Black officials, local, state, and federal, together to talk about common problems and goals; it was not to work out a strategy for the Presidential election. But, naturally, everybody was talking about Presidential politics, and the fact was inescapable that I was the only Black candidate moving at the time. The Caucus asked its members to choose what workshops they would like to take part in during the meeting and I, because of my background as an educator asked to be included in a workshop on early childhood education. When the meeting got under way, it developed that there was also a workshop on national politics, and that I had not been included in the panel. It seemed clear to me that there had been a subtle but unmistakable attempt to keep me out of the limelight and that there was no possibility that I would ever gain the unified backing of the Caucus."[51]

The omission of Chisholm from the panel was not a mistake. Congressmen Stokes and Clay were deliberately attempting to stifle her presidential aspirations by having her chair another session at the same time. The threat of Chisholm's supporters presenting her name at the conference as the candidate whom the black community should support was too big of a risk for many of her colleagues in the CBC. They knew she couldn't win, and they did not want to be caught on record not supporting another African American for the presidency. Although Chisholm did not wish to be held accountable during the season-long strategy sessions, her appearance at the conference was a last-ditch effort to win the support of her reluctant colleagues.

The next day the headline in the *New York Times* read: "Mrs. Chisholm Chides Black Caucus," and it went on to air publicly the dispute between Chisholm and her male colleagues. But Clay, Stokes, and many of their colleagues did not buy Chisholm's act. They thought it was political grandstanding in an effort to gather support for her fledgling campaign. "The vituperative outburst at the conference was vintage Shirley Chisholm. She was fully aware already two months prior that the session that I (Clay) moderated would be held. She knew for weeks that she was not scheduled to participate on the panel and chose not to make it an issue. Representative Stokes had written a memo to all CBC members announcing in detail the nature of each workshop and asking them to state their preferences. But rather than offer her critique then, she waited until the seminar was in process, under the beaming lights of television cameras and the sharpened pencils of nationally syndicated scribes, to charge that a plot had been concocted to deny her a platform for her presidential campaign."[52]

Many in attendance thought the outrage by Chisholm was planned because many reporters had seen her huddled up with Gwendolyn Cherry prior to the panel. Asked later about the incident, Cherry did not apologize and put it into a broader context of Chisholm's presidential campaign. "They were standing around peeing on their shoes, so Shirley finally said the hell with it and got a campaign going. If she hadn't we'd still be without a Black candidate." Julian Bond responded with disdain toward Chisholm's criticism of him and his colleagues. "She was absent from most discussions on strategy. We may have been peeing on our shoes, but if we were, she wasn't around to get splashed."[53]

Looking back at that period in her autobiography, Chisholm stated that she didn't immerse herself in the strategy sessions for two main reasons. First, she did not want to be a distraction. "Had I gone to any of them (meetings), I would have been the focus for all of the frustrations that they resulted in. I would have been the scapegoat for their inability to agree on a program." Second, she really didn't want her name to emerge as the chosen "black" candidate because her appeal was broader than just to black people. "I would have been locked into a false and limiting role. My potential support went far beyond the Black community. I was far and away the strongest Black candidate, because I was not solely a Black candidate." If her contemporaries would have acknowledged this and supported her, she was confident that she would've received over 85 percent of the black vote. "But that was a fantasy then and later. They would never get behind me. Behind a woman? Unthinkable!"[54]

The Caucus's refusal to support Chisholm may have partly been motivated by her gender, but they had concrete reasons not to support her candidacy. First, Chisholm was not strongly in favor of creating the Congressional Black Caucus and she rarely supported its programs. Second, Chisholm was difficult to work with. One CBC member described her as "self-centered, opportunistic, indifferent, and aloof—lacking in leadership qualities." Congressman Clay acknowledged that all elected officials, black or white, have "unusually large egos," but their disagreement with Chisholm was a matter of politics and not male chauvinism. After her public outburst at the conference, Chisholm lost virtually any black support she had, and her campaign for the presidency would be an exercise in symbolic politics.[55]

But the Chisholm controversy made it clear that the CBC was in trouble. The strategy sessions were now in shambles, and the idea of a black political strategy for 1972 was shrinking fast. This public debate allowed Baraka to once again push the idea of a black political convention, a gathering that the CBC wanted to avoid at all costs. During the panel session Baraka reiterated a point he had made at the Black Elected Officials meeting weeks earlier: if the Caucus did not call for a convention, then the black nationalists would call their own convention without them. "From early in '71 we had put forward the idea of the convention, and had generally met resistance or disregard. Some nationalists and Pan-Africanists rejected the idea because they felt that, in such a diverse setting, no real work could get done, the various contradictory ideologies finally almost neutralizing each other." But Baraka noticed after the Chisholm affair that the idea of a convention seemed like a good solution for the CBC, which was now trapped. "All that evening various speakers had challenged each other, actually challenging the conveners of the conference to set some outline for a Black strategy in 1972. After the Chisholm exchange the question of Black strategy was raised again. And we raised, again, the issue of a Black convention. Why not? What else had been settled? What other plan had been arrived at? It was generally agreed that none had." After the panel discussion Baraka, Hatcher, Diggs, Jesse Jackson, and the entire Congressional Black Caucus met privately to discuss the next steps. In that meeting Baraka stressed the idea of creating an "African People's Party," with the idea of running black candidates for every office where there was a sizeable black majority. This proposal did not sit well with members of the Caucus, but they did go along with the idea for a convention, which satisfied the more radically elected officials at the conference. Before deciding on a convention, Diggs appointed a committee to look at all of the options on the table. It included several Caucus members but also James Gibson of the Potomac Institute in Washington; Antonio Harrison of the National League of Cities/National Conference of Mayors; and Howard T. Robinson, executive director of the Black Caucus staff. Baraka convinced them to hold a convention, and they would make the announcement at the conference dinner that evening.[56]

Historian Lerone Bennett's keynote address at the conference dinner was titled, "A Black Agenda for the Seventies." Bennett opened by stating that a black agenda for 1972 was paramount. "We can no longer avoid the challenge of creating and disseminating a common Black agenda. It is imperative, it is a matter of life and death, for us to develop a series of comprehensive plans identifying the Black interest and Black position in every field." He then went on to mention that there were "at least five items" on the black agenda of the seventies: survival; empowerment; black renewal; "a massive mobilization of all the resources of the Black community"; and "the transformation of the institutions of American society." Bennett went on to echo the idea that what was needed was for black politicians and black people to work within the system to bring about change and to forgo all else. "By this I mean a strategy of working inside institutions with the express purpose of pushing them leftwards and backwards. In general terms this means using the legitimacy of the system to de-legitimize the system."[57]

The Call for a Convention

After Bennett's keynote, Congressman Diggs made the call for a convention: "For 300 years Black people have been the victims and pawns of the American political process. The political representatives of the Black community, meeting in Washington, D.C., in November 1971, have concluded that we still wear the shackles of political bondage. Tonight, the Congressional Black Caucus issues a call to the Black people of the United States for a national political convention to be held in April or early May of 1972, for the purpose of developing a national Black agenda and the crystallization of a national Black strategy for the 1972 elections and beyond." The press release also mentioned that the CBC would call for regional meetings in the Northeast, the South, and the Midwest and on the West Coast, "to bring together representatives of local jurisdictions who would enlarge the basis for involvement in developing the national convention and its programs." He also mentioned that the convention would crystallize strategies for "maximum practical unity in the national participation of Blacks in the Democratic and Republican conventions in local, state, and national elections." Then the release spoke to how the convention would have every ideology of the black community represented. "The deliberations and planning which would design and ratify a unified program must be opened to all Black people, regardless of party affiliation or ideology, to reflect the full diversity of interests among the nation's 25 million Blacks."[58]

It was not an easy decision to call for a convention because some CBC members did not want to get linked up with Baraka and his people. Julian Bond sent Baraka a letter asking why he (Bond) should be put in a position of having to be held responsible for some views that he might not agree with. Further, some black elected officials felt like many of the so-called activists did not have to answer to a particular constituency. Baraka had a good response to this line of thinking: "And this answer is always given by Black elected officials—that they have constituencies to be responsive and responsible to, whereas nationalists, activists, other radicals, 'have no constituencies,' therefore they can feel freer in taking way-out positions." Baraka questioned the degree and extent to which "the average Black elected official is totally responsive to his constituency. In most instances, Black elected officials who make statements like this . . . make these copouts because they are afraid of some national white backlash and the tarnishing of their image in white folks' eyes." Despite the Caucus's calling for a convention, Baraka believed that Louis Stokes and Bill Clay never felt comfortable with the idea. In fact, he believed that the CBC tried to sabotage the entire endeavor. To his credit, Clay recalls that the Caucus did spend a great deal of time discussing the feasibility of a national black political convention. In his words, it was a "bold move" for the Caucus to lend its name and credibility to the idea.[59]

3

WE ARE DEVELOPING A BLACK POLITICAL STRUCTURE

Making the National Black Political Convention a Reality

On January 30, 1972, Congressman Diggs announced that the "first Black political convention" would be held March 10–12 in Gary, Indiana. Diggs went on to say that the Convention organizers expected to seek 4,000 delegates who would "identify and ratify a national Black political agenda for 1972 and beyond." The convention would be chaired by three people: Diggs, Richard Hatcher, and Amiri Baraka. This three-headed form of leadership was strategic. Hatcher recalled that meeting: "And the decision was made that there ought to be three conveners. Congressman Diggs was at that time a very prominent member of Congress and he was a logical person to select, if you were talking about an elected official at the federal level. Amiri Baraka was clearly at that time the leader of the nationalist movement in this country although Maulana Karenga was also very prominent." Hatcher was not initially clear why he was selected as one of the conveners. "Aside from the fact that the decision was made to hold the meeting in Gary, I'm not quite sure why I was selected as sort of a third of the in-between person, other than, this feeling that I was quite comfortable talking to both sides, and relating to both sides."[1]

Hatcher was selected because of his strong civil rights credentials, his commitment to Black Power, and his 1967 mayoral election, which represented a black political takeover. Unlike Carl Stokes, who won election in Cleveland with the support of the white Democratic machine, Hatcher challenged the machine and won by capturing over 96 percent of the black vote in the general election. Born in 1933 in Michigan City, Indiana, Hatcher was one of thirteen children of two hard-working parents. Upon graduating from Indiana University he earned a law degree from Valparaiso before moving to Gary to open a law practice. There, Hatcher got involved in local freedom struggles, as he used his legal training to attack police brutality and school segregation. He further raised his profile among Gary's black residents as chair of Gary's NAACP Youth Council and as founder of Muigwithania, Swahili for "We are Together," an organization of young black professionals who were dedicated to black liberation. He entered local politics as a city councilman in 1963, and in 1967 he ran for mayor and won. At his inauguration, the 34-year-old Hatcher promised to bring about a "healthy, vital Black nationalism."[2]

Although upon reflection it appears that Hatcher, Diggs, and Baraka were good friends, they actually did not really know each other. "There was some distress," Hatcher recalled. "The three of us did not know each other very well. But, in the process we got to know each other very well. And I think we got to like each other quite a lot. We understood each other better and I think particularly between Congressman Diggs and Amiri Baraka, I think they came much closer together."[3]

Throughout 1971–1972 there was a schism between black nationalists and black elected officials, and Hatcher represented a bridge between the two. Hatcher recalled the schism: "There was a tremendous amount of distress between the nationalists and the elected officials, Black officials, and people who operated in the electoral arena and in the civil rights arena. The leadership of the civil rights community saw many of these nationalists almost as anarchists, and as people who were interested in 'Burn, Baby, Burn,' rather than 'Build, Baby, Build.' And so, there was this kind of division, this schism, within the Black community. And one of the reasons that I found myself in meetings with nationalists and with others was that I, I saw the damage that this, and other people saw it too, the kind of damage that this division was doing to the whole movement, to the whole effort to improve the lot of Black people in this country."[4]

The newly created coalition was a gamble for both the elected officials and the nationalists. For the black elected officials the gamble was easy to see. Many of them believed in changing the system from the inside, and now they were linking up with those who had no faith that the system would change. The gamble for black nationalists was whether, by linking up with the CBC, they were suggesting that the system could be transformed. Or were they thinking that they could transform conservative black elected officials into race-conscious liberators? The reality is that black nationalists needed the credibility of the CBC more than the CBC needed them. Yes, Baraka and the Congress of African Peoples could've continued holding their meetings and gatherings where they discussed solutions. But those events would've been just that, events. With the credibility of the CBC, Baraka and CAP were also able to speak to a much wider audience. Although people sympathized with the nationalists, the majority of black folks believed that the system worked, and that black elected officials would make the system work for them.[5]

In a closed-door meeting on January 30, 1972, with approximately seventy-five black leaders in attendance, there was a considerable debate about the time and place of the Convention. Gary was indeed an odd place for a convention. It was a medium-sized city, not home to a major airport, and it did not have a major convention center or adequate hotel space. Despite its shortcomings, Gary was chosen because of what it represented: black political empowerment. At his weekly news conference Richard Hatcher announced Gary as the host. "We are pleased and honored and proud that Gary has been considered the site for the most historic meeting of this type in the country." He then explained why Gary was chosen: "The request came through the Black Caucus body. I believe the basic reasoning on the part of those who made that decision was that Gary, in a sense, does represent and is symbolic of what organized Black political involvement can accomplish. And for that reason, it was felt that Gary would be an excellent site, the jumping off point, for what is of course being attempted nationally. And that is simply, for Blacks to have their fair share of the pie."[6]

Plus, there were practical reasons to come to Gary. It had a black mayor, black police, and a black infrastructure. "We should do it at a place where Black people from all over the country could come and feel comfortable. Wouldn't have to worry about the police beating them. Wouldn't have to worry about getting cooperation from city officials. And also the fact that Gary was located geographically pretty much in the center of the country," Hatcher recalled. But Gary had only "one viable hotel" with just three hundred rooms, and that concerned many of the planners. Where would the people sleep? "But the decision was made that the positives outweighed the negatives, and then of course once we knew that there was interest in coming to Gary, city officials and civic leaders in Gary assumed the leadership of the planning committee that would do whatever was necessary to accommodate this meeting."[7]

When the Caucus approached Hatcher, he not only pledged his support for having the Convention in his city, but he also pledged the support of his office toward making the Convention successful. Hatcher told them the only two places in Gary that could accommodate a large gathering: West Side High School gymnasium and the assembly hall at Gary Career High School. No, this meeting would not be held in the Hilton, Marriott, or Waldorf Astoria; rather, it would be held amongst the masses in a black city where everyone from members of Congress to street gang members from Chicago would feel welcome. The setting of the Convention sent a strong message that this was a grassroots effort designed to meet the needs of the black masses and not the needs of the black elite. The Convention would be accessible and practical, and it would have the feel of a family reunion.

While some understood the selection of Gary as the Convention site, there was much debate about when to hold the Convention. Some argued that they needed at least five to six months to plan a successful convention just from a logistical perspective. However, the New York delegation at the meeting argued vociferously for a March date so that they could take maximum advantage of the Democratic primary convention and delegate selection. They decided on March. This gave them six weeks to plan the National Black Political Convention. This would be a herculean task.[8]

The Baraka Formula for Delegate Selection

Discussions at the January 30 meeting also centered on the matter of who would attend the Convention and how delegates would be selected. The organizers wanted the Convention to mirror the Democratic and Republican Conventions: complete with delegates, a platform committee, state caucuses, resolutions, and so forth. On the matter of selecting delegates, a number of suggestions were made: (1) naming all black elected officials as delegates; (2) forming a bonus delegation based upon black elected officials by state; (3) making a selection of delegates based upon black populations in states or cities; and (4) selecting a representative number of delegates from national black organizations. After much debate, Congressman Walter Fauntroy presented the selection process for delegates as follows:

- Each state and the District of Columbia would have a minimum of five delegate votes.
- There would be a 2,000 vote spread over the entire United States based on proportional black representation reflecting the number of black people living in each state.
- Each black elected official from each state would be an automatic delegate.
- One hundred fifty votes would be equally divided among the following "recognized" national black organizations: Congress of African People; NAACP; CORE; National Welfare Rights Organization; SCLC; and Operation PUSH (People United to Save Humanity).

Based upon the above formula, New York would have the largest delegation, with 339 delegates; Michigan, 311; Illinois, 235; California, 224; Alabama, 217; and Ohio, 201. The Black Belt would be well represented: Mississippi, 191 delegates; Louisiana, 175; Texas, 173; and Arkansas, 153. Some of the states with smaller black populations had significantly less representation, such as Montana and Idaho with five delegates each.[9]

The delegation formula was significant for several reasons: first, there was a genuine desire to have every black voice represented at the Convention. Second, the organizers wanted to ensure that the Deep South was well represented since so much of the energy for the Convention came from black folks in the Northeast and the Midwest. And third, they wanted to make sure that black nationalists and other perceived black radical organizations had a seat at the table. Quite simply this would be one of the most inclusive political gatherings ever. The organizers were brilliant in that they knew they needed to be intentional about creating space at the Convention for black nationalists, activists, and community leaders.[10]

In addition to creating a delegate selection formula. those gathered also selected committee chairs. Jesse Jackson was named chair of the National Support Committee, while *Ebony*'s Lerone Bennett and Vincent Harding from the Institute of the Black World were put in charge of drafting the agenda. Ed Sylvester of Washington, DC, was named chair of the Rules Committee and would be responsible for the rules and procedures used on the floor of the Convention. Congressmen Walter Fauntroy was named chair of the Platform Committee, which would determine the all-important content of the National Black Political Agenda. In charge of the Credentials Committee was George Brown of Colorado. The constitution of the NBPC stated that this committee chair "develops a process in which challengers from states can resolve their differences with state delegations in order to obtain a single delegation from every state." Al Boutte of Chicago and Dr. Frank Lloyd of Indianapolis were in charge of the Finance Committee. Its work was a critical undertaking. Despite calling a conference, neither the CBC nor the other organizers had any money to host a conference.[11]

Jesse Bell, the comptroller of Gary, agreed to make all of the physical arrangements for the Convention. Mayor Hatcher put Bell in charge of this massive undertaking. In fact, the National Black Political Convention's mailing address was City Hall, 401 Broadway, Gary, Indiana. Bell would be assisted by some of Baraka's CAP staff in Newark and others in Washington, DC. California's Mervyn Dymally was named convener of the regional and state chairpersons "in order to assume maximum state and regional activity before the Convention." In a strange move, Julian Bond was put in charge of "Press Relations," and Barbara Jordan was announced as chair of the Resolutions Committee. A National Support Committee was formed shortly after this meeting in an effort to enlist the best of black America behind the Convention effort. Just weeks after the meeting the following individuals agreed to be on the National Support Committee. Their names would be placed on the Convention letterhead and stationery. The list reads like a who's who of black America:

Ralph Abernathy	Jesse Jackson	Carl Stokes
Harry Belafonte	Vernon Jordan	Leon Sullivan
Tom Bradley	Coretta Scott King	Percy Sutton
Yvonne Braithwaite	John Lewis	C. Delores Tucker
Howard Fuller	Betty Shabazz	Coleman Young

Despite its revolutionary overtures the structure of the NBPC mirrored that of the Democratic and Republican Party Conventions. The different committees, the delegate formula, voting by state, etc., were exactly the same. Moreover, Robert's Rules of Order and other formalities would set the NBPC up for problems. Although black nationalists often talked in terms of African consensus, the organizers could not think of a better apparatus that was inclusive of all ideologies. With just five weeks to plan a historic convention the organizers had to move quickly, or else it would be a debacle. Despite the public announcement of the Convention, some of the black elected officials had major concerns about moving forward with an event that they had actually co-opted from Baraka and the nationalists. It was too late to back out now. So, privately some were hoping that the event would either be canceled or would be a disaster. Reflecting on the decision to have the conference, Congressman William Clay recalled that the participation of CBC members was the drawing card. He was not convinced that Baraka could get that many black elected officials to attend without the CBC's involvement.[12]

The State Conventions
Representatives at the meeting were given three important dates for delegate selection. By February 15 the state conveners were to "form a state caucus for the purpose of planning and organizing the state-wide meeting." March 1 was the deadline by which state-wide meetings were to be held. Last, March 3 was the date that each state caucus "shall have selected and certified" their delegates to the Convention. The organizers made it clear that ALL black people were welcome to attend, even black Republicans.[13]

The state conventions were somewhat haphazard. Some states held conventions; others did not. Leaders of the Louisiana delegation, for example, went on radio and television to solicit people to come to the Convention. As expected, New York, with the largest delegation, had a very thorough state convention. State Senator Waldaba Stewart was the state convener, and he made it clear why the state convention was important. "The purpose of these conventions is not just to elect people, but also to develop a program for Black people which will become the basis for our participation in Gary and for our involvement together when we return from Gary." He was confident that the efforts of both the state and national convention would bear fruit. "We are developing a Black political structure, which will deal with the needs of our people unlike any other structure we have known." The state leadership also consisted of Sonny Carson as New York City area coordinator, while Hannibal Ahmed was youth coordinator and H. Carl McCall was in charge of public information.[14]

Black politics in New York was probably more complex than in any other state. With more than 2.4 million black folks in the Empire State, virtually every major political ideology was well represented. How would they work out their ideological differences? How could they agree upon a strategy? Who would compromise? What would be the points of agreement and the non-negotiables? In early February, planning meetings involving elected public officials, community representatives, youth and seniors, and males and females started gathering input on what the New York delegation would look like. This was intense work. Some days, the state leadership would travel to all five of the New York City boroughs in an effort to make sure all voices were heard before they announced the structure and date of the state convention. One particular meeting in Brooklyn started at 5:00 p.m. and was not over until 12:30 a.m. Much of the debate at the meeting centered around the question of nationalists vs. non-nationalists. After hours of debate in which the participants attempted to define the loosely defined terms, they passed a resolution stating that the delegation would be equally divided between black nationalists and non-nationalists.[15]

February 28 was the date of the New York convention, and all interested parties could vote at locations in Brooklyn, Bronx, Manhattan, Queens, Staten Island, Nassau, and Suffolk County. At a news conference prior to the February 28 vote, Stewart was adamant about the importance of the state convention to the Gary process. As the largest delegation in the Convention, it was essential that the New York delegation have a great turnout for the vote. The news conference was attended by a mixture of both black nationalists and black moderates, including Sonny Carson, chairman of the New York Congress of African People, who also had a considerable following. Roy Innis, who would later find himself in the middle of controversy at Gary, predicted that the Convention would be a turning point. "For the first time Black people stand a chance to convene for a common cause. Regardless of what comes out of the convention it will be the greatest contribution of Black people since we've been in the country." Innis was exaggerating because he, along with Stewart, wanted to ensure a huge turnout. A weak turnout for the New York delegation would be an ominous sign for the upcoming Gary Convention. "No longer will we allow brokers of the power structure—Black or white, Democrat or Republican, to sell Black people down the river for money or interests." When discussing the potential platform for the New York delegation, Stewart stated that the first order of the Convention was to "find out the things that bind Black people together." The issue of black unity would plague the Convention from its inception. Black New York was divided into countless ideological camps, precisely because the city was home to many people who had their own ideas about the key to black liberation. It was for this reason that the New York delegation decided to divide delegates into two camps: black nationalists and non-nationalists.[16]

Over 5,000 New Yorkers voted to select the 167 delegates that would represent New York City as part of the New York State delegation in Gary. That evening approximately 3,000 people voted in Brooklyn; 1,000 in Manhattan; and another 1,000 across the NYC area. Bryant Rollins of the *New York Amsterdam News* described the large Brooklyn gathering as "discord and a balloting process that required two days to tally." Similarly, the Manhattan meeting was "wildly confused and rancorous," with the counting of the ballots going on until 7:00 a.m. the next day. While some considered the meetings in NYC progressive because of the decision to divide the camp into nationalist vs. non-nationalist, others felt that ideological divisions would be a detriment to the overall goal of black political unity. State Convener Waldaba Stewart stated that the "dual status" was necessary because the traditional black leadership class had historically left out the Nationalists. He then mentioned that "this would not be the case when we got to Gary. We are going to Gary as a unified group of Black people seeking the same purpose, a solid Black political base on a national level." Still, others felt that the use of labels signaled nothing more than the "too damn long division of Black people." While the New York delegation appeared to be committed to the ideological division, the leadership of the delegation was overwhelmingly represented by members of the traditional black leadership class.[17]

Others believed that despite the Convention's desire to be inclusive, the entire idea was a charade. One attendee who voted was open about his suspicions: "These dudes ain't gonna do nothing but sell us out to the Democratic Party . . . that's what this is about." When one looks at the final New York delegation it was populated by very few black nationalists. The decision to divide the delegation into nationalists vs. non-nationalists gave previously excluded groups a voice at the table, yet the traditional leaders were still in charge, with the exception of avowed nationalist Sonny Carson, whose title was "New York City Area Co-Coordinator." In an effort to unify the New York delegation, Bryant Rollins gave the delegation a strict mandate: "Adopt and carry to Gary a resolution calling for the formation of a national Black Political Party." This was based upon the history of American politics. "It is time to dispense," he said, "with the fantasy that the Democratic or Republican Parties are willing or able to seriously and consistently deal with the critical survival issues that affect Black communities."[18]

If the New York delegation and subsequent convening was marked by the nationalist vs. non-nationalist divide, then the Cleveland delegation was marked by unity, cohesion, and consensus. Led by brothers Carl and Louis Stokes, the Stokes machine ran the Cleveland delegation, and it was a model of efficiency. As expected, the Ohio delegation was dominated by Clevelanders, the majority of whom were political players in the Stokes machine, the Twenty-First District Democratic Caucus. Congressman Stokes controlled the Ohio delegation such that he set the tone, tenor, mood, and platform of the state delegation. In what appears to have been a shrewd attempt at outlining the parameters for the state's platform, the Ohio delegation would use their state convention "updating, localizing, and expanding the recommendations made by the Congressional Black Caucus to President Nixon in 1971." Considering the range of issues, topics, and political ideologies across the state, this was puzzling. In a letter sent to potential delegates Stokes included a copy of the CBC resolutions that were sent to Nixon. The delegation met for consecutive days in late February. One of the meetings was led by "consultants" who met to plan for revisions to the document, and an initial planning meeting the next day set the stage for the state convention on March 4. The Ohio delegation was basically the Cleveland delegation and vice versa. Meeting at the historic Olivet Institutional Baptist Church on Cleveland's black East Side just a week before the Gary Convention, the Ohio delegates devoted themselves to updating the CBC recommendations. This was done to prevent any radical proposals or measures, such as the possibility of an all-black political party, from forming. By determining the rules of the game, Louis Stokes could determine the winner.[19]

The seven original recommendations to the CBC dealt with the following topics: manpower development and employment, health and welfare, minority economic development, education, housing, the drug crisis, the judicial system, civil rights, foreign affairs, the armed services, and foreign affairs. Some of the additional recommendations were as follows:

- Insuring that the appointed heads of the Departments of Labor, Justice, and Health, Education, and Welfare be approved by the Black Caucus
- Universal health care for all Americans
- Increased representation of welfare recipients on all policymaking boards, with respect to welfare reform
- The creation of a national development corporation with $5 billion capitalization for new and existing institutions and businesses geared to black economic development; assist black farmers in forming co-ops
- Open admissions at all public colleges and universities
- The dispersal of section 8 housing to suburban areas
- The penalty for drug usage "be treatment, not penalization as a felony since it is an illness which society has created by not attacking the problem of drug abuse in minority groups"
- Vigorous recruitment of blacks for law schools
- "The procedure for administrative discharge be re-evaluated and revised to suit the needs of Black servicemen; the threat of court martial and possible imprisonment is used to persuade them to accept such a discharge"

- That immigration quotas for African or third world countries
  should be established on parity with European nations

The proposed amendments to the CBC list of recommendations were
logical, expected, and not necessarily radical. They fit the mood and tem-
per of elected black officials who wanted to reform the system but in no
way overturn it.[20]

In addition to selecting the official Ohio delegation, the state convention had vigorous debates over whether or not it would endorse a
presidential candidate. Predictably, the Ohio delegation followed the
opinion of Carl Stokes, who had made it clear back in the fall of 1971 that
to endorse a candidate at Gary would be political suicide. They agreed
that they would not endorse a candidate because it would be "inimical
to the historic meeting in arriving at a common accord on the problems
from which all Americans suffered." The Ohio delegation believed that
the "development of the Black agenda is its sole purpose for attending
the National Black Political Convention."[21]

Carl Stokes was adamant that the National Black Political Convention not endorse a presidential candidate. In a letter to Hatcher, Diggs,
and Baraka, Stokes wrote that the Gary gathering "should not leave itself exposed to the ill-disguised efforts of a few persons to exploit this
great gathering for the purpose of their particular candidate." Stokes felt
strongly that the endorsement of a candidate "would render meaningless
all the magnificent work which has gone into developing a National Black
Agenda—to which all presidential candidates should have to respond."
In the eyes of the former mayor, an endorsement would reduce the Convention "to divisive bitterness and destroy chances of a solid front in the
1972 general election." Stokes was right. As the Convention approached,
there were camps of supporters promoting the declared candidacy of
Shirley Chisholm, who stood zero chance of winning the Democratic
nomination. If they weren't careful, Stokes thought, then the Convention
could potentially turn into a rally for Chisholm. "I'm concerned that a
lot of people will be there who are committed to candidates and causes
that won't permit them to go along with the recommendations of the full
body. And I am going to ask those people to stand, identify themselves,
and indicate whether or not they intend to do so."[22]

While New York and Ohio represented two examples of state delegation politics, there were others that had their own unique culture as well. The Mississippi delegation focused its attention on the "failing state economy and land reform," and they wanted the NBPC to support the Republic of New Afrika and other political prisoners." As expected, some of the Midwest delegations had ideological splits such as in Illinois, but they were able to reconcile their differences before the Convention. Half of South Carolina's delegation consisted of college students. Similarly, in the nation's capital, students from Howard University attended the state convention en masse and were able to secure a majority of the delegate seats. After bearing the brunt of criticism from their elders, they agreed to relinquish some seats to others. The DC delegation was also unique in that the leadership of their delegation consisted of local political rivals. Walter Fauntroy, who was the DC representative in Congress, chaired the delegation, along with his political rival, Rev. Douglas B. Moore, head of the local Black United Front. The DC contingent had a meeting in February attended by more than 1,000 people. They voted to send 21 delegates to Gary, including "Howard and Federal City College students, federal employees, PTA leaders and welfare recipients, many who have not been active politically before." Rev. Douglas Moore, who ran for Congress from DC in 1971, yet only got 1 percent of the vote, somehow resurrected his political career and was now apparently a major player in the political life of black people living in the District. Moore was ecstatic at the makeup of the delegation from the District, saying, "This slate was put together without any interference from white people." Moore was an outspoken black nationalist who had on more than one occasion called Fauntroy a sellout, and he was eager to see the nationalists carry the day at Gary. "Black nationalists will have a pretty powerful voice. Nationalists will be in just about every delegation and by the time we put all of them together we'll have a powerful delegation. It is our time now." Moore was vocal during the DC meeting, and his comments foreshadowed what would happen in Gary. In fact, the tensions that shaped many of the state conventions—the endorsement of a presidential candidate; forming an all-black political party; and staying within the existing two-party structure vs. withdrawing from the political process altogether—would come to Gary.[23]

California state senator Mervyn Dymally led the California delegation with future San Francisco mayor Willie Brown, and it was a model of efficiency. It was unified, diverse, and organized. California's delegation reflected "youth and effective leadership input." Members of the Western Region of CAP were well represented at the state convention and at smaller meetings held in Long Beach, Sacramento, Los Angeles, and East Palo Alto. Dymally and Brown made certain that all black citizens across the state had access to the convention apparatus. Dymally also invited and welcomed the involvement of college students, although some students looked at the invitation with suspicion. Members of the Black Student Union at San Francisco State University were hesitant to accept the invitation because "in the past students and community people have been used" to further the agenda of the black bourgeoisie. "After the Black bourgeoisie or Black so-called leaders" had achieved their goal, the interests of the community were "shunned aside and we are left right where we started, with nothing." If the goals were sincere, then the students would work with the NBPC "whole heartily." If the goals were only for a small clique of black bourgeoisie, then they would organize "whole heartily against you." Nonetheless, the California delegation was cochaired by Lamar Lyons, the 23-year-old black student body president at UCLA.[24]

In all, thirty-four states held conventions, including Hawaii, Maine, and Utah. Alabama, New Mexico, South Carolina, and Virginia chose to select delegates by a committee system; Alaska, Idaho, Rhode Island, Vermont, and Wyoming did not hold a convention nor select delegates; Kansas, Nevada, and Oregon "were still trying to decide what to do"; and NBPC organizers had no contact with representatives from Montana, New Hampshire, and North and South Dakota.[25]

On to Gary

With just five days between the end of the last state convention and the opening session in Gary, the organizers and hosts had a ton of ground to cover. Who would pay for the Convention costs? How could they prepare logistically for 8,000–10,000 visitors to a city with very few hotels? Where would people sleep? Where would they eat? Where would the actual Convention be held? How would the Agenda be created? How would the Convention program get printed? All of these logistics were necessary to nail down, and on a shoestring budget, no less. Financing the National Black Political Convention became more of a challenge after the CBC backed off on its commitment to secure funding for the Convention, fearing that they had lost control over the event to Baraka.[26]

Gary seemed to be an odd place for a convention. And with reticent corporate support, Mayor Hatcher and his team would be challenged to pull it off. Hatcher dedicated much of his mayoral staff to the Convention, and Amiri Baraka sent members of CAP to Gary to assist with the planning effort. Since the city did not have meeting space to accommodate the Convention, Gary West Side High School became the de facto Gary convention center. Organizers would use the gym for the plenary sessions, and they would use the classrooms for committee meetings and as meeting space for the state delegations. The bigger question for the Convention organizers, after meeting space had been found, was the housing situation. Where would the delegates, attendees, and journalists sleep?

During the preparation period Hatcher wasn't sure how much support he would get from the Gary business community: "The White business community in Gary had these extreme fears about this large number of Blacks coming to town. They thought in terms of crime and all kinds of horrible things. It was almost as if someone had just announced that the Vietcong was coming to Gary. Their initial reaction was very apprehensive and there were a number of meetings held and they eventually said, 'Well, we'll see what happens.'" Things went surprisingly well. "It ultimately turned out that the white business community as well as the leadership of the Black community in Gary opened up their arms and welcomed the delegates to town."[27]

Convention attendees were given a welcome packet from the black business community which encouraged them to spend their money with black-owned businesses in the area. The Host Committee also planned a slew of recreational activities such as a tour of the city and a card party, probably spades or bid wist, at the YMCA. Attendees were also given a special handout from the *Gary Post-Tribune* titled "What to Know About Gary," and featured in the paper was a story on an emerging singing group from Gary called the Jackson Five.[28]

Armed with the support of the white business community, Hatcher and other Convention organizers could now deal with the utter reality that Gary did not have the hotel capacity to host such a large gathering. Since the Gary area only had six hotels, attendees were forced to stay as far away as Chicago and in rural Portage, Indiana. Although Hatcher was able to secure 2,400 hotel rooms, this was not enough, so he made a plea for local residents to open up their homes to guests, and they did. Visitors were charged $15 a day for a single room and $20 a day for a double room, which included breakfast on the first day of the Convention. In addition to utilizing private homes, the Convention secured dorm space at nearby Indiana University–Northwest and at two boarding schools in the area. "We called upon the citizens of Gary to open their homes to the delegates who were coming to the convention. And they did it with relish. There were just wonderful stories that were told as the delegates lived with Gary families, and over the period of the time of the convention got to be friends, and friendships were established that continue even to this day as a result of the people of Gary opening up their arms and their homes."[29]

Transitioning West Side High School into a convention center would be much more challenging. Since school was in session, organizers could not get access to the gymnasium and classrooms until the school day ended. Students watched construction workers build a platform and "decorate the gym with red, Black, and green—the Black liberation colors." The haphazard nature of the lodging and meeting space was a result of the shoestring budget and the short planning time. Hatcher recalls that if it weren't for CAP members coming to Gary, the Convention would've been a logistical disaster. The impact of Baraka's staff on the Convention was priceless: "They were very hard-working and would work for hours on end, without any relief. But if you watched them back in the rooms at this huge high school where the Convention was held they would work for maybe an hour or two hours. Then they would take a fifteen-minute break, and the break would be to form a circle holding hands, and then they would begin to do chants and sing for about fifteen minutes. And it seemed that the music, the singing, the chants refreshed them, and then they would go back to the typewriters and work for another two hours. It was a pretty incredible sight and most of them wore these long white, full-length gowns and turbans." Baraka's staff had significant experience with the logistics of convention planning since the Congress of African Peoples held both national and regional meetings.[30]

The White Media Controversy

Even before the Convention opened its doors, it found itself in the midst of controversy. The first controversy dealt with the potential exclusion of white media from the Convention proceedings. The overly nationalistic New York City delegation held a news conference before departing for Gary, and a reporter from the *New York Times,* Edward Hudson, was barred from attending the event held at the Harlem YMCA on 125th street. Hudson was apparently handed the following press release: "No Caucasian reporters and/or staff people will be permitted to cover press conferences sponsored by the New York delegation to the Black National Political Convention. Black staff from all media are welcome." Roger Clevending, chairman of the Public Information Committee of the delegation, issued a statement so there would be no confusion as the Convention approached: "All media must in fact, send only Black representatives, reporters, staff and/or technicians to cover the delegation's events. All media must use the term 'Black' in referring to people of African descent who are involved in and with the New York delegation to the Black National Political Convention. There will be no exceptions to this mandate." The *New York Times* followed up with Rev. H. Carl McCall, chair of the editorial board of the black *New York Amsterdam News,* to see if this was indeed the policy. "I would expect anything he says is the official policy of the Steering Committee, McCall replied." Manhattan borough president Percy E. Sutton was shocked when he heard that white reporters would not be allowed to cover their events. "One of the purposes is to bring attention to the plight of the Black community. I don't think it will be the policy of the national convention." The exclusion of white journalists from the New York delegation's events made sense. The delegates understood that the white press had rarely covered black community events in a way that was fair, objective, and empowering. It was often the opposite: slanted, distorted, and presented in a way to make the black community appear dysfunctional. The second reason for the exclusion is that the New York delegation wanted to highlight the lack of black journalists at major media outlets. As expected, A. M. Rosenthal, managing editor of the *New York Times*, responded. "The *New York Times* will not assign reporters to the New York State Delegations to the Black National Political Convention as long as these conditions exist. The *Times* does not accept imposed racial restrictions on news coverage."[31]

The next day Baraka stated that Convention press credentials would be determined by the Convention's public relations staff and that they would not "discriminate against legitimate members of the press." The Convention was in a quandary. While it publicly proclaimed the white press was welcomed, Baraka and the nationalists were thinking of ways to exclude them. Baraka understood the manipulative practices of the white media, and the nationalists did not want the historic Convention to be distorted in the press. They knew that the white press would tell anything except what actually went on in Gary.[32]

The fears of Baraka and his disciples were confirmed in the days leading up to the Convention, when the press began to highlight stories about leading black political figures who would not be attending the Convention. "Shirley will miss Gary Parley," read one headline in the *Chicago Tribune*. Written in a tone to suggest that the Convention must not be that important if Chisholm didn't attend, the article referred to her decision not to come as "an unexpected setback for the convention." When asked why she wouldn't attend, Chisholm gave the excuse that she needed to campaign. "I am going after delegates, not endorsements, and time is short. My commitment to be in Florida March 9th through 14th was made long ago, and I don't see at this time how I can be in Gary."[33]

The real reason she did not plan to come was that her candidacy had very little support among black politicos. To come to Gary and not get endorsed would have been the ultimate rejection of her campaign. Similarly, the *Gary Post-Tribune* ran an article letting its readers know that Georgia state representative Julian Bond probably "would not make it to the Black National Political Convention until its last day." But unlike Chisholm, Bond had a strong reason to come late: the National Black Political Convention was being held on the same weekend that the Georgia Democrats were meeting to select their delegates to the Democratic National Convention in Miami.[34]

Comparatively, the black press, which was optimistic about the gathering, questioned what involvement civil rights groups such as the NAACP and National Urban League would have in Gary. In an effort to be inclusive, the NBPC allotted 150 delegate seats to the NAACP, SCLC, CORE, Urban League, and Jesse Jackson's Operation Push. The NAACP, which was never on board with the idea of the NBPC, confirmed that they were sending fifteen delegates, but they quickly made a disclaimer: "They understand that they are not to commit the NAACP to any position, nor endorsement of any kind," said Roy Wilkins, NAACP executive director. Wilkins, who wanted no part of any coalition with black nationalists, was conveniently out of the country and not scheduled to return until after the Convention. In his place, John Morsell, assistant executive director of the NAACP, would keep a close eye on the Gary proceedings and a close eye on the NAACP delegation. "Our policies are set by our annual convention. But we are certainly interested in making whatever kind of contribution we can to the [Gary] Convention." Vernon Jordan, director of the National Urban League, stated that his organization's tax-exempt status prevented them from sending delegates because it prohibited active involvement in political activities. However, Jordan stated that he "planned to attend the meeting briefly, although not in an official capacity." Jesse Jackson said that PUSH would have representation, while SCLC's Ralph Abernathy said that his group "will be amply represented at the Convention."[35]

The black press also played up the importance of the event, with numerous articles highlighting the possibilities of black political transformation. One article in the *Chicago Defender* spoke of how the event would be "the most important political convention in the U.S. in 1972." Chicago congressman Ralph Metcalfe believed that the Convention represented "the development of a new political awareness among Black people," while Chicago alderman William Cousins suggested that "for too long we Blacks have been party directed instead of issue directed. Now we're getting ourselves together to work in unity and we are forgetting those party labels."

On the eve of the Convention, Hatcher, Diggs, Baraka, Barbara Jordan, Jesse Jackson, and Walter Fauntroy held a press conference in

Chicago "to secure national attention for what is certainly the most significant gathering of Black people to be held in many years. Perhaps it is the most significant. The political diversity of the conveners has been consciously proposed in order that a similarly diverse and broad based section of the Black National Political Convention be represented at the Convention. The concrete idea of the Convention itself was the result of many meetings held throughout 1971 among much larger versions of the same conveners group all over the country, including Democrats, Republicans, other Black elected officials, Nationalists, Civil Rights organizations, activists, etc."[36]

It continued: "The purpose of the National Black Political Convention is to promote National Black Political Unity and create a Black political agenda and set priorities for the 1972 election year, and begin to establish a political direction for the national Black community, for the year to come. It is the hope of the conveners to transform Black political potential through structure into political power commensurate with our members in America. For this reason the Convention will also seek to crystallize strategies for maximum practical unity in the national participation of Black people in the Democratic and Republican Conventions and in local, state, and national elections this year." If only it were that easy.[37]

With the Convention just days away, organizers got disturbing news that violence might play a role in the Convention. It was reported that the Black P Stone Rangers, a Chicago street gang, planned to kidnap a prominent delegate to hold hostage until the release of jailed P Stone leader Jeff Fort. Diggs was not worried: "They'll have to deal with the Gary Godfathers and they aren't about to let any outsiders mess up their town." The issue of political violence was real. With a large delegation of black nationalists expected to attend, it was not beyond the realm of possibilities to think that West Side High School could be the scene of black-on-black political violence.[38]

With just two days before the start of the Convention, organizers released the Convention schedule. Betty Shabazz and Coretta Scott King were named honorary secretaries of the Convention. The speakers represented the diversity of black political thought: Hatcher, Jackson, Congresswoman Yvonne Braithwaite, and Shirley Chisholm (if she came) would provide keynote addresses, while other speakers included Bobby

Seale, Louis Farrakhan, and others. All of the committee assignments were set. However, Baraka asked Diggs and Hatcher if they would appoint an 18-year-old from New York City who had recently formed an organization to empower young people to the Platform Committee: his name, Al Sharpton. It was also announced that the proceedings would be televised on cable television in New York City, with eighteen hours of live coverage moderated by Clarence B. Jones, editor/publisher of the *New York Amsterdam News.* Teleprompter would be producing the show in conjunction with WTTW, Chicago's public television station, which was broadcasting the event live in Chicago and Gary. Live television coverage of the event suggests that there was a great deal of interest in the Convention, particularly in the Northeast and Midwest, where black viewers had been exposed to black-centered public affairs programming.[39]

As the delegates poured into Gary on Thursday evening, they were given an enthusiastic welcome by the city of Gary. Rev. Benjamin Chavis from Wilmington, North Carolina, vividly remembers the moment. "Well, our preparation to go to Gary, Indiana, was enormous. And of course we sent hundreds of delegates from across the state of North Carolina to Gary. I had never been to Gary before. Some went by bus, some went by car, and some went by plane. We drove up and all the way up we were thinking about what we were going to see when we arrived in Gary. And I remember when we first saw the sign saying 'Welcome to Gary' and we get to downtown Gary, I mean, we thought we were in a different country. I mean to see a city in the United States, given now of all this Nixon repression going on, all this sense of disillusionment in some quarters of the nation, to drive to Gary, Indiana, and see streams, red, Black and green, and 'Welcome, Black National Political Convention,' and then we found our way to city hall. And the city hall was decorated with red, Black, and green banners. It was a fulfillment of what a lot of our dreams were. And we knew that the Gary Convention was time limited. But it was important to have that time to come into a city and that place. It made us feel good. It made us see visibly with our eyes that the struggle had not been in vain. That at least in one municipality, there had been some control to the extent to which a National Black Convention could be welcomed. But not only just welcomed. And affirmed the cause of the struggle into the welcome. I think that was very important."[40]

4

THE MONUMENTAL TASK OF DRAFTING AN AGENDA WE ALL CAN AGREE UPON

Black Politics at the Crossroads

The Convention opened quietly on Friday afternoon with a press conference held by Hatcher, Diggs, and Baraka. The bulk of Friday's time was spent in state caucuses as they began to think about what specific agenda items they wanted the Convention to adopt. As mayor of Gary, Hatcher had some city business to take care of on the opening day of the Convention. As he was out that morning, Hatcher had two major thoughts in his head: would he make it across town to West Side High School in time for the opening of the Convention; and would people even show up for the event. They did. At the press conference the leadership trio was joined at the podium by Jesse Jackson, who would use the Convention to steal the spotlight in hopes of setting himself up as the leader of black America. All four men were dressed in garb appropriate to their constituency: Diggs in a conservative suit as representative of the Congressional Black Caucus; Hatcher in an expensive tailor-made suit exemplifying the new generation of young, educated, urban mayors, controlling majority-black cities; Baraka in his dashiki representing black nationalists; and Jesse Jackson dressed like Superfly—wide collar shirt, vest, with a large medallion engraved with the image of Martin Luther King Jr. hanging from his neck.[1]

At the press conference scores of media heard the conveners talk about the importance of Gary and what they hoped to accomplish. Diggs, the elder statesman, likened the Convention to the founding of the Democratic and Republican parties and the founding of the NAACP. To confirm the importance of the NBPC, Diggs told the media that the Nixon administration asked if it could have representation in Gary. This request affirmed in his mind the importance of the NBPC to white politicians. "I don't think there is any question about the recognition of the Convention. The major political forces and personalities have already provided ample evidence that from the White House to various statehouses and courthouses around the country they are fully cognizant of the implications of the movement, are nervous about it and obviously see this is a new criteria for approval in the political arena." He continued, "there is no question in my mind that this reflects the attitude of the Democratic and Republican parties, because in the last two or three days certain people have indicated that they want in—they want recognition here. Nobody of any significance wants to be excluded." In fact, the Nixon administration's black appointees and other black Republicans were well represented in Gary. Art Fletcher, "the father of affirmative action," headed the Washington State delegation; Samuel Jackson, assistant secretary of HUD, chaired the Platform Committee; and Assistant Secretary of HEW Edward Sylvester was in charge of the Rules Committee. Their presence and active involvement was an indication of Nixon's interest in the proceedings. Additionally, members of the newly created National Council of Concerned Afro-Republicans were active throughout the weekend on the Convention floor.[2]

Mayor Hatcher told the press that Gary was about leveraging black political strength. "We recognize as Black politicians that in terms of our numbers, we have not been compensated or reimbursed in any measure commensurate with our contribution. We are here in Gary to say that this is over." Echoing Hatcher but with a bit more militancy was Baraka, the organizer of the event. He didn't try to be conciliatory or diplomatic; he was straightforward about the goal of the NBPC: the unification of black people. "The delegates will seek the creation of a unified political culture and the transformation of our potential through structure to power. We will be dealing with the shaping of a concrete and specific means of gaining political power for Black people." Although the idea of creating an all-black political party was a strong outcome of the NBPC, Jesse Jackson was the only one at the press conference who mentioned this possibility. "The Convention may very well evolve into a Black political party. But we would not like to restrict ourselves by calling it a force or a party. It will evolve into some form. We are concerned about the success of this particular meeting but we certainly recognize we cannot yet get what we want in a one-shot proposition. This is certainly not the last time you will hear of the Black political movement." From the press conference it was apparent that Baraka and Jackson would push a nationalist ideology over the weekend; Diggs would be the resident political conservative; and Hatcher would occupy the middle ground.[3]

The most exciting moment of a relatively mundane press conference came when Hatcher was asked if members of the white media would be allowed to cover the gathering (although they were at the press conference). Hatcher "looked around and tossed the question to Baraka." Obviously prepared for the question, Baraka stated that it was politically necessary to allow white media access. "Part of the idea of community is there has to be communications. In order to have a movement, you have to have an ideology, organization, communications, and resources. What we're trying to do is reach the maximum of Black people so we can have communications and unity, so we can have community. We must be realistic . . . most of our people will read about this Convention in the white media."[4]

Baraka's response came as a shock to black nationalists. Prior to the Convention they were told the white media would not be allowed to cover the proceedings. But Baraka soon realized that he wasn't chairing a CAP meeting, but a meeting with a broad spectrum of black America. Further, he understood that limiting coverage to black journalists would restrict the broader impact of the Convention if black people could only read about it in the black press. Some die-hard nationalists began to question Baraka's commitment to their ideology, and throughout the Convention what Baraka considered a compromise with black elected officials would be considered selling out by his fellow black nationalists.

On the eve of the Convention, Vincent Harding and Bill Strickland of the Institute of the Black World predicted that Gary would represent a marker for a new black politics. "The hour of potential political Black independence is now: we can no longer afford to place our trust in white-dominated parties, platforms, and policies that have nothing to do with our growth and well-being or even with our minimal human requirements. We cannot stand idly for a white awakening to our demands. Implementation must come through Black leadership."[5]

Arriving in Gary

Across from city hall, thousands of delegates gathered in the lobby of the Holiday Inn, and it was a sight to behold. CBC member Bill Clay of St. Louis called the atmosphere "bazaar-like" in one sense, bizarre in another. "Vendors sold balloons, t-shirts, and Afro combs. Others stood on sidewalks reciting poetry about the struggle for freedom and hawking books about Marcus Garvey and Malcolm X. Caterers with food carts offered such soul food delicacies as pigeon sandwiches, chitterlings, and red beans and rice. Delegates were frocked in assorted dress. Ivy League suits, button-down collar, freedom fighter dungarees, cotton dresses, dashikis, and other elaborate African garb. Colorful boubous of traditional African cloth and smartly wrapped gelees bedecked the ladies and heads of beautiful, stately Black women." Queen Mother Moore, the longtime civil rights activist and nationalist, was hawking her pamphlet on black reparations. "Stop begging. Stop begging. Stop begging for a better house, a better job, a better this and that. Get your reparations. Don't settle for less. Get your share. Take it." At one booth they were selling red, black, and green Convention posters; at another, African books, records, and poetry; and at another table a group of performers solicited donations for the fight against sickle-cell anemia. One observer remarked that in addition to conservative-looking black men, they were outnumbered by "bushes, beads, and beards." Indeed, as the conveners looked at the delegates scattered across the hotel lobby, they knew they had achieved something historic. High school and college students were also highly visible in the Convention lobby, many of whom had been active in campus and community struggles. Student journalists from HBCUs in attendance were angry when they could not get media credentials to cover the event, although white news outlets had them. They were given just one pass to share on a rotating basis, making it hard for them to adequately cover the event.[6]

It would be a monumental task to chart an agenda that the masses could agree upon. An unnamed 72-year-old grandmother from New York City took the train to Gary just to observe. "I just decided I wanted to come and see what the trend is. I really don't think there is going to be a trend because there's going to be too many different opinions." While she believed in nonviolence, she also believed in getting things done

because "the politicians aren't going to do that much. They're more interested in themselves than in the people." Charlotte Shropshire of Omaha,
Nebraska, made the trip to Gary "because it's time to get the Black nation together. We've been down too long and we shall move up from
here." Others attended out of genuine self-interest, such as C. Ronald
McCants, a member of Local 777 Seafarers Union in Chicago. "Many
times when issues come like this Black labor is not represented and that
is why I am here. I feel it is absolutely necessary that those who work
are represented. We want to get rid of the union shop because it has
locked us out of the race." Many of the delegates from Washington, DC,
such as Aurelia Corbett, came to convince other delegates to support
statehood for the District. "I'm here because we want self-determination
in Washington, DC, and we want the support of delegates from all of
the states represented here. We want them to press their congressmen
for our self-determination." Charles Evers, brother of Medgar, told one
reporter that he was there first and foremost to get support for John
Lindsay's presidential bid.[7]

Unbeknownst to those in attendance at the convention was that the
FBI had a significant number of informants in Gary. Virtually every major state delegation had been infiltrated at the deepest level. The NBPC's
FBI file is filled with memos from informants on state meetings and
specific travel information on delegates. The Cairo, Illinois, delegation
had an informant on the train with them to Gary, and even the overly nationalistic New York delegation had an informant on their charter flight
from New York City. Despite the significant presence of informants, it
appears they merely relayed information that was easily accessible to
the general public.[8]

Committee Meetings

The first day of the convention was filled with state caucus meetings,
leadership meetings, and committee meetings. The most important of
these were Credentials, Resolutions, and the all-important Platform
Committee. The Credentials Committee was responsible for using the
Baraka formula to register official delegations; the Resolutions Committee would hold hearings from state caucuses and organizations on
specific items to go into the agenda; and the Platform Committee was

responsible for putting together an agenda that the black community could agree upon despite their deep ideological divisions. Many state caucuses held tense meetings upon arriving in Gary because they simply did not have adequate time to meet prior to the Convention. There were the predictable divisions between nationalists and integrationists; between those who favored an all-black third party and those who did not; between those who wanted to endorse Shirley Chisholm and those who didn't; between those who wanted the Convention to support busing and those who didn't; and between those who objected to Baraka letting white journalists cover the Convention and those who didn't.[9]

In some caucuses tensions ran so high that enforcers, usually nationalist in orientation, "kept a lot of folks from leaving the caucus room until the finer details were worked out." This tactic proved successful because much of the tension within state delegations never reached the Convention floor. There appeared to be a consensus among delegates that their homework should have been done at home before the Convention. In addition to hammering out their ideological differences, the state caucuses also spent a great deal of time on logistics—the things that were not sexy. They had to adopt a draft preamble and rules of formation, tackle the question of how the Convention would proceed, and more importantly, plan for what would happen after the National Black Political Convention. One of the main fissures in many of the caucuses was the demand by nationalist factions that they make up half of the convention's decision-making apparatus, although it was unclear how big or who their constituency was. Black elected officials objected to this by arguing that they themselves were the only ones with a voting constituency.

The battle for chairmanship of the New York delegation provides a telling example. State senator Waldaba Stewart was challenged for his position as chair of the delegation by CORE's Roy Innis, an unpredictable and avowed nationalist. When Innis was defeated by Stewart "he was seen walking in the hallway in suspended animation . . . not wanting to accept his defeat." In fact, Livingston Wingate of the New York Urban League had to separate the factions within his delegation after one delegate threatened another.[10]

Black nationalists were highly visible in Gary with their requisite "honor guards" or security personnel escorting them around the Convention. One reporter took note of this and called it laughable: "Then there was the gesture, the arms-waving, the loud talking, of the various chiefs of states whose honor guards shuttled them up and down the Convention floor to various hallways and caucus rooms."[11]

One thing that integrationists were not prepared for was the issue of busing. In the New York, South Carolina, and Florida state caucuses, nationalists were adamant about making the busing controversy a central factor in the Convention. They were in favor of community control of schools rather than busing black kids across town to schools where they weren't wanted. Two days later the issue of school busing would literally tear the Convention apart.

With just a short time to plan a national Convention, chaos was inevitable, and the Credentials Committee had its hands full trying to register almost 4,000 delegates. The initial problems arose over just who was a delegate. Under the Baraka formula each state had a minimum of five delegates and after that the delegation was based upon the total black population in each state. Additionally, certain black organizations such as the NAACP, CAP, Black Panthers, etc., each had ten delegate slots allotted to them. Some delegates had been elected in elaborate state caucuses, others just showed up and registered. Another concern for the committee was the $25.00 registration fee. This was high for students and elderly delegates, plus the collection of the money was chaotic as well, such that the Convention leadership decided to waive the fee altogether on the second day of the Convention. The Credentials Committee also heard criticism about the entire structure of the NBPC. In particular, nationalists wanted to know who chose Diggs, Hatcher, and Baraka to be in charge? Who picked the committee chairs? Who made committee assignments? Who would be in charge of the NBPC after the Convention? Would nationalists be excluded? The Credentials Committee felt the full brunt of this anger. Students also grew frustrated when they discovered that they had little representation on Convention committees and within state delegations. They felt excluded, and throughout the weekend the NBPC did not provide an outlet for the views of black youth, thus missing an opportunity to transform their experiences into broader social and political action.[12]

The two most important committees at the Convention were Resolutions and Platform. They would play the central role at the Convention. Barbara Jordan of Texas chaired the Resolutions Committee, and throughout Friday's activities they were bombarded with resolutions "reflecting virtually every spectrum of political thought from far left to far right." During the four-hour committee meeting at the Holiday Inn, the Resolutions Committee had to work at a record pace since the deadline for submission was the next morning. The three most controversial resolutions dealt with abortion, busing, and the endorsement of Shirley Chisholm. As chairlady of the Gary Commission on the Status of Women, Yvonne Day created a firestorm in the committee meeting when she submitted a resolution calling for abortion on demand. That triggered an emotional debate when several of the male delegates objected by calling abortion a form of genocide. She responded by arguing that their point of view was a "black male" opinion and that her proposal would be a "woman's choice" in safe and sanitary hospitals.

Proposals were presented both for and against busing. Some delegates argued that busing was not the ideal solution but it was the only way to guarantee educational equity. This was the viewpoint of many black southerners. Black folk from the Midwest and Northeast, however, felt that busing was an educational experiment that used black kids like lab rats. Busing them out of their own community schools to schools in communities across town where they weren't wanted and where they didn't want to be was not a solution to the problem of school segregation. In turn, these delegates advocated community control of schools. In their eyes the solution was not to think that something magical would happen to black kids once they sat next to white kids in school. The solution was a community school in their neighborhood with faculty and staff that knew and loved the students. Equally debated were opposing proposals "one to endorse and another not to endorse" the candidacy of Shirley Chisholm. Percy Sutton and a nationalist faction from New York City were pushing the Chisholm campaign based upon black solidarity more than anything else. With Chisholm's absence from the National Black Political Convention, it would be hard for any of her supporters to generate considerable interest in her campaign at Gary. Other resolutions submitted were:

- Economic, political, and educational empowerment for women
- Boycotting firms doing business in South Africa
- A fixed income of $6,500 per year for a family of four
- Twenty-four-hour day care centers
- Reducing the minimum age to receive Social Security benefits
- A United Nations investigation of US prisons
- Support of an RNA proposal to establish a plebiscite on an 11,000-square-mile piece of land in Mississippi
- Improved health care
- Increased channeling of federal housing funds into inner-city areas
- More high-ranking black officials in the federal government
- Job training programs
- Stronger anti-pollution laws

In addition, the delegations from Cairo, Illinois, and Wilmington, North Carolina, submitted a joint resolution asking the NBPC to endorse armed self-defense. The committee had a lot to digest after a full day of hearings.[13]

It was up to the committee to determine what they would "sort out, distill, agree upon, or toss out." During the committee proceedings there appeared to be a ton of confusion over the difference between the Resolutions Committee and the Platform Committee, the group responsible for putting the Black Agenda together. Delegates didn't know the distinctions between the two committees. To clarify things, the NBPC circulated a memo to delegates, which stated that the Platform Committee was explicitly responsible for developing the Black National Political Agenda, an agenda meant to state "the program this Convention believes to be necessary to create to see fundamental changes in the life of Black and White America which must take place to move us toward Black empowerment, Black self-determination, Black liberation." This agenda would speak to the question of "why such change is necessary and how it can take place." This programmatic emphasis was to be the major role of the Platform Committee's work. Conversely, the Resolutions Committee would deal with "positions and points of views" on issues and events concerning the life and future of black people. Another distinction was that the Platform Committee would focus on national issues, while the Resolutions Committee would take up local and statewide concerns.[14]

The Convention would rise and fall on the work of the Platform Committee. This group would draw up the agenda that the nation's 22 million black folk would follow toward liberation. Chaired by Walter Fauntroy with considerable input from Carl Stokes, the Platform Committee would find itself swamped over the weekend. Working closely with the Platform Committee were a group of intellectuals whose job was to draft and write the actual agenda. Leading these efforts were Vincent Harding and Bill Strickland from the Institute of the Black World (IBW), an independent black think tank located in Atlanta, Georgia.

Established in the aftermath of Martin Luther King's assassination, the IBW was for activist intellectuals who wanted to devote their time to serious analysis of the problems facing black America. Not content to produce esoteric ivory tower research, this group of black scholars saw it as their role to find solutions to these problems. When the leadership of the NBPC approached Harding and Strickland, and the staff of the IBW, about drafting the convention call and a black political agenda, the IBW had a structure in place to make it happen. In 1970 the IBW convened eight groups of ten to fifteen scholars each and charged them with developing programmatic proposals in the areas of education, economic development, political organization, health and welfare, communications, Pan-Africanism, and religion. As Derrick White notes in his book on the IBW, each group was asked to develop a "larger plan of analysis" and programs in these eight areas. While this analysis would be used in a broader framework of public policy and grassroots initiatives, the 1972 elections gave the IBW an opportunity to use these proposals as the foundation of the black political agenda. Within these groups were some of the leading scholars in the African American community.

The IBW used the framework of structural racism when examining issues facing black communities, and they relied heavily upon the collective scholarship of their researchers, many of whom were donating their time and intellectual resources to the IBW. Although the IBW spent a considerable amount of time working to establish black studies programs at the university level, black elected officials soon looked to them as a resource. Newly elected black politicians often called upon the IBW to help them strategize around solving urban problems and meeting concerns.[15]

Strickland and Harding were eager to work with the Convention because they realized that the split between nationalists and black elected
officials hindered black progress. While black elected officials considered
themselves the spokespersons for the black community, since they were
elected by the people in a democratic process, many of their supporters felt that they had compromised their political vision once in office.
Some critics argued that black elected officials used the energy of the
Black Power movement to get elected, only to then seek to silence that
energy upon assuming office. But black nationalists were not completely
innocent. Their narrow, vague, utopian, and out-of-touch-with-reality
dreams of a black nationalist takeover made them irrelevant to the ev-
eryday struggles of black people. Quite simply, the nationalists did not
have a vision of how to improve the material conditions of black people.
So, the IBW warmly embraced the opportunity to work with the NBPC
in hopes of building a bridge between the two camps by providing a
workable roadmap of black liberation.[16]

Armed with the monumental task of putting together an agenda,
the committee got off to a late start. Vincent Harding was not asked to
serve on the Drafting Committee until ten days before the start of the
Convention. Included in his written invitation was a plea that he attend
a meeting the weekend of March 3–4 in Washington, DC, to work on a
first draft of the agenda. That weekend the committee met at Howard
University and essentially laid out 90 percent of the agenda, which was
centered around seven topical areas that were the summation of discussions during the 1971–1972 strategy sessions; organizational input from
the CBC, CAP, and the Institute of the Black World; and discussions from
the state and regional caucuses. In a letter sent to Platform Committee
members, the committee was to be guided by the following questions
of principle:

- Can the platform serve to unify and be representative of the ideological spectrum and regions without the danger of being a bland
  political mixture as before?
- Can it challenge nonblack perspectives in such a way as to test the
  seriousness of delegates, candidates, and black voters regarding the
  future of blacks in this country and abroad?

- Can it be a black political liberation charter without seeming to black people to be unpragmatic and unachievable?

Harding and Strickland worked feverishly throughout the Convention to put together a document that spoke to the above parameters.[17]

The agenda would focus on the following seven areas:

- Economic empowerment
- Political empowerment
- Human development
- Environmental development or protection
- Rural development
- Overseas relations
- Communications

With specific draft committees for each area made up of some of the leading black researchers, scholars, and thought leaders on each issue, the Platform Committee and its drafting group got down to work. Over the two-day period at Howard University they created a "shopping list" of agenda items that dealt with the full range of black life. They brought this skeleton agenda to Gary with the goal of incorporating last-minute items into the agenda after it completed its hearings on the first two days of the Convention. On the opening day of the Convention the Platform Committee met with the state delegations, who brought a wide range of issues such as prisoners' rights, busing, US foreign policy toward Africa, congressional redistricting, and other issues. The committee also heard from organizational spokespersons as they began to shape and narrow the platform. One observer noted about the work of the committee: "They held hearings for eight solid hours on the first day listening to every state delegation that had something to say, to every accredited national organization, to community groups and to interested individuals. When they were through with their hearings they worked all-night to condense the draft while trying to incorporate the multiplicity of ideas that they had heard, but which were not in their drafts."[18]

The platform hearings were intense yet respectful, but the Oregon delegation erupted in anger when they realized the Platform Committee had compiled much of the agenda prior to Gary. Their spokesperson told the committee: "We protest the way the platform committee has already met and presumably prepared policy recommendations. We had hoped to have a voice in the platform committee actions here, we don't want to be dragged along by the big states." The Oregon folks had a point. They had only seven days to select delegates and get to Gary. It was literally no time for them to put together policy recommendations. But Carl Stokes didn't buy their excuse: "Ohio had no more time than you. And if any other delegations had more time than you or we I'd like to know it.[19]

The Preamble: "Black Politics at the Crossroads"

Toward the end of Friday's business, the Platform Committee released the Draft Preamble—The Call to Convention. It was titled: "What Time is It: The Gary Declaration—Black Politics at the Crossroads." Written by Vincent Harding and Bill Strickland, this document "would set the tone for the Convention," and it "would place in historical perspective where Black people and their concerns are politically in 1972. This portion of the document should not only frame what is to come thereafter, but should inevitably contrast rather sharply with what is likely to be said in either the democratic or republican platform and campaign documents." The draft preamble was simply to state the overall meaning of the NBPC and set the ideological mood of the Convention.[20]

The title, "Black Politics at the Crossroads," suggested that the black electorate was entering a crucial moment that would determine whether the community would remain dependent upon the current political system and work within it, or whether they would strike out on their own, close ranks, and create an all-black political party. Harding and Strickland opened the preamble by arguing that the NBPC was coming to Gary "in an hour of great promise for Black America." Since the "white nation" stood on the brink of chaos, and white politicians "offer no hope of real change," the black community was faced with both an "amazing" and a frightening choice: "We may choose in 1972 to slip back into the decadent white politics of American life, or we may press forward, moving relentlessly from Gary to the creation of our own Black life. The choice is large but the time is very short." The document suggested that black people "from every rural community in Alabama, to the high rise compounds of Chicago" were in crisis. "From the sprawling Black cities in Watts and Nairobi in the West, to the decay of Harlem in the East, the testimony we bear is the same. We are witnesses to social disaster." Because US cities had become "crime-haunted dying grounds," black folks faced a range of problems: unemployment, poor schools, an unfavorable criminal justice system, and "the officially approved epidemic of drugs" that threatened to "wipe out the minds and strength of our best young warriors." These conditions were the twin products of American capitalism and white supremacy.[21]

These twin powers extended well beyond the borders of the United States and all the way to the African diaspora. "For while we are pressed down under all the dying weight of a bloated, inwardly decaying white civilization, many of our brothers in Africa and the rest of the Third World have fallen prey to the same powers of exploitation and deceit." But, the preamble insisted, "Americans cannot hide." The crisis faced by America's black citizens was the "crisis of the entire society." It went deep, to the very bones and marrow, "to the essential nature of America's economic, political, and cultural systems." The complexity of the problems would not be altered one bit "by new faces in the old places" in Washington, DC. What was needed was a black political Convention that would operate from the following truth: "The American system does not work for the masses of our people, and it cannot be made to work without radical, fundamental change." In light of those "realities," black folk could either stay the course and remain dependent or do something to bring about political independence. The authors suggested that Woodrow Wilson, FDR, Truman, and Eisenhower all received the support of black folks, yet in return black voters received nothing. "We were wooed like many others by the superficial liberalism of John F. Kennedy and the make believe populism of Lyndon Johnson. Let there be no more of that."[22]

The second part of the document had the subheading "Both Parties Have Betrayed Us." Whether Democrat or Republican, in peace or war, and in depression or prosperity, "both parties have betrayed us whenever their interests conflicted with ours (which was most of the time), and whenever our forces were unorganized and dependent, quiescent and compliant." But this shouldn't be a surprise since the US political system "was designed to operate for the benefit of the white race; it was never meant to do anything else." White liberalism, as so many suggested, was not the key to liberating black people. If so, Lincoln, Roosevelt, Kennedy, and LBJ "would have done so." Relying upon white politicians was a waste of time since what was needed was a change in the system.[23]

The Gary Convention was not about "the old Convention questions of which candidate we shall support," but rather "whether we will move to organize independently." This new independent black political thrust would accept the responsibility for creating both the "atmosphere" and the "program" for fundamental change in America. "Such responsibility is ours because it is our people who are most deeply hurt and ravaged by the present systems of society." On the question of independent black politics, the preamble made it clear, "there can be no equivocation on that issue. History leaves us no other choice. White politics has not and cannot bring the changes we need." But in order to bring about this change, black politicians and black activists needed to transform from "favor-seeking vassals and loud-talking militant pawns" into ambassadors of "the unorganized masses of our people." This, "the Black Politics of Gary" would place "community before individualism, love before sexual exploitation, a living environment before profits, peace before war, justice before unjust order, and morality before expediency." A prerequisite to such an ideology required a "determined national Black power." The preamble closed with a brief discussion on the soon-to-come Black Agenda. Recognizing that no one else could represent black interests but black people, "the agenda we now press for at Gary is not only for the future of the Black community but is probably the only way that the rest of America can save itself from the harvest of its criminal past." It closed with a strong appeal to the delegates: "So, brothers and sisters of our developing Black nation, we now stand at Gary as a people whose time has come. From every corner of Black America, from all liberation movements of the Third World, from the graves of our fathers and the coming world of our children, we are faced with a challenge and a call. Though the moment is perilous we will not despair. We must seize the time, for the time is ours."[24]

The Gary Declaration and its fundamental critique of white America, white liberals, and the American political system was greeted warmly by Convention delegates. It was arguably one of the best Convention calls of all time. However, as delegates basked in the declaration, the nation's largest civil rights organization vigorously denounced it. In a widely distributed memo to the NAACP's ten at-large delegates, Roy Wilkins's assistant, John Morsell, insisted that the NAACP would not and could not be a part of a process that promoted independent black politics, the idea of a black third party, or a withdrawal from the current political system. "The draft preamble is rooted in the concept of separate nationhood for Black Americans. It calls for withdrawal from the American political process on the theory that this is white politics. It proclaims the doctrine of racial superiority in that it holds that only persons of African descent are capable of spearheading movement toward desirable change in society. Its rhetoric is that of revolution rather than reform." The memo argued that the logical conclusion of the preamble was "revolt aimed at setting up a new nation with its own territorial base." Any NAACP member was entitled to their own opinions, it said, but the preamble did not reflect the "philosophy" and "position" of the NAACP. It closed by mentioning that the NAACP was committed to a "practical politics" of accomplishment within the current political system.[25]

Privately, Carl Stokes also had a problem with the preamble. He basically told the Ohio delegation that if the NAACP could not support the preamble then neither could he. Stokes agreed to support the preamble only after the Ohio delegation had a team of lawyers examine it, who then told Stokes that he should accept it.[26]

Understandably, the NAACP and some of its older black members from the South were frightened at some of the language in the preamble. The idea of independent black politics was indeed threatening to those who were still celebrating the legislative victories around integration and voting rights. When Hatcher was asked about the NAACP memo he shrugged it off, saying "perhaps unity will not be possible. But what is important is that we try. If it isn't possible, it's important that we find out." Writing in the aftermath of the Convention, Baraka had this to say about the NAACP's actions: "Before the gavel had wrapped down on the first session of the Gary Convention, ol' Roy Wilkins had issued his customary disclaimer and vicious putdown of what had been said at Gary, when, in fact, nothing had yet been said. He put down through his boy Morsell, the preface of the Gary Declaration of the soon to be created Black Agenda, just to let white people know he wasn't in with some of that 'Black Stuff.'"[27]

The NAACP critique was a blow for the Convention and especially for Baraka, who was really hoping for the creation of an all-black party and an independent black political mechanism. But Baraka was not surprised. In an article written about a month before the NBPC, Roy Wilkins had conveyed his thoughts on the Convention in an op-ed titled "Minorities are the Losers When they Play Ethnic Politics." Wilkins spoke out against the NBPC by arguing that the concept of racial unity is a deception and that an all-black political party was not feasible simply because black voters did not have the numbers. Despite the NAACP's conservatism, reticence, and lack of aggressiveness, they were still the largest civil rights organization in the country. In fact, they were the de facto voice of black America. In defense of Wilkins, he was accurately expressing the views of his constituency. In 1972 the overwhelming majority of black folks wanted to work within the system to bring about change, and they had very little interest in the abstract notion of revolution.[28]

Jesse Jackson's Party in Chicago

After a lengthy day of intense meetings, state caucuses, and committee hearings, many delegates were excited about being invited to Jesse Jackson's party in downtown Chicago at the McCormick Place. As the initial event in the Jesse Jackson coming-out party, Jackson hosted approximately 10,000 people that evening for an Operation PUSH fund-raiser. It was dubbed "A Family Affair."

Delegates traveled the forty-odd miles from Gary, unknowingly participating in the first soul food dinner ever served at McCormick Place. On the menu was ham hocks, red beans and rice, pickled beets, corn muffins, and sweet potato pie. With Harry Belafonte providing the evening's entertainment, delegates enjoyed themselves, and as they headed back up the interstate late that night they reflected upon the day's activities and were optimistic about the second day of the Convention.[29]

5

NATIONTIME!

The Politics of Forming an Independent Black Political Party

As Convention-goers prepared for the day's activities, they were greeted with the following headlines in both the local and national press:

- "Black Convention Split"
- "NAACP Blasts Preamble"
- "Gary: Odd Place for a Convention"
- "Blacks Marching to Different Drums"
- "NAACP Opposition to Militants Issue Threatens Parley Split"
- "Discord is the Key for Black Convention"
- "NAACP Aide Opposes Draft of Black Preamble"

Diggs, Hatcher, and Baraka were not shocked at the portrayal of the convention in the press. In fact, they expected it. Conversely, the black press was much more favorable to the events of the first day, leading with such headlines as, "Blacks Make History in Gary" and "Convention Debates Black Goals." In an effort to shape public opinion and diminish the effect of the gathering, the white press would unfortunately highlight the negative throughout the weekend. Members of major media organizations looked to highlight discord as a sort of payback for the Convention's attitude toward white reporters. Second, the lack of black journalists at major media outlets also played a role in the negative coverage. Throughout the weekend the relationship between the NBPC and the media would be a contentious one; whatever happened at the Convention would be covered negatively by the media in attendance.[1]

Saturday's proceedings got underway five hours late as the various caucuses, committees, and groups were meeting, and because it took the Credentials Committee a while to certify delegates and to give the delegates a chance to make it in from their hotels in the area. The Convention opened with a thunderous rendition of the Black National Anthem as 7,000 people "lifted their clinched fists in pride as they sang 'Lift, Every, Voice, and Sing." Representative Diggs then followed with a quick discussion of US foreign policy toward Africa, which as chair of the House Foreign Affairs Committee he was more than qualified to do. During his speech, attendees demanded that the scores of news media in attendance move from their constructed platform, since it was blocking their view. "We can't see, we can't see," they shouted. Diggs politely asked the crowd to move to another area of the gym, but they refused. Diggs did not want to ask the camera crews to move from their constructed space because he knew that the Convention needed maximum media coverage. "The logistics arrangement for the television cameras involved a long thought out process that can't be worked out any other way," Diggs told the shouting audience. He pleaded with them to allow the opening session but they didn't budge. Hatcher eventually asked the cameras to move to another area of the gymnasium. One reporter remarked that the new location did not allow him to get shots of the crowd, just shots of the podium and people's crotches.[2]

"History Will Be Our Judge"

With five precious hours lost because of the late start, the delegates had a ton of work to complete if they were going to make the Convention a success. Hatcher delivered the Convention's first address and he would not disappoint. He went straight to the Old Testament as he began his speech by comparing the assemblage before him to how the people of Israel felt "when they witnessed the parting of the Red Sea." He knew his audience wanted a word and he gave them more by comparing their jubilation to that of "Joshua and his soldiers" at Jericho, and recalling the "exultation of Noah when he gazed at Mount Ararat as the clouds parted and the sun shone down." And then he got a bit more contemporary, citing how W. E. B. DuBois "and his fellow members" felt at the first gathering of the Niagara Movement.[3]

Hatcher then shifted gears and attacked the news media for being critical of the Convention and for playing up divisions like the NAACP critique. "It is our Convention. We shall determine who attends it. All

Black people are welcome. Thousands strong, we warmly embrace Angela Davis and Bobby Seale." But he reminded them that they needed a productive Convention and not just rhetoric when he said, "we must emerge from this Convention with an independent national Black political agenda, a dynamic program for Black liberation, that put into process will liberate America from its current decadence. Equally important we must not leave this Convention until we have built the mechanism to implement our program. Program must mesh with action. For this plan, as we work the banner waving over our head must proclaim 'unity.'"⁴

As an elected official, Hatcher knew the importance of political power, but he also knew its limitations when he remarked, to the delight of the nationalists, "we support radical action. We support all avenues to liberation. We know full well that political action is not the whole answer, but political action is an essential part of our ultimate liberation. And it is these political questions we shall pursue at this historic Convention." He cautioned his audience not to waste time at the NBPC "in fruitless debates, ego trips, self-aggrandizement, or rhetoric uninformed by thought. Every word, every moment, we shall invest with the utmost meaning."⁵

Hatcher then took the attendees on a history lesson detailing how, prior to the New Deal, black people supported Republicans only to get nothing in return, and then after switching their allegiance to the Democrats during the reign of FDR they still received crumbs in return. Those days of unwavering loyalty were over. "We have tried year after year, election after election, to work with the two major political parties, each time hoping they would come true. We are through believing. We are through hoping. We are through trusting in the two major white American political parties. Hereafter we shall rely on the power of our own Black unity. We shall no longer bargain away our support for petty jobs or symbolic offices." These words echoed nicely in the ears of those who wanted the NBPC to launch an all-black political party, and they frightened many of the black elected officials in attendance who, unlike Hatcher, did not come from safe, majority-black areas.⁶

Then Hatcher gave the following conditions for how black folk would pledge their political allegiance. First, black people would need to have a vote in the decision-making body of the party. "We emphatically reject the role of adviser to the party's circles," he said. Second, that power-sharing be the rule from the neighborhood/ward level up to the presidential cabinet. Third, that black voters have a proportional share in the party commensurate with their vote. Fourth, that black voters pick their own candidates. "No political party to which we attach ourselves may any longer pick and choose the Toms and Sallys among us." Fifth, that the party "work from the grassroots up" before critical national decisions were made; "they must be discussed in every nook and cranny of this country from the tarpaper shacks in the Mississippi Delta, to the pine hovels in the Appalachian Hills, from the rank and fetid basement apartments of 47th street to the barrios of Spanish Harlem." But the most crucial questions related to party support and affiliation were a bit more simplistic. "Who does the party represent? For whose benefit does it exist? What does the political party stand for? What is its ideology?"[7]

If both the Republicans and Democrats wanted black voters, then they needed to pursue platforms that led to "the immediate liberation of Black people from their long night of relentless indignities" and covered employment, education, drug abuse, corporate exploitation, and Vietnam. Since black soldiers were disproportionately sent to Vietnam, Hatcher knew that many of those in attendance could relate. "This horrible war, the ugliest page in our foreign history, could never have taken place without the overwhelming complicity of both political parties. And it could not continue for another day without the same complicity." He remained on the foreign policy subject by mentioning some of the regimes the United States had propped up—Taiwan, Argentina, and South Korea—and the governments the CIA had toppled in Iran, Guatemala, El Salvador, Ecuador, Honduras, Peru, and the Congo, where Lumumba "was butchered because he refused to orbit within the American sphere." Further, the American corporate support of South Africa, Angola, Rhodesia, and Mozambique was further proof that US foreign policy needed a drastic overhaul. "No self-respecting Afro-American can, without a sense of profound betrayal, offer one iota of further support to any political party which does not condemn American foreign policy with abhorrence."[8]

Toward the end of his address Hatcher provided the call for what many assumed was the gavel to launch an all-black independent party. "This Convention signals the end of hip-pocket politics. We ain't in nobody's hip-pocket no more! We are through with any political party and, many of us, with any political system which is not irrevocably committed to our first principles, pursued in tenacious action: the liberation of Black people at home and the end of exploitation abroad." He then made a U-turn and suggested that black America give the two major parties one more chance before black folks "crossed the rubicon and formed a third party political movement." Hatcher was willing to give them "one more chance" in the 1972 elections. But if the parties did not address black concerns then black people would organize independently and "take with us, Chicanos, Puerto Ricans, Indians, Orientals," a veritable rainbow coalition. But the rainbow would not stop with people of color. "We shall take with us the best of white America," which included youths, intellectuals, the poor, veterans, and the blue-collar white man like Archie Bunker." The crowd booed loudly because the NBPC was not about forming coalitions, it was for black people to work on their issues. After losing the crowd, Hatcher recaptured it as he closed out the fifty-seven-minute speech. "The seventies will be the decade of an independent Black political thrust. Its destiny will depend on us. How shall we respond? Will we walk in unity or disperse in a thousand different directions? Will we stand for principle or settle for a mess of pottage? Will we maintain our integrity or succumb to the man's temptations? Will we act like free Black men or timid shivering chattels? Will we do what must be done? These are the questions confronting this Convention. And only we can answer them. History will be our judge."[9]

The speech was a work of art. Hatcher's ability to speak to the central issues of the Convention was amazing. His critique of America, his analysis of black political history, and his flirting with the idea of calling for a black political party were timely, on point, and warmly received . . . and this was not an easy audience to impress.

Jesse Jackson was next up at the podium. The young 30-year-old lieutenant of MLK and the founder of the recently created PUSH organization could not wait to take the microphone. He would be the heir apparent to MLK and the voice of black America, and he would give one of the most memorable speeches in the history of black America. As Jackson began his address to the Convention, a group of delegates from Washington, DC, grew tired of all the talk. They wanted to get to the business of the Convention, which was principally concerned with drafting an agenda. They were tired of rhetoric and emotional speeches. They wanted to get to work. To show their frustration, one delegate shouted, "no more speeches. We want to take something home. We can't take speeches home." Others chimed in with "we want Jesse." Jesse fought through the shouting match and quickly energized the crowd.[10]

"Nationtime"

The young country preacher opened his speech by comparing the NBPC to a family reunion. "Brother Hatcher came up North and got a new house in Gary and said to all the scattered tribes around the nation come home. I know my home is too small but come home. We could've went to New York City or L.A. but we didn't have a home there. Come home. Over in this smoke-filled city called Gary one of our Black brothers said 'Tribe' come home." This coming together was like reuniting a family that had been broken up. "The tribe in Mississippi does not know the tribe in California. The tribe in New York does not know the tribe in Georgia." This reunification of the black community, he said, "was so great until nobody has the right to deny this tribe the opportunity to organize political power." Then Jesse surprised many in the audience when he affirmed the nationalist call, "Nationtime."[11]

"Brothers and Sisters, what time is it?"

"Nationtime," the crowd responded.

"For 7.5 million registered Black voters and 6 million unregistered Black voters, what time is it?"

"Nationtime."

"For Black democrats, Black republicans, Black panthers, Black Muslims, Black independents, Black businessmen, Black professionals, Black mothers on welfare, what time is it?"

"Nationtime."

This affirming of the black nationalist call was an entrée into a discussion on the need for black folks to become politically unified despite their differences. "Black is our common denominator. As Brother Malcolm X said on more than one occasion, we saw ourselves as house slaves, field slaves, and yard slaves, but the common denominator was slavery and our numerator didn't make any difference."[12]

While Hatcher wanted to give the Republicans and Democrats one more chance to do right by black voters, Jesse was ready for an all-black political party. "I don't want to be the grey shadow of the white elephant or the grey shadow of a white donkey. I am a Black man and I want a Black party. I do not trust white republicans or white democrats," he said, as the crowd roared its approval. However, in order for black folks to maximize political opportunities they had to get themselves together morally and mentally. "We are not gonna take over this nation drunk or on dope. We gotta be sober. We gotta know what's going down. You gotta clean up your mind. It's your thought pattern." This included undergoing a de-brainwashing against the process that taught white superiority. "Some of us believe that the white man's ice is colder, his sugar is sweeter, and his medicine is better. We gotta clean off our minds. Put our minds inside our body. If your body is here and your mind is in some white camp you are a schizophrenic."[13]

For Jesse, black folks were crazy to let other people represent their interests. To him it was a sign of low self-esteem. What was needed was for black people to step up and have some ego. "We don't have enough ego," he preached, "when you sit here with your healthy Black body and developed Black mind and put your confidence, creativity, and belief in somebody else who is less intelligent than you, to represent you, your ego has been castrated."

"What time is it?"

"Nationtime!"

In describing some of the political infighting and confusion that was present at the NBPC, Jesse compared it to a new baby being born. "This is a beautiful occasion. When the baby is gonna be born, everybody gets scared. I know some of y'all are jumpy, your white folks are waiting for you to call them on the phone. We are pregnant, we are ready for change and whether a doctor is there or not the water has broke, the blood has spilled, and a new Black baby is about to be born." He continued, "We know who our parents are, their baby has now been born, we are grown, we ain't taking it no more. No more 'yassah boss,' no more bowin' and scrapin'. We are 25 million strong. Cut us in or cut it out, it is a new ballgame."

He closed his speech in the rhetorical tradition of the black church.

"When we come together, what time is it?"

"Nationtime!"

"When we respect each other, what time is it?"

"Nationtime!"

"When we get ourselves confident, what time is it?"

"Nationtime!"

"When we form our own political party, what time is it?"

"Nationtime!"

He then stepped away from the podium with his large MLK medallion swaying from his neck to a thunderous applause.[14]

Jesse's speech was not just motivational, inspiring, and exciting, it pointed to the development of a new black political culture. The growing black electorate, the rising number of black officials, combined with continued white flight, made Jesse realize that black people would control the nation's urban areas, and he wanted them to seize that opportunity. Years later Jesse reflected on the speech. "Well, I sensed that I was speaking to the alienation but giving it some sense of direction. I had drawn much of the strength of Nation Time from a poem written by LeRoi Jones, Amiri Baraka at that time. The sense of people saying, what's happening? Saying, nothing's happening man. Say, what's really happening? It's nation time, it's time to come together. It's time to organize politically. It's time for partnership. It is indeed, whether you're in California or Mississippi, it is nation time. And out of that speech many young people around the country began to gravitate toward a sense of national, indeed international consciousness."[15]

Delegates who listened closely to both Hatcher and Jackson were confused by the two contradictory messages: Hatcher suggesting that blacks give the Democratic Party one more chance, and Jesse calling for an independent black nation. Since these two messages seemed to contradict each other, both men held a hastily called news conference during the recess to clarify their positions and make it known that their messages were not in conflict, but complementary. At the news conference Hatcher said there was no difference between his and Jackson's views. "The two parties have one more chance to show if they will let Blacks participate. If that response is similar to the response we have received in the past, we will have no choice." Jackson agreed that he and Hatcher both wanted the same thing but he didn't feel that either party would respond to black demands, and his call for an all-black third party just put him one step ahead of Hatcher. "There is no disagreement that is as strong as our unity," he stated.[16]

The different strategies expressed by Hatcher and Jackson appeared contradictory but they weren't. They were just two ideologies expressed by two different men based upon their political stations. Hatcher was a well-educated elected official who governed a majority-black city. So in Hatcher's mind, staying with the major political parties for now made sense. Jesse, who was an itinerant preacher and full-time civil rights activist, preferred to work outside of the mainstream of the system. He liked the idea of being a free agent and a political maverick. Plus, Hatcher knew the simple reality that black folks did not have the infrastructure to launch an all-black third party; nor could they expect the millions of black folks across the country to essentially forfeit their vote in the name of revolution. One attendee remarked that the speeches were more like sermons rather than representative of a deep political divide.

"All Hell Broke Loose"

After the Saturday keynotes the Convention got down to the business of the day with Congressman Diggs chairing the proceedings, and things quickly went bad. There was a considerable debate over whether or not to endorse a presidential candidate, with Carl Stokes and Percy Sutton representing opposite sides. Stokes believed that an endorsement would do nothing but "cause bitterness among those who more than ever before need to be united." Sutton disagreed on the basis that the purpose of the convention was to endorse candidates. "How much validity can a Black Convention have if it does not evaluate and then endorse the only Black candidate running for President? I take opposition with the coordinators who have said they will make no endorsements. I think we should endorse Shirley Chisholm but I'm not going to push it because it might cause dissension." Disputes also erupted over the naming of a permanent chair or chairs of the NBPC when Diggs entertained a motion to close the nomination process after he, Hatcher, and Baraka had been nominated. A stickler for process, Diggs used Robert's Rules of Order during his chair of the proceedings. When the voice vote was given there was an overwhelming response of "nays"; delegates wanted to keep the nominations open, particularly the delegations from Louisiana and Connecticut. When Diggs said "the nominations are closed," all hell broke loose. "In a matter of a few words, the Convention exploded. There were jeers, boos, and a sudden outpouring from the delegations." Ben Chavis of Wilmington, North Carolina, was in the audience, and he suggested that the response was not directed against Diggs personally, but against what his misreading of the voice vote represented, political repression. "People were insulted because they didn't want the Convention to start on a point which they had just left in all the repression. We wanted an open Convention, not an oppressed Convention. And so Diggs got himself in some hot water." Baraka and Hatcher desperately wanted to recess the Convention so the leadership could tighten up the platform rules for Sunday's all-important closing session.[17]

With tensions already high, the frustration over how to set up a permanent organization and who would lead it threatened to derail the entire NBPC, with some state delegations ready to pull out and go home. A bit later a group of delegates from New York stormed the stage to take the microphone from Diggs. "Security men ringed the stage and quieted the participants as others roared 'unity,' and the session resumed. But Diggs never recovered and he recessed the Convention for the day with its delegates "visibly disturbed and depressed, and its brokers disillusioned. The dream of holding such a super political parley, momentarily at least, was in pieces."[18]

Since the NBPC was Baraka's brainchild he was determined not to let the Convention fall apart on Saturday night. That night he worked tirelessly trying to get frustrated delegates to understand the Convention slogan "Unity without Uniformity." Baraka vividly recalled that night when it seemed that it would fall apart: "I wasn't a mayor or a congressmen, but

I was a Black Nationalist. I was an activist. And I thought a lot of those people had come to Gary because of our organizing, our pleading with people to come and be part of a whole Black political development. And I thought it was important that the thing not fall apart, that we talk to the people and find out what could be done other than just walking out."[19]

That night Baraka and others kept the Convention together by visiting the various state caucuses and Convention committees. Baraka couldn't believe that there was tension even before they had a chance to discuss the agenda draft that was being finalized by the Platform Committee. Since Baraka's role at the NBPC was to keep the nationalists at the table, he had to keep them, as well as the more traditional delegations, engaged. One of the Convention organizers said that Baraka was able to earn the respect of the people because "he was the only man who had no political ambition and no desire for publicity. He knows politics and he knows people. And he was more concerned about making the Convention a success than he was being the leader of a particular group."[20]

The complex late-night sessions consisted of state caucuses, subcaucuses within state delegations, splinter groups of black elected officials, black nationalists, and Marxists. Reflecting on that night years later, Baraka recalled, "So, I'd have to get to the various kind of power factions and find out what each thought they were going to do and whether we were going to have some kind of accord. Whether there was going to be a united front or what they were going to do." Writing just several months after the Convention, Professor Ronald Walters wrote this about Baraka's work that night: "It was his skill and respect among the masses which moved the business of the Convention along in a way which others could not."[21]

That night the tension within the delegations was lessened to a great extent with the release of a draft of the National Black Political Agenda, the document that would serve as the guidebook for black politics in 1972 and beyond. With the Convention scheduled to end at noon on Sunday, delegates were up all night reviewing the document and suggesting revisions and/or additions both in open and "in secret, all-night meetings," in hopes of developing an acceptable program. Throughout the night, state caucuses sent recommendations to committees and the committee chairs began to revise the proposed agenda.[22]

Some delegates took a break from reading the agenda to have a party. It was billed as a fund-raiser to benefit the NBPC, and delegates were treated to a live concert by Isaac Hayes, a comedy show by Dick Gregory, and appearances by Harry Belafonte and Coretta Scott King. Held at Roosevelt High School on the other side of Gary, it was attended by over 3,000 people. Guests were surprised when Bobby Seale of the Black Panther Party made a surprise visit, and minutes before the show got underway, he encouraged them to use the political process to acquire power. "If you are participating in changing the system in any way, you are a revolutionary, too. Use your vote like a shot in the forest. Aim and fire only when you expect to bag what you need." Seale went on to mention that he would not refer to any of Gary's black police officers as "pigs" since they treated him well, and he would only refer to them as "brothers." Coretta Scott King, who was described as "weary but exuberant" that night, was swamped by journalists who wanted to know what she thought about the Convention. "This is a historic event," she said. "We are here on very serious business. What we do at this Convention will be judged by future generations of the Black liberation struggle."[23]

6

WE WILL WALK OUT OF HERE WITH A PROGRAM

Ratifying the National Black Political Agenda

The only important item on Sunday's agenda was the ratification of the National Black Political Agenda, which delegates were poring over in their respective state caucuses, hotel rooms, and whatever other space they could find. As on Saturday, the headlines in Sunday's major papers once again stressed the negative at Gary. "Disorganization Plagues Blacks at Gary Convention"; "Observers Criticize Planning"; "Hatcher, Jesse, in Policy Split"; "Black 3d Party—Now? Wait?" As a response to the critics Alvin Boutte, chair of the Convention's Finance Committee and member of the Chicago school board, dismissed it. "There is no more confusion here than anywhere else, certainly not more than at white political Conventions. There have been a few schedule delays, but generally it's going well. The main point is that we walk out of here with a program, and Monday morning you can bet we will." Jesse agreed. "The white press has described us as having dissension and diversity here, but you see we have come from different families across the nation and this is the first time that many of us have met, we've only known each other through the same white press which distorts the picture here. Now we're here, we've met and we all have the same goals." The white press was not accustomed to being in an environment where black folks debated, argued, and expressed different positions. The black community was not monolithic. Although there were things that were universally agreed upon, the white press came to Gary expecting groupthink, only to get confused when they realized that these delegates were intellectually complex.[1]

The National Black Political Agenda

Released in tabloid form to only a few select Convention leaders on Saturday evening, the long-awaited National Black Political Agenda was twelve pages in length, and it represented a culmination of months of complex work. Under the direction of Walter Fauntroy's Platform Committee, Bill Strickland and Vincent Harding of the Institute of the Black World assembled some of the best scholars in black America to do the heavy research on the document. The Agenda addressed seven areas critical to the future of black America: (1) political empowerment; (2) economic empowerment; (3) human development; (4) rural development; (5) foreign policy and black people; (6) environmental protection; and (7) communications. Investigation of each topic was led by a committee who compiled exhaustive data, reports, and analysis, which served as the foundation for that portion of the Agenda. The reports represent some of the best research compiled on the black experience. They are exhaustive, detailed, and dense, yet written in a clear language that all could understand.[2]

The controversial preamble which the NAACP still did not approve of led off the document, and what followed was arguably the best black political statement in all of US history. The "Black Agenda for Action" in its opening pages tackled the complex issue of political empowerment. Since the American political system was "dedicated to the presentation of white power," and white politics was "the politics of racism," it could not be made to work for black folks. "It cannot deliver Black folks from the clutches of Babylon." It was precisely in view of this reality "at this moment in history" that the black community needed to decide whose side they were on. "Are they for or against this system?" What was needed was a "Black politics" that went far beyond electoral politics and beyond 1972. As it had been discussed throughout the 1971–1972 strategy sessions and proposed by Baraka and the nationalist contingent of the NBPC, black people needed something radically different. "We need a permanent political movement that addresses itself to the basic control and reshaping of American institutions that currently exploit Black America and threaten the whole society." This permanent structure would offer a meaningful alternative "to the existing American political, economic and cultural systems."[3]

Political Empowerment

Delegates made eight demands of the federal government that would address the political servitude of black voters. The Agenda's first demand was proportional representation in Congress based upon population figures. "We are at least fifteen percent of the population . . . we ought to have a minimum of sixty-six representatives and fifteen senators." Until Congress passed a law to make this the law of the land, Congress was to be filled by persons elected at-large by the "national Black community." The second demand was that proportional black employment and control "at every level" of the federal government structures was needed to ensure that black folks were getting their rightful share of the jobs in the public sector. Third, the Agenda demanded "a national constitutional Convention" for the United States in the next twelve months. "The existing system cannot effect the changes that are necessary. It must be changed."[4]

Since gerrymandering was being used "to destroy Black political power," an executive order was necessary to end it. Home Rule for the District of Columbia, a plank that Walter Fauntroy spent much time championing, was listed fifth. Since the District was now majority-black, what existed was an apartheid-type system. "A Black majority in the nation's capital is now controlled by a white-dominated Congressional Committee and a set of presidential appointees. We must have Black self-determination in Washington, D.C." Similarly, to address the persistent issue of police brutality, the Agenda pressed for residency requirements for local police officers. Delegates believed that those policing black neighborhoods should live there. "A Bill of Rights for All Black People" in the criminal justice system was listed seventh. This meant: the right to a speedy trial, fair bail procedures, "full human rights while in jail and prisons," due process, and a fair shot in society once one had paid their debt to society.[5]

If there were any disagreements on the above-mentioned demands, virtually all of the delegates were in agreement with the demand that the FBI end its illegal COINTELPRO program, a J. Edgar Hoover initiative that treated many black political operatives as a threat to national security. Instead of the FBI using its energy to illegally spy on and harass black activists, it read, the Convention wanted the bureau "to shift its attention to ending the drug traffic in the U.S." If they couldn't make this transition then the FBI "needed to be phased out of existence as an irrelevant and worthless tax liability."[6]

The NBPC was under no illusion that the white political structure would act on these demands. "That is up to us," it read. For this aspect of the Agenda to become "real," dedicated activists needed to organize, not as "a temporary protest" or a "pressure group faction," but as a new political force in American life "whose time has come."[7]

Economic Empowerment

Economic empowerment was discussed at length in the Agenda. Considering that African Americans represented America's underclass, it was imperative that a focus on money occupy a central place in the overall black strategy for liberation. Since race and economics were inextricably connected because of the exploitation of slave labor, America owed "a debt" to black people. "While the moral horrors of slavery and the human indignities visited upon our people by racial discrimination can never really be compensated for—and certainly never with money alone—we must not rest until American society has recognized our valid, historic, right to reparations, to a massive claim on the financial assets of the American economy."[8]

With an eye toward reparations, the Agenda demanded that the White House establish a majority-black commission to study how much black America should be given in terms of "land, capital, and cash" as restitution for enslavement, Jim Crow, and racial discrimination. One component of the reparations strategy was for the federal government to budget $5 billion a year for an independent black development agency which would facilitate black ownership of a full range of "business and service enterprises now serving ghetto communities." The $5 billion would be awarded through local community development corporations.[9]

To address the issue of low-income housing, "the creation of a new urban homestead act" would better utilize publicly owned land for housing than if it moved "into private hands." Pension funds "holding sizable Black assets" should be controlled by black investment managers, and private foundations needed to be "obligated by law" to give at least 10 percent of their assets every year, with at least one-half of that coming to the black community. Other demands included an annual income of $6,400 for a family of four; the closing of federal loopholes for the rich; a 50 percent cut in the nation's defense budget; the ending of corporate welfare; expanded block grants; and the enforcement of antitrust legislation. The only aspect of the economic empowerment strategy that focused on what black people could do for themselves dealt with better spending habits and the development of a black fund. Conspicuous consumption, crass materialism, and "excessive frivolities" needed to stop. Then, black folk could support a "Black United Fund," which all black people "will be expected to contribute to in proportion to their income." The proceeds of the fund would be used for "Black charitable and developmental purposes."[10]

If there was any question about the Agenda being a black nationalist document, the sections on political and economic empowerment settled that debate. The nationalists were clearly in control of the Agenda, and it did not bode well for the future of the Convention and the permanent political structure nationalists hoped to create. Demanding a constitutional Convention to address black issues and demanding reparations were pipedreams. It seemed as if Baraka and the nationalists in Gary liked the idea of shock value over political pragmatism. Further, what is also puzzling is that much of the first two parts of the Agenda focused on what they demanded of the government and not what they could do for themselves. So while they were critical of the government and preferred to work outside the system, the plans for dealing with political and economic empowerment seem to suggest that despite all of their critiques they still had faith in the system. The remaining five areas of the Agenda would not be nearly as controversial as the first two.[11]

Human Development

In the area of human development ten suggestions were listed to help black folks "define the human development we need" and the "necessary conditions for its realization." The demands included tuition-free college education; black control of schools; a 100 percent increase in Social Security benefits; publicly owned, twenty-four-hour day care centers; the elimination of capital punishment; and the creation of a national health care system, which included a national network of community health centers "to deal with the problems of the delivery of health care services to Black communities." These were items that both civil rights activists and Black Power apostles could agree upon. They jointly rallied around the creation of a National Federation of Black Education, "funded from our own and public sources," which would function like a research center with a strong focus on the black family. Unlike some of the proposals dealing with political and economic empowerment, these agenda items were thoughtful, practical, and reasonable. In fact, in later years liberals would actually embrace these ideas as public policy initiatives.[12]

Rural Development

Southern delegates were excited when they read the platform on rural development. While the NBPC was dominated by delegations from the Northeast and Midwest, they understood that a huge number of black folks still resided in the rural South, and their concerns needed to be addressed within the NBPC and the subsequent Agenda. To acquaint the Convention with their plight, draftees of the Agenda included a three-paragraph first-person description of life in the rural South. "Our material environment is characterized by the worst the American social system has to offer. Our housing is poor and structurally unsound and we control none of the housing production process. We are mainly tenants rather than owners. Even the land we toiled for centuries has seldom been ours to own, control, or pass on to our heirs. Healthy services, when they are available, are of low quality, high cost and outside the control of our communities. The rather recent technological revolution in agriculture has been particularly vexing for Black agricultural labor. This labor, long a saleable commodity, has been rendered virtually useless. When other jobs are available for Blacks, they are generally low-waged, debasing, and short-lived. Many of us are without any income at all. Faced with these conditions, we are left with few real options. Millions have fled in a forced removal from the rural South, seeking refuge in northern cities. Others, perhaps a quarter of the nation's Black population have remained to eke out a living as a landless class, with no rights that must be respected by the dominant society."[13]

While this vivid description of white oppression moved the readers, the document also suggested that black folk could do more for themselves. "Far too often we choose to support economically white enterprises, ideas, plans and programs, which are detrimental to our own self-interest as a people." What was required to reverse the declining quality of life for rural black southerners was a broad land reform policy that would provide "tracts of sufficient size to be economically viable."

Second, the USDA needed to reorganize to better meet the needs of small and medium-sized farms. Third, every rural black family should be given a "sound, safe, and sanitary home," based on need rather than ability to pay. They also called for a quasi–Tennessee Valley Authority type of program to work on issues of rural industrial development "in the Black Belt." In closing, readers were asked to consider the possibilities if black northerners and black southerners in rural areas could establish a "vertically integrated food processing and distribution network." While the majority of delegates were urbanites reading about the plight of black folk in the rural South, it triggered memories of what they and their families escaped during periods of migration.[14]

Foreign Policy

While the Convention was principally focused on domestic concerns, "Foreign Policy and Black Policy" was given considerable attention in the Agenda. Congressman Diggs spent much of his congressional time on issues affecting the African diaspora, and many delegates had a deep love and affection for their African brothers and sisters. When Congressman Diggs mentioned to the NBPC that their work didn't stop at the water's edge, he foreshadowed what was to come. Little did he know that one foreign policy issue would eventually split the Convention. Throughout its history black America had always paid attention to foreign policy matters, but this would be one of the first times black folks articulated a foreign policy statement.[15]

Calling US foreign policy "world-wide imperialism," this section of the Agenda discussed how African people "are dominated, exploited, and brutalized by Europeans." US complicity in these efforts to subjugate African people and forestall independence movements was an effort by white powers to maintain control of cheap labor, raw materials, and profits. Because the United States was so often involved in maintaining this dynamic, delegates understood that they could no longer "abdicate their international responsibilities." They had four goals: to further the progress of revolutionary movements in southern Africa; to assist African countries; to help newly independent countries become economically self-sufficient; and to stop European domination of African and "Third World" peoples. They were squarely committed to supporting the African revolution "by all means," demanding that the United States cease its complicity in imperialistic efforts; support the Organization of African Unity and a "Pan-African Philosophy" with concrete programs; and end the war in Vietnam by the end of 1973. The most controversial aspect of the foreign policy agenda dealt with the Israeli/Palestinian conflict, but this would not be introduced until the waning moments of the Convention. Writing after the Convention, Ron Walters boasted that this was "the most comprehensive and forceful foreign policy articulated by African peoples to date."[16]

Environmental Protection

Because many of the delegates lived in communities populated with toxic dump sites, landfills, industrial plants, and other environmental hazards, the Convention took up the issue of the environment. Unlike white environmental concerns such as forestation, recycling, and climate, black frustration with the environment was rooted in day-to-day health concerns. Black environmentalists didn't believe that the country's focus on the newly created "Earth Day" had a focus on the "critical impact of environmental pollution—noise, air, solid waste, sewage, rodents and pests, and lead poisoning in Black inner-city residents." One of the unfortunate consequences of living in poor inner-city neighborhoods was that their residents confronted pollution on a daily basis. For instance, "irregular and inadequate solid waste disposal" forced black residents to use DDT, a popular pesticide. The chemicals from DDT are "subsequently ingested by the household occupants" and it remains "in their tissues at levels which may eventually lead to death." City street noise, automobile exhaust, and food products "with excessive chemical additives" were all major items of concern. The Agenda made the following four recommendations:

- Educate black community residents on the causes and effects of pollution.
- Set community standards for air pollution, waste-efficient discharges, noise levels, and other sources of pollution with a focus on the special impact of all such pollutants separately and in combination with each other.

- Give local governments the authority to ban all through traffic from inner-city streets whenever air pollution levels "approach dangerous heights."
- Create employment opportunities for black residents in solid waste management, sanitation engineering, environmental health, and air pollution control. This would help develop an in-house expertise on these issues.[17]

Communications

The last major issue the Agenda addressed was "Communications." The debate over whether or not white reporters would be allowed to cover the Convention illustrated the importance of black media outlets and black journalists. Black newspapers, it said, throughout the history of our struggle became primary agents of communication. "They kept us informed about ourselves because we owned it. It brought us pouring into Northern cities and it helped us keep in touch with our brothers and sisters who had not left the South; it told us about lynching's, and our treatment in the Army; and it fought to preserve our culture." The Kerner Commission mentioned the lack of black media perspectives as one cause of the 1960s race riots that spread across nearly every major urban center.[18]

"The Black Agenda for Communications" argued that there was "no substitute for the control of our own institutions." As a catalyst for social change, the black press had a responsibility to the community to tell our people "what we need to know," and the black community had an obligation to support and strengthen black media companies. The issue of radio and television ownership was important since, of the 365 "Black-programmed radio stations in America," 345 were owned by whites, thereby enabling them to become millionaires "through the exploitation of the Black public." Until black folks could move into the ranks of radio and TV owners, they needed to form media watchdog groups "to document unfair media practices in hiring, news coverage, entertainment and advertising." Consistent with this idea was a warning that black people needed to control the fledgling cable television industry. This unregulated industry had the potential to do great damage. "We must see to it that no cable television comes into our communities unless we control it. Our minds and the minds of our children are at stake." In an effort to have some kind of media oversight, the Agenda called for three black persons to be appointed to the Federal Communications Commission to ensure monitoring at the highest levels. If black entrepreneurs didn't have sufficient capital to purchase an outlet, then the government should transfer certain stations to black community control. "We must tell our own story to our people."[19]

In sum, the Agenda was designed to lay out strategic areas of concern and focus for the well-being of the African American community. Both black nationalists and civil rights activists had worked since the fall of 1971 to determine the most pressing issues facing the community. However, even a cursory reading of the full Agenda makes it clear that this is the work of Baraka and black nationalist sympathizers. Much of the document seemed like a dream rather than a concrete action plan. While the Agenda addressed day-to-day issues, it did not make practical recommendations on how to solve them. These were the pragmatic issues that needed to be addressed because black people of all ideological persuasions could agree on the basic survival issues, whereas much of the Agenda is overly idealistic. Further, too much of the Agenda makes demands upon the US government. Would the US government really give five states to its black citizens? In addition to capital and cash? Some delegates were disappointed and rightfully so. Coleman Young, the leader of the Michigan delegation, the second largest, openly confronted Baraka about the Agenda, and the two of them would have a showdown on the last day of the Convention. In addition to ratifying the Agenda, the Convention also needed to act on a number of resolutions that were divisive, such as the endorsement of Shirley Chisholm; whether or not the Convention would endorse a third political party or some type of permanent political structure; questions around school busing; and a controversial resolution dealing with the Israeli/Palestinian conflict.

Baraka chaired Sunday's session, and he made it known that he would not adhere "slavishly" to Robert's Rules of Order, as Diggs had attempted to do the day before. "Since my own acquaintanceship with traditional politics is rather new, Robert's Rules of Order may not be adhered to like it is in Congress. However, there was a thing called African consensus which dated back a couple thousand years before Congress which meant that we had to agree [reach consensus] before we moved." Baraka was determined to get the Agenda ratified before the Convention adjourned. Not to get a ratification would make the entire exercise of political unity a monumental failure.[20]

"A Blatantly Separatist Document"

However, some delegates were not in favor of ratifying the document on site. Coleman Young expressed his anger at Baraka and tried to convince him to give the delegates some time to read and discuss the Agenda before he sought ratification. Young recalled telling Baraka that the delegates needed to take the Agenda home "to have a full discussion at the grass-roots level of our respective organizations." Young and the delegation dominated by the United Auto Workers (UAW) had several major issues with the "Black Magna Carta," as he called it. His principal concern was that the Agenda deserved "a greater and broader input from the total Black community." Young was convinced, and he was right, that the Agenda had largely been put together before the Convention. "It (the Agenda) was a grandiose idea, the problem being that the platform was already put together by the time we got to Gary. After some inane discussion we were handed a Black agenda, as the Baraka people called it—a document about the size of the *New York Daily News*—and told that we had two hours to digest it before the vote. I maintained that if they wanted us to consider their proposals seriously we should take them home and study them for a couple of weeks and then come back and have some more discussion then vote." Young told reporters that Baraka privately agreed to delay the vote, yet then proceeded to bring it to the floor for ratification.[21]

While Young and the Michigan delegation (along with the Illinois delegation) had serious concerns over certain aspects of the Agenda like the establishment of a black political party, the call for a constitutional Convention, and the entire plank around reparations, he had problems with the entire document. "As a political monograph the platform was completely off-target and unacceptable. It was a blatantly separatist document, the obvious work of Baraka, the misguided ramblings of a so-called artist who would be dictator. It consisted of bullshit like taking over five states for Black people." Not only did the Michigan group have problems with the issues mentioned above "but there were many more issues written into these basic documents, each of which collectively and individually are of sufficient importance to call for a pause." In an effort to appease Michigan and Illinois, Baraka appointed a special committee to work out a compromise with them. This was not only done to give Michigan more time to look at the Agenda but also to address concerns from those within the Michigan delegation who disagreed with Young and wanted to ratify the Agenda.[22]

The future mayor of Detroit felt, like many others, that the Agenda was hypocritical and contradictory. "These documents are a back and forth hodge-podge moving from participation in the system by changing the constitution to separation by forming a Black nation." But perhaps this was unavoidable. As Robert Smith notes, the Agenda was "internally contradictory." Since the NBPC wanted to be inclusive, "everyone's pet ideological or institutional position" was included for the sake of black unity. Young was also upset, like Roy Wilkins, that the Convention and Agenda failed to criticize President Nixon. "It is strange indeed that every progressive president of the democratic party was castigated, while little was said about Mr. Nixon in his attempt to turn back the clock on Black progress." He continued. "The Agenda assumes that 90% of white America is racist. I don't happen to believe that ninety percent of whites are racist."[23]

In a hastily prepared two-paragraph statement that the Michigan delegation gave to the press and other delegates, Young and his supporters explained their frustration. "The Michigan delegation, because of the shortness of time and its inability to thoroughly examine the National Black Political Agenda and resolutions as proposed, by this Convention, and because of serious principle reservations with specific proposals in the Preamble and the Program, as well as in certain resolutions, is not prepared at this time to fully endorse the proceedings in this area." The Michigan delegation read that statement to the crowd and then proceeded to walk out of the Convention both literally and figuratively. Young would say days later, "We went there to unite Black people, not to have shoved down our throats lengthy documents we had not seen until Saturday afternoon."[24]

As the Michigan delegation followed Young out of the building, Baraka pleaded with them to stay. "Michigan! Michigan! Michigan . . . ," he said, but they ignored his plea and kept moving toward the door. But as they left someone noticed that a small contingent of Michigan delegates were still seated, causing someone to yell into the microphone, "Michigan has not left the building." Ecstatic that the fractured coalition was not completely broken, the crowd started chanting "Nationtime!" The small group that stayed were critical of their fellow delegates and blamed the walkout on the UAW's control of black Detroit. "The Michigan delegation is highly organized and politically sophisticated, but largely reflects the so-called 'Friends of the Negro Group' like the UAW and the Democratic Party. Therefore, they have not dealt with the very fundamentals of the Gary experience." They were in favor of ratifying the Agenda because not to do so would "result in the continued castration of Black people's leadership capabilities. To postpone action today is to deny the historically important purpose for a vote." Illinois, the third largest delegation, supported Michigan and got the Convention to agree that Michigan's concerns be given full consideration before the Agenda was finalized later that spring. Since there was strong sentiment not to leave Gary without ratifying the Agenda, the Convention then spent several hours on resolutions, which would be added to the Agenda.[25]

As the Michigan delegation walked out the doors of West Side High School, some of Baraka's "henchmen" tried to stop them. "We were strapped down pretty well and showed them enough artillery to make it out of there," Young recalled. But trouble followed them to their hotel. "We closed ourselves off in our section of the hotel, and I contacted some trade union guys from Chicago who brought us some additional firepower. It was a tense and volatile situation, Baraka's followers were zealots, and he had brought a lot of muscle from New Jersey—but violence never broke out." Baraka recalled that Young's critique of the Agenda was a smokescreen. "He walked out because somebody had proposed a Black union," and he could not support that because he was controlled by the UAW. The threat of violence in this conflict explains why very few black elected officials challenged Baraka's authority at the NBPC. Baraka was not afraid to use tactics of intimidation to coerce his critics into supporting him. Young, however, was willing to meet violence with violence, and that deterred Baraka's lieutenants from any kind of violence toward Young and the other delegates from Michigan.[26]

While Coleman Young thought the Agenda was "separatist," ironically some black nationalists believed that the Agenda was an integrationist document. Midway through Sunday's session a bomb threat was called in, and Gary Fire Department officials had to evacuate the gymnasium. There was some speculation that an anonymous black nationalist phoned in the threat to prevent the NBPC from finishing its business, which included the ratification of the Agenda. Nationalists also accused Baraka of selling out. They felt that he had compromised them by seeking to ratify a watered-down integrationist platform. One of Baraka's biggest supporters came to his defense against these attacks by suggesting that Baraka was growing as a leader. "I don't think as some of the nationalists do, that he has compromised himself. He is moving to help Black people to get into the system so they can realize that once they get in they will see that it is good for them."

"We Want a Third Party"

One of the ongoing questions during the Convention was whether or not it would endorse a presidential candidate. Specifically, would the NBPC express its support for Shirley Chisholm, the only African American presidential candidate in the 1972 election. Manhattan borough president Percy Sutton, Chisholm's biggest supporter in Gary, encouraged the Convention to endorse her candidacy as a means of "solidifying Black voters." Jesse Jackson also voiced his support while suggesting, in addition, that black folks needed to form an independent political party. During the intense debate over endorsing presidential candidates, Ohio introduced a resolution against endorsement, while Louisiana delegates were in favor of endorsing. Sensing that the Convention would not endorse, Jesse quickly jumped on that bandwagon by stating an endorsement would "violate the spirit of our hosts," who in calling for the Convention stated that its intent was not to endorse. Ironically, during the debate Chisholm's name "never came up during the discussion." The resolution not to endorse was overwhelmingly passed by the Convention, and black women such as Coretta Scott King and Dorothy Height, president of the National Council of Negro Women, agreed. King believed that the Convention was about issues and not individuals, especially since they were trying to move toward broad-based leadership. "I can appreciate what

Shirley is doing and I support Shirley's efforts. I've talked with Shirley and she knows that, but personally I am not in a position to endorse anybody at this time. I take the position that this should be an issue-oriented thing because what you've got here is a lot of Black politicians who are committed and have to be committed to certain things and you put them in a bad position." Height stated that from an organizational standpoint the NCNW would not endorse candidates "but rather work to awaken women to action and get them to work in their communities. I personally don't think the purpose of this Convention is to endorse candidates," she said.[27]

With little to no support at Gary, the Chisholm campaign was virtually ignored. Carl Stokes actually made the point of no endorsement early in the 1972 black strategy sessions, and this view carried the day at Gary. In his autobiography Stokes wrote that this was precisely aimed at Chisholm. "This policy of no endorsement, admittedly, was to stop them from joining Congresswoman Shirley Chisholm on her ego trip in the presidential primaries. The view prevailed, but it was rough at first. I looked at the situation we faced in 1972, and it was exactly what it had been in 1968. We faced the probability of four more years of Richard M. Nixon. Yet many people were still out there playing games." The NBPC never considered Chisholm a serious candidate and not even someone who could get votes. Her election in Brooklyn, some believed, was not by "any particular mandate of the voters," but rather "due to the apathy and indifference of her Brooklyn constituency." They pointed out that each time she was elected to Congress, it was with fewer votes than any of the other 434 members of the House of Representatives.[28]

Although Chisholm was invited to Gary to address the Convention on Sunday, she never showed up. Her official excuse was that she was campaigning in Florida, but she never planned to attend despite the many times Convention organizers reached out to her. "I was not present at the Gary Convention," she said, "I didn't intend to present myself to a group of people who were just going to slash me left and right. Because they would laugh at me. I knew that and I didn't want to be wasting my time to have them laughing at me. I was on a mission. I saw myself on a mission. And that was all there was to it." Despite the ambivalence of many of her fellow black elected officials, Hatcher believed that if she would've showed up to Gary, the Convention would've endorsed her because of what her candidacy represented. "I absolutely believe that if Shirley Chisholm walked into that hall, just walked into that hall, she wouldn't have had to say a word, and the entire Convention would have gone up in smoke, because there was such a great sense of pride that a Black woman had the courage and fortitude to announce that she was running for the highest office in the country."[29]

Chisholm may not have ever received an endorsement even if she participated in the Convention, but her ego didn't help her gather much support. She expected support although she separated herself from the 1971–1972 strategy sessions and the broader black political apparatus. She also appeared to run as a woman's candidate rather than a black candidate. Without the support of mainstream black politicians, her candidacy quickly withered. For the NBPC to ignore the Chisholm candidacy was a sign of deep disrespect and a missed opportunity. Some believed that the Chisholm endorsement would have given the NBPC leverage at the Democratic Party Convention, while others felt that to support Chisholm the NBPC would risk fracturing the Convention since she did not have much of a political base in the black community. Further, some delegates believed that if the NBPC were to endorse Chisholm and she did not capture the nomination, then the Convention would lose any potential brokering opportunities. Instead, by not endorsing Chisholm they could use the NBPC as a tool, and whichever presidential candidate agreed to support the goals of the Convention, they would then broker deals for more black federal judges, black cabinet posts, and chairs of agencies such as the U.S. Securities and Exchange Commission (SEC), the Federal Trade Commission (FTC), the Federal Communications Commission (FCC), and the Federal Reserve Bank.[30]

Form a Third Party?

Whether to form an independent black political party or stay within the Democratic Party was arguably the underlying rationale and theme of the entire 1971–1972 strategy sessions. Nationalists came to Gary with the goal of launching an independent black political party, and black elected officials wanted the black community to unify. But the officials wanted to avoid any discussion of an all-black third party for two main reasons:

first, many of them enjoyed being Democratic officeholders—the perks, salary, clout, and popularity allowed them to have a good living. Second, and more pragmatically, they were not convinced that the votes of black people, who made up only 11 percent of the population, could leverage the value of a third party. Thus, they felt that it would be political suicide to launch a third-party effort. Since many delegates came to Gary "for the whole purpose" of forming a third party, there was much debate about it throughout the entire weekend. But black elected officials, those firmly entrenched within Democratic circles, fought it bitterly. Baraka recalled that it was "the electoral politicians, and the Black caucus, that mitigated the discussion."[31]

Throughout the weekend extensive lobbying took place, and when Jesse gave his "Nationtime" speech many were confident that a black political party would get launched on the Convention's last day. Even Jesse told Hatcher, "we ought to stop talking about it and just do it." But a wave of political conservatism slowed this momentum, largely out of self-interest. With so many black elected officials in attendance, they had a strong "stake in not seeing a third party form." Hatcher explained, "Some of them were very active and had relationships in that party they did not want to sever. And as a consequence, you know, they were opposed." Many like Hatcher were caught in the middle. They saw the necessity for a third party but were not convinced that it was "the right time," considering that the history of third parties in America had typically not been successful. One black elected official from the Midwest put it at an even more basic level. "You can be very Black and very unified in Gary, but when you get back home, your life, your patronage, and your political future, depend really on how well you fit into the pattern of a very white, regional machine."[32]

Those favoring a third party were black nationalists and young people who could not understand why black voters would give undying allegiance to both parties. Twenty-one-year-old L. P. Banks, a Georgia delegate, felt "there is no need to deal with Republicans or Democrats anymore." When a reporter followed up with him about whether or not a third party would be confusing to the masses of black voters, he said, "as long as we have to deal with white political parties, confusion is the price we must pay." Another young delegate, Ray Standard, 18, of Washington,

DC, did not see the value in working within the system. "The time of bargaining is long bankrupt. As I see it the problem is not in setting up an agenda with which to deal with the two parties, but to be about the business of what we're going to do in terms of a third party."[33]

Bill Crawford of the Indiana delegation was the only member of his state's delegation to vote for the creation of a third party. "When we talk about the ability to determine our own destiny, we can only be talking about the formation of a third political party. We should be going back to our communities from this Convention to teach 'Black party' because our people have to be educated to this." Those who made an argument based on black population numbers did not sway him. "Just because we are a minority, we get so hung up on numbers. If two percent of South Africa controls the whole country, then 6.5 percent (Indiana's Black population) can control, or at least be a strong determining factor in Indiana politics. All the whites are divided between the Democratic and Republican parties."[34]

The National Black Political Assembly

As sentiment swelled against forming a third party, Jesse Jackson changed his position "when he led the fight to block formation of a third party"—which had been his own idea! While the forming of a third party sounded good, it was simply impractical because the NBPC did not have the apparatus set up to institutionalize an effective third-party mechanism. So, Hatcher's idea of giving the major political parties one last chance won out. As a compromise measure the Convention voted to create the National Black Political Assembly, which some saw as a transitional form for a third party, "a kind of developmental outpost for a third party."[35]

As the brainchild of Baraka, the National Black Political Assembly would be the NBPC's permanent political structure. New York's Waldaba Stewart saw it as "moving from rhetoric to constructivism." The assembly would be made up of 427 members, which represented 10 percent of the total delegate count in Gary. Baraka predicted that the Assembly would function like a congressional body. "It would endorse candidates, support candidates, run national voter education and registration drives, lobby for Black interests, assess Black programs, make recommendations to the national Convention and in the Black community generally." Issue-

oriented, the Assembly would be the "chief brokerage operation" for dealing with the white power structure, and it would help build bridges between African Americans and "our brothers and sisters on the continent."
Carrying on the day-to-day business of the Assembly would be a Steering
Committee of forty-three people that would "fit" the following eleven
categories: North, South, East, West, Central, Black Elected Officials,
Nationalists, Activists, National Black Organization Representatives,
Youth, Women. The council would meet four times a year, the Assembly
once a year, and they would hold a black political convention every two
to four years.[36]

Creating a structure that would extend beyond the Convention was
important because it would allow the NBPC to move from talk to action.
Hatcher believed that the Assembly would "decide the tactics of the Black
political movement to be used from now on." It was also important because now black southerners had a voice in the Convention apparatus. In
fact, the NBPC was embarrassingly void of southern leadership. Jackson
told one reporter that the possibilities for the Assembly were endless.
"You may have people here who remain democrats or republicans, but
they're Black. This group might seek support from a third party, or it
might run its own slate. It is a new structure for youth to come in and
may even inspire them to vote. Youth don't relate well to either of the
two major parties."[37]

By moving toward a politics based on race, the creation of the National Black Political Assembly was greeted warmly by delegates. Many
delegates felt that the Assembly could be a bridge to a third party because it would give them some time to "do some organizing and some
hard work," and it would also allow time "to convince a lot of brothers
and sisters who aren't here and who are bound to existing party structures." This was a bold, innovative, and creative attempt by Baraka to
pull black voters together nationally. It was a structure that even the
most diehard integrationist and committed black nationalist could agree
upon. With the defeat of the third-party resolution, the Agenda would
now be used as a platform to take to the Democratic Party Convention
in Miami to broker with Democratic candidates. In essence the NBPC
leadership would pledge black support to the candidate that supported
the Agenda.[38]

Looking back at the convention months later, Baraka was convinced that the NBPC's "most essential" accomplishment was the creation of the Assembly. He said that as a structure, it "would function in all the ways the national Black community needed it to function, to gain, maintain and use power . . . which is my understanding of what politics is." He also suggested that the Assembly would be capable of "criticism, and of self-criticism, growth and influence. This was a critical lesson he learned at Gary. "If one ideology moved to dominate the Convention or follow-up assembly, we would all be lost, because no Assembly would be formed, but only another collection of opportunists at worst, or at best, another of the endless critics of intellectuals . . . debating the perfect way to solve problems—while at all points of street reality the problems get observably worse."[39]

The Debate Over School Busing

The most controversial resolutions passed in Gary came at the end of Sunday's ten-hour session, when some delegations had already headed home and others were preparing to leave. Chuck Anderson of the *New York Amsterdam News* stated that as the Convention appeared to be coming to a close, several resolutions "came to the floor in a pell mell, chaotic fashion," leaving many delegates and observers "wondering what exactly was going on." School busing and Israel were two of those resolutions. The controversial practice of school busing was something black nationalists were determined to end. The idea of busing black kids to white schools where neither the faculty, staff, or students necessarily wanted them was absurd. Why would black parents send their kids to an environment where they were not wanted, they asked. Further, could the black community really accept the notion that black kids would do better academically just because they were sitting next to a white kid? Finally, could white teachers, who had very little experience teaching black children, and probably very little interaction with black people in general, effectively teach black children?[40]

These concerns were not only voiced at Gary by black nationalists but also spoken privately by some black elected officials and black parents. However, because the NAACP and other liberal organizations championed school busing as an easy solution to end school segregation, many critics of busing did not feel comfortable speaking against it openly. The convention gave the critics of busing an opportunity to bring this discussion into the public discourse and make it a plank of the National Black Political Agenda. Many southerners privately disliked busing because it hastened the closing of previously all-black schools and led to the firing of black teachers. So now they had a friendly environment in which to voice their displeasure.[41]

Roy Innis of CORE was active throughout the convention, and he was determined to get his antibusing resolution onto the floor. After working with the youthful delegations from the states of South Carolina, Florida, Wisconsin, and Oregon, the South Carolina delegation presented the following resolution:

> We condemn forced racial integration of schools as a bankrupt, suicidal method of desegregating schools, based on the false notion that Black children are unable to learn unless they are in the same setting as white children. As an alternative to busing of Black children to achieve total racial balance, we demand quality education in the Black community through the control of our school system, school districts and a guarantee of an equal share of the money.[42]

After the resolution was read, Henry Marsh of Richmond, Virginia, moved to reconsider the motion. Marsh was the vice mayor of Richmond, and ironically the leading attorney in a lawsuit against the Richmond Board of Education, which sought to use busing as a means to foster school integration. He was just one of many Virginia delegates who were leaders of that state's school desegregation cases. Despite Marsh's plea against the South Carolina–sponsored antibusing resolution, the resolution overwhelmingly passed, putting the Convention on record as being against busing.[43]

When the resolution passed, Roy Innis and his lieutenants ran out of the gymnasium and held a press conference to announce what had just happened. "This is a historic moment for Black people in America. It is the first recorded change in educational policy since 1954." He continued, "Busing is obsolete and dangerous to Black people. We are ready to control our own destiny." In the eyes of antibusing proponents, the issue was not sitting next to white kids, but rather it was about community control of schools and school financing. CORE envisioned a community school structure with federal funding coming to the black community directly, "not through white school boards." They wanted an equal share of the money, not forced integration. This was part of CORE's unitary school plan. "We're going to draw lines for the first time to have Black school boards and Black control where Blacks are in the majority."[44]

CORE's national deputy director Victor Solomon also appeared at the press conference and explained a bit more the importance of the resolution. "Before we thought it was a move toward equality to have Black kids sitting next to white kids. Now we feel differently. Where are the Black school boards?" Solomon was then asked how he felt the NAACP would respond to the resolution since it had come out against the preamble days earlier. He said, "The NAACP is dying and so are its integrationist policies in the Black community."[45]

As Innis and Solomon and other CORE members engaged the press, some probusing delegates inside the Convention hall stayed and proceeded to draft a less-condemning resolution for several reasons. First, they understood that white liberals had provided strong support to the black freedom struggle and for school busing, so they did not feel free to critique it. Second, some saw the antibusing resolution as playing into the hands of Richard Nixon and George Wallace, who were both against school busing albeit for reasons vastly different from black people's. Last, they knew that the white media would focus on the singular issue of busing at the exclusion of everything else that went on at the convention. For the above-mentioned reasons, the New York delegation offered a "resolution of clarification," which reiterated their rejection of busing, but for different reasons. "We demand that all monies that will be used for busing be spent in Black communities to achieve quality education." But it was simply too late. The antibusing forces had won out and Innis believed that the CORE-sponsored resolution "made it crystal clear that the Black community is tired of forced integration and ready to govern our own educational institutions."[46]

The Question of Israel

The last resolution that caused a great deal of turmoil at the NBPC was the issue of Israel. Black nationalists had long supported the idea of a Palestinian homeland. Peniel Joseph writes that many black radicals "identified Palestine as a colony and its people as a community of color under siege." So throughout the Black Power era, Jews and black nationalists would have a tense relationship. Jewish support for black civil rights issues was expected to be repaid with unequivocal black support for Israel. With this backdrop, Rev. Douglas Moore, a staunch black nationalist and head of the local Black United Front, introduced a resolution calling for the destruction of Israel. It read:

> Whereas the establishment of the Jewish State of Israel in 1948 constituted a clear violation of the Palestinian traditional right to life in their own homeland,
> Whereas thousands of Palestinians have been killed, thousands have been left homeless by the illegal establishment of the state of Israel,
> Whereas Jews ruling Israel have demonstrated fascist desires through the occupation of other Palestinian and Arab lands,
> Whereas Israeli agents are working hand-in-hand with other imperialistic interests in Africa,
> Be it therefore resolved:
>
> • that the U.S. government end immediately its economic and military support of the Israeli regime;
> • that the U.S. government should withdraw its military forces from the Middle East area;
> • that the historical land of Palestinian and Arab people be returned to them;
> • that negotiations be ended with the freedom of the representatives of the Palestinians to establish a second state based on the historical right of the Palestinian people for self-government in their land.

The resolution passed handily without much opposition.[47]

Predictably, black elected officials and their Jewish supporters were furious. Ronald Walters recalled that some representatives of Jewish groups were so upset that they called members of the Convention staff "to discover the specific source of the resolution." This was the last item of business for the National Black Political Convention as it adjourned at 9:30 p.m., and as delegates headed home there would be mixed opinions over whether or not it was a success.[48]

7

WHAT WE WARNED AGAINST HAS HAPPENED

The Withdrawal of the Congressional Black Caucus

As delegates said their good-byes and exited Gary's West Side High School, the conveners celebrated what had been accomplished. First, they were successful in bringing black folks from all walks of life and every political leaning together under one roof at one time to discuss a black political strategy. Second, they achieved their ultimate goal, ratifying a black political agenda that the masses could agree upon. And third, they created a permanent political structure, the National Black Political Assembly, to carry on the business of the National Black Political Convention. All three of these accomplishments were remarkable and it was a testament to both groups: integrationists and separatists. Mayor Hatcher saw the significance in the Convention: "But what has happened here is that every spectrum of political thought and political ideology has been put into one building and in one room, and in fact, are holding a Convention where they are making decisions jointly that will affect all groups, all philosophies, all ideologies in the future, and I think that it is highly significant not only for Black people but for this country." Congressman Diggs told reporters that he was "very much gratified" with the results, which exceeded his expectations. In the eyes of Jesse Jackson, "What has happened here has been a rather extraordinary situation. We pulled off a lightweight miracle here with the most credible Black Convention in history." Notably absent from the post-Convention press conference was Baraka. He would not comment on the Convention until weeks later.[1]

It did not take long for a reporter to bring up the idea that the Convention was chaotic, intense, and full of confusion. Hatcher anticipated the question and he gave an excellent response. "I think if you were to take the John Birch society on the one hand and the Americans for

Democratic Action on the other and put 3,000 of them in the same room you would have total chaos and I'm sure you could not possibly hold a Convention."[2]

As expected, just three days after the close of the Convention both Richard Hatcher and the Congressional Black Caucus came under intense pressure from white liberals and Jewish groups to denounce the Convention in light of the controversial resolutions on busing and Israel. On the issue of Israel, Hatcher called the resolution "a most unfortunate incident." When pressed by reporters about how it got passed he said simply, "I think it was snuck through." As reporters continued to probe to assess whether or not black folks supported Israel, Hatcher told them that the resolution passed late in the session with less than half the delegates in attendance and that the resolution did not reflect the overall views of the black community. "I didn't see any strong anti-Israel sentiments on the floor." Hatcher was prepared for the volley of questions because Jewish money had supported and funded civil rights activity throughout much of the twentieth century. When asked about the busing resolution, Hatcher expressed frustration that the media played up the resolution and ignored the subsequent resolution that supported busing only in situations where black kids could not get a quality education. Later that day the Congressional Black Caucus came out publicly against the antibusing measure at a press conference in Washington, DC. The thirteen-member delegation reaffirmed their support for busing "as one of the many ways to implement the constitutional requirement of equal educational opportunities in education." But they did state that if done correctly, "most schools could be integrated without massive busing." The CBC's statement was not only important in light of the convention resolutions but also because the day before, black voters in Gadsden County, Florida, had supported a constitutional amendment against forced busing by a 3 to 1 margin. The Caucus avoided making any reference to the Gary Convention, but one journalist felt that the statement in support of busing was designed to show that the National Black Political Convention was not necessarily representative of black opinion. Roy Innis of CORE wasn't buying it. In his mind the Convention was the voice of the people, and the people made it clear that they didn't want busing. "The anti-busing resolution was a mandate from Black folks, proving they support this approach. Now we know we are on the right road. We will go back into the South and redouble our efforts against busing from our new moral position. We can now claim broad-based support for nationalism, and Black people cannot be bulldozed anymore by the integrationists." Despite Innis's pronouncements, there was some talk that white conservative interests were bankrolling CORE, and others wanted to know the size of CORE's membership in light of their apparent influence within the NBPC.[3]

Journalists offered their opinions on the Convention in its immediate aftermath. Thomas Johnson of the *New York Times* said the National Black Political Convention showed off the "complexity and vitality" of black America "by having a meeting of 8000 people show up representing a wide variety of political interests." In Johnson's opinion, black elected officials and civil rights veterans won in Gary by defeating proposals that called for blacks to pull out of the two major political parties and form an all-black party. Readers of the *New York Amsterdam News* noticed that Carlos Russell was equally celebratory after the Convention. Amidst the "carnivalesque" and "chaotic" atmosphere of Gary, serious business was done. "There were the hucksters hawking their wares—beads, buttons, posters, and incense—while on the floor Black men and women wrestled with concepts which they felt would bring us, as a nation of Blacks, closer together." He then spoke to those who complained about the Convention being unorganized and messy. "To expect order, clarity, and organiza-tion, at an initial meeting where there are varied elements, ideologies, positions, self interests, programs, and even provocateurs is to expect too much." He then reminded his readers, "we, as Blacks sometimes tend to be hard on ourselves." He saw the Convention as black folks forging a new political movement."[4]

Someone else described the Gary Convention as "Black people at their best, and Black people at their worst." At our best was a general com-mitment to improve black people's quality of life; and at our worst there was "viciousness, division, jealousy, rhetoric rather than hard working reality; confusion, disorganization and poor planning." Yet the Gary Con-vention was "a soulful new beginning" as black folks spent three days wrestling with "crucial political issues in our own way." Similarly, Roger Wilkins of the *Washington Post* believed that the National Black Political

Convention "served notice" to the nation that "Blacks intend to become a serious political force in this country and that they have the skill and the determination to do it."[5]

But not everyone looked at the Convention as a success. Bayard Rustin was extremely critical about it and its desire for black political unity. He felt that the ideological divide between integrationists and black nationalists was too wide for them to find common ground, and that the only positive to come out of Gary was that 4,000 people showed up. Rustin believed that the conveners should've spent time on more practical issues. "No major steps were taken that had anything to do with the education of our children, the building of homes, the elimination of slums, and no groundwork was laid for any constructive activity." Many journalists, both black and white, ignored the fact that the delegates produced an agenda where they agreed on all but three or four items, and created a permanent political structure. Instead they focused solely on the busing issue and Israel. The editor of the *Chicago Defender* provided perhaps the most vicious critique of the Convention, solely because of busing. "The Convention was a Babel of ideologies, half-baked dilettantism and infantile assumptions. It did not live up to its roseate promise. It had a chance to be a force in the conversation of American politics, it has muffed it."[6]

Revisiting the Busing and Israel Controversies

Two weeks after the close of the Convention, the NBPC held a Steering Committee meeting of state chairpersons in Washington, DC, principally to address the busing and Israeli resolutions. The Steering Committee was created as a go-between to connect delegates and the NBPC leadership, and they would have to satisfy the demands of the NAACP and CORE, who were at opposite ends of the black political continuum. Thus, attendees were hopeful that the committee would come up with a more pragmatic document even though the nationalist contingent would probably oppose it. But black elected officials did not despair about a probusing or pro-Israel resolution because they understood that black nationalists were always more active and vocal than moderates. The controversy wouldn't go away because of pressure from white liberals and longtime Jewish supporters of civil rights. Relative to busing, the NBPC came under attack from those who suggested that the resolution gave

ammunition to both George Wallace and President Nixon, who vociferously opposed busing. In an attempt to address these concerns the
Steering Committee decided to "soften" the resolution by introducing
and passing a substitute resolution that clearly separated their position
from those of Wallace and Nixon. They added the following sentence to
the original resolution: "We disassociate ourselves from the positions set
forth by Wallace." This slight modification did nothing to silence their
critics. On the Israeli question the Steering Committee also rewrote the
resolution by removing the language calling for Israel to be dissolved.
Instead it stated that the NBPC position on Israel was the same as those
of the Organization of African Unity and the UN Commission on Human Rights. However, the CBC released its own statement on Israel that
reaffirmed their commitment: "We fully respect the right of the Jewish
people to have their own state in their historic national homeland. We
vigorously oppose the efforts of any group that would seek to weaken
or undermine Israeli's right to existence."[7]

At the close of the March 24 meeting, the leadership of the Convention reaffirmed their unity in the midst of the controversy surrounding
the busing and Israel resolutions. Diggs, Hatcher, and Baraka believed
that they could work through their issues and satisfy all parties involved,
including the NAACP. They cited the substitute resolutions and their
working to bring Michigan back into the fold, and they announced that
additional committee meetings would be held so any and all parties could
submit resolutions and agenda items before the Steering Committee met
on May 6, 1972, in Greensboro, North Carolina, to ratify the final agenda.[8]

Despite these genuine efforts designed to satisfy the concerns of white
liberals and Jewish supporters, it didn't work. The initial resolutions
concerning Israel and busing had set the tone. Baraka recalled that even
though the two resolutions were "softened" and "compromised" in the
name of black unity, they were still not acceptable to the NAACP and
black elected officials. "They still publicly ran and disclaimed," Baraka recalled. The NAACP stated that in essence the two new resolutions meant
nothing. "It (the NAACP pullout) is based squarely upon basic division
between a belief in racial separatism and nationhood." Since both of the
revised resolutions were contained in the final National Black Political
Agenda, which was scheduled to be released on May 19, the birthday of

Malcolm X, both Hatcher and Diggs disassociated themselves from the resolutions. In a joint statement they said: "We feel obligated to point out that in our judgment the resolution regarding Israel and the busing element . . . are not representative of the sentiments of the vast majority of Black Americans." But Walter Fauntroy, who was also in attendance at the press conference, affirmed his signature to the statement as well. So now, two of the three conveners of the National Black Political Convention had effectively withdrawn from the Convention effort largely because of the busing and Israel issues.[9]

The NAACP Pullout

As the NBPC prepared to release the final version of the Agenda, the NAACP officially withdrew its support from the Convention. In a letter to Hatcher and Baraka, Roy Wilkins explained in a paternalistic tone that he "warned them" that if the "Agenda adopted by the Convention turns out to be consistent with the draft preamble, the Agenda will be impossible to endorse." He then mentioned that "what we warned against has happened." Wilkins told the conveners that the "true spirit of Gary" had been "badly served" by the draft preamble, the forthcoming Agenda, and the resolutions on Israel and busing. And that despite the post-Convention Steering Committee meetings, "no thorough ongoing modifications in tone, language, or meaning can be expected." However, while the NAACP did agree with many of the planks in the Agenda, the NBPC did not spend enough time on issues "upon which there is genuine consensus in the Black community." For Wilkins, the Agenda was openly separatist and nationalistic. "It envisages a separate Black nation, a separate Black politics, and the establishment (with the help ironically, of the rejected white nation) of separate Black institutions. It was empty rhetoric at its best." The busing and Israel resolutions were "repugnant" to Wilkins, and in his mind they should have been completely erased from the Agenda. For these reasons the NAACP would have no further involvement with the National Black Political Convention. Eugene T. Reed, state chair of New York's NAACP chapter, ignored Wilkins's statement. "I respect the authority of the executive director and I'll conform within the framework of he organization, but individually I will do as I please. I was a Black man before I was a member of the NAACP." Following the NAACP's lead, Diggs,

Hatcher, Fauntroy, Barbara Jordan, Charlie Rangel, and the entire Congressional Black Caucus all distanced themselves from the resolutions, but in essence they were effectively leaving the NBPC and its theme of "unity without uniformity." Thus, when the final National Black Political Agenda was released on Malcolm X's birthday, it was just an afterthought. While black elected officials did not openly oppose the Agenda when it was released, they never embraced it or even mentioned it.[10]

Baraka was livid and he had the right to be. How could the NAACP denounce the National Black Political Agenda when it came out against the Convention with its critique of the preamble? Baraka believed that Wilkins often "expresses the bias of an old white man and not the Black people he was supposed to represent." As it stood, Baraka was now the only convener and literally the only person with a national following that embraced the Agenda. He could not understand why the Convention participants could not embrace tension and disagree with one another like other political bodies. "It is stupid to me to destroy our own institutions because we can't agree on Israel. We have to agree as a people that we have got to become mature enough to maintain our basic institutions and not destroy them because we disagree." He then complained that white politicians are not asked to "resign from Congress" because they disagree with their party colleagues over a particular piece of legislation. This confirmed to him that black elected officials never really embraced the Convention, so when their friends and supporters got "offended" or "threatened" by portions of the Agenda, they were forced to pull out. Wilkins responded to Baraka's charge that the NAACP had basically sold out to white interests by suggesting that "liberals like Senator Edward Kennedy and Senator Hruska both believe in the American system. Neither wants to destroy it, or withdraw from it, in order to form a new nation, separate from the American nation." Writing in the *New York Amsterdam News* the day after the Agenda was ratified, Baraka felt the black community had a decision to make. "From this point we can either pull together, build and rise, or else we can draw apart, splinter, or polarize."[11]

Post-Gary

Baraka got his answer two weeks later when the Congressional Black Caucus issued a "Black Declaration of Independence" and a "Black Bill of Rights" at a news conference on June 1, 1972. Both documents were eerily similar to the National Black Political Agenda, except that the Caucus's "lacked the fiery rhetoric and nationalist orientation" of the Gary document. Caucus members said they would take their demands to the Democratic Platform Committee. That was the plan of the National Black Political Convention! How then could both the NBPC and the CBC take their plans to the Democrats? How could Diggs be a leader in both organizations and go along with this arrangement and essentially render the work of the NBPC meaningless? Ironically, in the CBC press conference members of Congress did not make a single mention of the Gary Convention. When asked about his involvement in both groups, Diggs said that he was hopeful that the CBC and the NBPC could get together and form a single proposal. Was he serious? That was the entire purpose of the NBPC! It was later learned that a group of black Republicans jumped on the "agenda" bandwagon as well by presenting the Republican leadership with a list of concerns. In the aftermath of the CBC press conference, one black nationalist summed it up best: "It appears that groups are trying to maintain their own power rather than working for the common good."[12]

The CBC-issued "Black Bill of Rights" was the last power play issued by civil rights activists, and it effectively ended any hopes of black political unity, in favor of a strategy that favored black elected officials. Baraka provided an excellent analysis of that decision. "The 'Black Bill of Rights' is frankly a co-opt attempt. It takes many of the concerns, and even the phrasing of the Agenda, but waters them down for white delectation. It is a document which screams out loud to be considered 'reasonable' by white folks. This 'Black Bill of Rights' is a mimeographed clutch of papers gotten together hurriedly to be put in the path of the Black Agenda." But Baraka wasn't surprised at the actions of the Congressional Black Caucus. He knew that they were using the Bill of Rights as a "bargaining document" to secure some goods and services from the eventual Democratic nominee. Although Baraka had previously been critical of the "Black Brokerage" approach, he evolved to the point that he believed "there is a legitimate 'brokerage' function that can be pursued, involving some of the goods and services that the community needs." But, he wrote, "such a function can only be legitimately pursued by a representative permanent political structure created to gain, maintain, and use power for all Black people and not a narrow Washington-based elite."[13]

To Baraka, the Congressional Black Caucus was a typical example of "bourgeoisie sellout nigger politics," because they claimed to be the "only formalized structure of Black politics." Although Baraka's language is harsh, his critique is accurate. Since its creation in 1969 the CBC did see itself as the voice of black America, and they actually saw themselves as the spokespersons for the masses, who in fact put them in office. So, while black congressional representatives used the energy of grassroots activism to gain elective office, they did not feel accountable to the community.

With the NBPC on life support, Floyd McKissick told 2,500 black Republicans that black folks needed to stop "sucking the tit of Democratic Party rhetoric and to work within the Republican party." He felt that the GOP was best for those interested in black self-determination. Although black voters were frustrated with the Democrats, under no circumstances would they leave en masse to support the Republican Party.[14]

As black elected officials and Baraka looked to the Democratic National Convention in Miami that summer, the central question was brokerage. The idea of black unity was clearly a lost cause, so as Miami approached, black elected officials began jockeying for position, using the Black Bill of Rights as a bargaining tool with the two Democratic candidates, George McGovern and Hubert Humphrey. Congressmen Walter Fauntroy, Louis Stokes, and William Clay were in the McGovern camp, while Arnold Pinkney of Cleveland and Charles Evers of Mississippi were supporting Humphrey. Somehow Fauntroy positioned himself as chief broker, even telling McGovern that he could deliver black delegates. But Baraka could not understand all the jockeying. "What is to be gained by Black support for a Democratic presidential nominee? And to whom would it accrue? Would it be cabinet posts, Secretaries of Housing and Urban Development or the Secretary of Health Education and Welfare? Would these be the Black prices for Black support? Who would name these Black cabinet secretaries if this was part of the price of 'delivering' the Black vote, and who would these Black folk be? Whose constituency would they be a part of, or what constituency would they be related to? The same small elite of D.C.-based bourgeois negroes most likely."[15]

Fauntroy emerged as the black broker in the weeks leading up to the Convention by using his role within the NBPC and his standing with the Congressional Black Caucus. He assumed this role without the permission of the NBPC or the CBC when he, Stokes, and Clay called a press conference on June 26 telling reporters that they had secured enough uncommitted delegates to give the nomination to McGovern. In turn, they said, he agreed to endorse the Gary Agenda. Of the 452 black delegates in Miami, 90 had been at Gary. However, after witnessing black elected officials sell out the NBPC, black nationalists saw no need to make the trip to Miami. Instead of rallying around the idea of black unity in Miami, black elected officials and politicos were still lobbying for McGovern, Chisholm, and Humphrey at the expense of a united black front. The actions of black elected officials at Miami triggered Baraka's wrath. Writing in the *Black World* several months after Gary, Baraka openly expressed how he felt about Fauntroy and others betraying the spirit of the NBPC. "Walter Fauntroy of D.C. should be looked at closely in this regard. His moves should be studied for he is truly as slippery as a traditional Black-eel politician, though faced with new challenges, which he is still young enough to try to master rather than openly cop out of, such as the National Black Political Agenda. He has managed to slip back and forth between the Congressional Black Caucus and the National Black Political Convention, wearing both hats, or anything else he needed to place himself at the core of any brokerage with the Democratic nominee." But Baraka wasn't done. "But in Miami it was ugly to see how the sellout works. Niggers ranted and raved about white folks and Shirley Chisholm. Black people in Miami acted about Mrs. Chisholm as if she were actually running for president, and not in reality running to line up at the McGovern pay window!" He saved his worst insults for Humphrey's black supporters. "But some other niggers were even more reprehensible. The Humphrey niggers led by Arnold Pinkney of Cleveland and Charles Evers of Mississippi were the lowest of all. They shit physically! Like old winded rats dizzy from their treadmills they bumped into people trying to form the words Black on their shitted-out mouths." But Baraka saved his most insulting critique for Evers. "Charles Evers was such a bold-faced 'ho' it was embarrassing, switching from candidate to candidate, with his hand out and his butt cocked for ready access."[16]

When McGovern won the Democratic nomination, black elected officials threw their support behind him, hoping that a McGovern presidential victory would elevate them individually, and perhaps, extend some patronage to the black community. But when McGovern lost in the general election to Richard Nixon, black elected officials were left out in the cold. This, combined with the departure of black elected officials from the NBPC, essentially rendered the extensive 1971–1972 strategy sessions a failure. By withdrawing from the NBPC, black elected officials had summarily rejected the slogan "unity without uniformity." Instead they chose to put all of their proverbial eggs into the basket of the Democratic Party, forgoing any notion of a black united front. With Nixon's victory, black politics was right where it had been prior to the strategy sessions. Although civil rights activists and black elected officials were rightfully disappointed that they were unable to leverage their power in Miami, they could at least claim a victory over the black nationalists. Not only did they strategize to render the NBPC meaningless, they also managed to push black nationalist ideology and black nationalists out of the political mainstream into the desert of political irrelevance.[17]

EPILOGUE

BLACK NATIONALISTS DON'T DELIVER VOTES

The Legacy of the National Black Political Convention

With the Congressional Black Caucus pullout from the National Black Political Convention, the NBPC was virtually on life support after the 1972 elections. Nonetheless, Richard Hatcher and Amiri Baraka remained hopeful that the fractured coalition could reconcile. In 1973 the National Black Political Assembly held regional meetings in Atlanta, Detroit, San Diego, and Greenville, Mississippi, before announcing that the second gathering of the NBPC would take place in 1974 in Little Rock, Arkansas. Unlike Gary, the convention would primarily devote its time in Little Rock to the issue of political mobilization.[1]

Because of the deep divisions that became exposed in the aftermath of Gary, the grassroots work at the local and state assembly level did not get done. Black elected officials did not engage in the local political work that was necessary to make the National Black Political Assembly an effective body. They were occupied with reelection campaigns, legislation, working within their larger party structures, and winning. Therefore, the work of local organizing fell to black nationalists who had the time to devote to the effort but who did not know the basics of effective community organizing. Plus, since many black nationalists had no desire to work within the existing party structure to bring about change, they were not able to connect to the masses of black people.[2]

Since black elected officials were preoccupied with carrying out the duties of their office, black nationalists handled much of the planning for Little Rock, and this convinced many black politicians to stay home. Black elected officials had four major concerns about going to Little Rock. First, they didn't know how they would be treated by the nationalist contingent. Second, they did not want to find themselves embroiled in controversy as they had been in Gary when the antibusing and pro-

Palestinian resolutions were passed. Third, there was a deep belief among them that the NBPC was a totally ineffective mechanism. Last, many black elected officials saw no need to work with black nationalists since they could not deliver votes. Why waste time with them when they did not believe the political system could bring about change, they thought.[3]

The challenge at Little Rock was for delegates to develop an ideology that could attract mass black support and bring black elected officials back into the fold. This would be a monumental undertaking considering that Congressmen Charles Diggs, one of the three cochairs of the NBPC, resigned his position with the Convention one week before the start of the 1974 meeting, leaving Congressmen John Conyers and Ron Dellums as the only two CBC members in attendance. Predictably, the NAACP and National Urban League made it public that they were not participating, while prominent figures such as Vernon Jordan, Floyd McKissick, Senator Edward Brooke, Julian Bond, Andrew Young, Willie Brown, and newly elected Los Angeles mayor Tom Bradley made the decision not to go to Little Rock. Although the Convention leadership did not invite Jesse Jackson to Little Rock, he showed up anyway.[4]

With so many of the prominent BEOs avoiding Little Rock, it was clear that the entire Convention effort would be on its last breath if they did not return to the fold. In a keynote address at Little Rock, Hatcher struck a harsh tone: "We need Roy Wilkins now. It's time that Mr. Wilkins stopped defending our grandfathers and started defending our children. We need Vernon Jordan now. We need Ed Brooke now. We need Charles Diggs and Floyd McKissick and we need Tom Bradley. We need Coleman Young and we need every Black man and woman who has risen from the ranks. If our leaders abandon us, we are lost. Everyone must be brought into the fold. In the name of all Black Americans who have been abandoned, in the name of all of the dispossessed and disenfranchised, I summon our leaders back to our ranks." Unfortunately, black elected officials were long gone and they weren't coming back.[5]

While the most obvious remaining groups were black nationalists and a small contingent of relatively obscure black elected officials, the majority of the 1,700 delegates did not fit into either category. "They were school teachers, students, librarians, workers, parents, welfare recipients, postal clerks, reporters, waitresses, maids, and executives," who were more interested in gaining political power in their local communities than anything else. Consequently, there were no fireworks or controversies in Little Rock. One reporter referred to it as a "Low-Key Black Meeting," absent large-scale division and conflict. Delegates passed a total of nine resolutions, and people went home thinking less about creating a black political party and more about how to get black people into public office.[6]

The "Low-Key" 1974 National Black Political Convention effectively ended the work of the Convention, although its remnants would stretch throughout the 1970s. As the Convention experiment flickered out, black elected officials increased their numbers by the thousands as they took the spirit of the NBPC and elected mayors, city councilpersons, school board members, state senators, state representatives, sheriffs, constables, judges, members of Congress, and countless other positions at all levels of government. The total number of black elected officials in the country grew from 1,469 in 1970 to 4,890 by 1980, with approximately 50 percent of these positions at the local level. As black nationalists still remained skeptical about working within the system to bring about change throughout the 1970s, the overwhelming majority of black America "expressed great faith in the ability of black elected officials," and the running of black candidates for office became a source of racial pride in itself. In that spirit, black politicians created several organizations modeled after the Congressional Black Caucus: the National Black Caucus of State Legislators; the National Black Caucus of Local Elected Officials; the National Council of Black Mayors; the National Association of Black County Officials; and in virtually every state, a black caucus within its state legislature. These organizations provided a mechanism for crafting black political agendas at the local, county, and state levels, and they exercised power especially in places with a sizeable black population.[7]

The defeat of black nationalists at Gary was all too predictable. As political scientist Robert Smith noted, "The black community is too ideologically diverse to operate for long in a single, all-inclusive, organization capable of representing the interests of the race in its relationship to whites or to the larger external political order." Baraka and other black nationalists didn't know this. They looked at the black takeover of Cleveland and Newark and assumed that it could be carried out on a national level. What they didn't realize was that in those mayoral elections, both black moderates and black radicals had a singular purpose of electing a black mayor. Gary also revealed that Black Power apostles never had large-scale support among rank-and-file black people, and that black America favored integration and assimilation over the concept of racial separatism. While nationalists did have sympathizers and those who agreed with portions of their ideology, the card-carrying membership of both national and local Black Power organizations remained relatively small, and they never challenged black elected officials in elections, nor did they ever run for political office to garner mass support for their programs. In the eyes of black elected officials, this diminished their credibility. Congressman William Clay of St. Louis put it bluntly: "My district is 49 percent black and 51 percent white and I get elected every two years. Baraka's district is 65 percent black and they send Peter Rodin, a white man, to Congress. Now tell me, what business do I have letting him tell me about political power and political organization?" Despite their shortcomings, the black nationalists' critique of American society along with their heroic, selfless, and courageous acts of protest scared white America, and in the process made it easier for black elected officials and other black moderates to access power. Nonetheless, the popularity of black nationalist organizations can partially be attributed to the massive amounts of media attention they received. Talk of overthrowing the government, creating a separate black nation, returning to Africa, demanding reparations, embracing African names and values, and stressing black political and cultural unity made Black Power more popular in the imagination than in reality. Black nationalists were fun, provocative, interesting, and unpredictable. Black elected officials and those who favored integration were not really that exciting by comparison.[8]

Indeed there were varying degrees of Black Power and black nationalist ideology. Groups like the Black Panther Party advocated a socialist overthrow of the US government; the Republic of New Afrika wanted the United States to cede several states in the Black Belt to form a separate black nation; and Maulana Karenga's US organization believed that reclaiming African values was the key to black liberation. At the other end of the spectrum, black students at elite universities demanded a buffet of blackness: black studies classes, more black faculty and administrators, special admissions programs, and black dorms. These ideologies were held together by a common belief: that the American system would never work for black people.

Looking back, black nationalism was simply an unrealistic concept for the masses of black Americans, whose blood, sweat, and tears were woven into the mortar and fabric of American society. With African Americans gaining political power in the early 1970s, black nationalists did not evolve with the times. Their narrow beliefs and outlook made it impossible for them to embrace the most basic form of electoral politics, since they considered voting to be a waste of time. They were skeptical and suspicious of black elected officials and those seeking political office. As a result they often held black politicians to unrealistic standards and expectations.[9]

After Gary the concept of black nationalism underwent a rapid decline. With black mayors gaining power in nearly every major city in America by the mid-1980s, they were able to address black material concerns and issues such as housing and employment, whereas black nationalists had little to offer in terms of practical benefits to the black masses. Black nationalists failed to realize that the black masses were not "fighting for ideas, for the things in anyone's head," as the Guinean revolutionary Amilcar Cabral noted. Rather, "they are fighting to win material benefits, to live better and in peace, to see their lives go forward, to guarantee the future of their children." By the 1980s, Louis Farrakhan and the sectarian Nation of Islam (NOI) would emerge as the most prominent black nationalist organization in the country. Farrakhan galvanized thousands of listeners in arenas and venues across the country as he promoted the NOI's doctrine of black self-help and racial separatism with his indictment of America. However, the same people who listened to Farrakhan and read *The Final Call,* the NOI's newspaper, also actively supported Jesse Jackson's presidential campaigns in 1984 and 1988, and they did not see a contradiction in their actions. Why? Because they believed the system could act in their best interests if it were in black hands. This political complexity illustrates that black voters have the ability to both critique the system while at the same time having faith in their ability to change it from the inside. Despite the collapse of the National Black Political Convention, it galvanized entire communities around the possibilities of black political power and "people went back home, rolled up their sleeves and ran for public office in a way that Blacks had never thought about running for public office before." Thus, the presidential victories of Barack Hussein Obama can trace their lineage to Gary West Side High School, where black folk met in 1972 under the banner of the National Black Political Convention.[10]

APPENDIX I

FOUNDING MEMBERS OF THE CONGRESSIONAL BLACK CAUCUS

Shirley Chisholm	Brooklyn (NY)
William Clay	St. Louis
George Collins	Chicago
John Conyers	Detroit
Ron Dellums	Oakland
Charles Diggs	Detroit
Walter Fauntroy	Washington, DC (delegate)
Augustus Hawkins	Los Angeles
Ralph Metcalfe	Chicago
Parren Mitchell	Baltimore
Robert Nix	Philadelphia
Charles Rangel	Harlem
Louis Stokes	Cleveland

APPENDIX II

NATIONAL BLACK POLITICAL CONVENTION SUPPORT COMMITTEE

Ralph Abernathy
Harry Belafonte
Tom Bradley
Yvonne Braithwaite
Wiley Branton
Willie Brown
Sammy Davis Jr.
Nelson J. Edwards
Charles Evers
Howard Fuller
Jesse Gray
Dorothy Height
Haywood Henry
Aileen Hernandez
Carl Holman
Roy Innis
Marcellus Ivory
Jesse Jackson

Vernon Jordan
Coretta Scott King
Howard Lee
Alma Lewis
John Lewis
Huey Newton
A. Phillip Randolph
Frank Reeves
Betty Shabazz
Carl Stokes
Leon Sullivan
Percy Sutton
Jonnie Tillman
C. Delores Tucker
George Wiley
Roy Wilkins
Coleman Young

APPENDIX III

NATIONAL BLACK POLITICAL CONVENTION LEADERSHIP AND COMMITTEE CHAIRS

COCHAIRMEN
Imamu Amiri Baraka
Charles Diggs
Richard Hatcher

CREDENTIALS COMMITTEE
George Brown

RULES COMMITTEE
Ed Sylvester

FINANCE COMMITTEE
Al Boutte
Frank Lloyd

ARRANGEMENTS COMMITTEE
Richard Hatcher

PRESS RELATIONS COMMITTEE
Julian Bond

PLATFORM COMMITTEE
Walter Fauntroy

REGIONAL COORDINATION
Mervin Dymally

RESOLUTIONS COMMITTEE
Barbara Jordan

APPENDIX IV

NATIONAL BLACK POLITICAL CONVENTION STATE CONVENERS

ALABAMA
John Cashin
Fred Gray

ARIZONA
Clovis Campbell

ARKANSAS
John Walker

CALIFORNIA
Mervyn Dymally
Imamu Sukumu

COLORADO
George Brown

CONNECTICUT
Wilbur Smith

DELAWARE
James Sills
Lew Gothard
Herman Holloway

DISTRICT OF COLUMBIA
Walter Fauntroy

FLORIDA
Boisy Waiters
Joe Waller

GEORGIA
Julian Bond
Maynard Jackson

HAWAII
Charles Campbell

ILLINOIS
Richard Newhouse
Jesse Jackson
Sonni Adika
Ruwa Chiri

INDIANA
Richard Hatcher

IOWA
June Franklin

KANSAS
Billy McCray
Chester Lewis

KENTUCKY
Harry Sykes
Georgia Davis
Raoul Cunningham
Lois Morris

LOUISIANA
Dorothy Taylor
Nils Douglas
Alex Willingham

MAINE
Gerald Lewis

MARYLAND
Parren Mitchell
Decatur Trotter
Art King
Bill Perry

MASSACHUSETTS
Royal Boiling

MICHIGAN
Charles Diggs
David Holmes

MINNESOTA
Bill Smith
Raymond Pleasant

MISSOURI
William Clay

MISSISSIPPI
Aaron Henry
Robert Clark
Charles Bannerman

NEBRASKA
Ernest Chambers

NEVADA
Woodrow Wilson
Leonard Mason

NEW JERSEY
Imamu Baraka
William Hart

NEW YORK
Waldaba Stewart
Tom Fortune

NORTH CAROLINA
Howard Clement
Rex Harris

OHIO
Louis Stokes
C. J. Mclin
Ron Daniels

OKLAHOMA
Hannah Atkins

PENNSYLVANIA
Hardy Williams
Richard Traylor
Leroy Patrick

RHODE ISLAND
Larry Brown

SOUTH CAROLINA
John Harper
James Clyburn

TENNESSEE
Harold Ford
Robbo Jumatatu
Avon Williams

TEXAS
Gene Locke
Curtis Graves
Barbara Jordan
Zan Holmes

VIRGINIA
Henry Marsh
Ruth Harvey Charity
Bill Robinson
Val Merritt

WASHINGTON
Arthur Fletcher
George Fleming

WISCONSIN
Lloyd Barbee

VIRGIN ISLANDS
Cyril King

APPENDIX V

NATIONAL BLACK POLITICAL AGENDA RESEARCH TEAMS

POLITICAL EMPOWERMENT

Matt Holden, University of Wisconsin
Mack Jones, Atlanta University
Jim Turner, Cornell University
Charles Hamilton, Colgate University
Roger Wilkins, *Washington Post*
Will Usery, Black Urban Systems

RURAL DEVELOPMENT

Charles Prejean, Federation of Southern Cooperatives
Danny Mitchell, Newark, NJ
Randy Blackwell, Highland Park, MI
Charles Sherrod, New Communities
Jesse Morris, Delta Ministry

ECONOMIC EMPOWERMENT

Robert S. Browne, Black Economic Research Center
James Hefner, Princeton University
Karl Gregory, Detroit, MI
Vivian Henderson, Clark College
Frank Davis, Howard University
Thaddeus Spratling, UCLA

HUMAN DEVELOPMENT

Andrew Billingsley, Howard University
James Comer, Yale University
Lisle Carter, Cornell University
Joyce Ladner, Howard University
Preston Wilcox, AFRAM Associates, Inc.

Jean Fairfax, NAACP Legal Defense Fund
Don Harris, US Senate Committee for Education

INTERNATIONAL RELATIONS AND DEFENSE POLICY

Charles Diggs, US Congress
Ronald Walters, Howard University
Tilden LeMille, Hunter College
Herschelle S. Challenor, Brooklyn College
Hugh Smith, Brooklyn College
Howard Fuller, Malcolm X University
Leonard Jefferies, San Jose State University

ENVIRONMENTAL DEVELOPMENT OR PROTECTION

Al Fisher, Urban Coalition
Gus Heningburg, Greater Newark Urban Coalition
Alvin Poussaint, Harvard Medical School
Lilia Ann Abron, Tennessee State University
J. Herman Blake, UC–Santa Cruz

COMMUNICATIONS

Carlton Goodlet, San Francisco
Bill Strickland, Dartmouth University
Bill Wright, Black Efforts for Soul in Television
Austin Scott, Associated Press
Vincent Harding, Institute of the Black World
Gerald Fraser, *New York Times*
Tom Johnson, *New York Times*
Lerone Bennett, *Ebony*
Robert Maynard

APPENDIX VI

THE GARY DECLARATION

Black Politics at the Crossroads

The Black Agenda is addressed primarily to Black people in America. It rises naturally out of the bloody decades and centuries of our people's struggle on these shores. It flows from the most recent surgings of our own cultural and political consciousness. It is our attempt to define some of the essential changes which must take place in this land as we and our children move to self-determination and true independence.

The Black Agenda assumes that no truly basic change for our benefit takes place in Black or white America unless we Black people organize to initiate that change. It assumes that we must have some essential agreement on overall goals, even though we may differ on many specific strategies.

Therefore, this is an initial statement of goals and directions for our own generation, some first definitions of crucial issues around which Black people must organize and move in 1972 and beyond. Anyone who claims to be serious about the survival and liberation of Black people must be serious about the implementation of the Black Agenda.

WHAT TIME IS IT?

We come to Gary in an hour of great crisis and tremendous promise for Black America. While the white nation hovers on the brink of chaos, while its politicians offer no hope of real change, we stand on the edge of history and are faced with an amazing and frightening choice: We may choose in 1972 to slip back into the decadent white politics of American life, or we may press forward, moving relentlessly from Gary to the creation of our own Black life. The choice is large, but the time is very short.

Let there be no mistake. We come to Gary in a time of unrelieved crisis for our people. From every rural community in Alabama to the high-rise compounds of Chicago, we bring to this Convention the agonies of the masses of our people. From the sprawling Black cities of Watts and Nairobi in the West to the decay of Harlem and Roxbury in the East, the testimony we bear is the same. We are the witnesses to social disaster.

Our cities are crime-haunted dying grounds. Huge sectors of our youth—and countless others—face permanent unemployment. Those of us who work find our paychecks able to purchase less and less. Neither the courts nor the prisons contribute to anything resembling justice or reformation. The schools are unable—or unwilling—to educate our children for the real world of our struggles. Meanwhile, the officially approved epidemic of drugs threatens to wipe out the minds and strength of our best young warriors.

Economic, cultural, and spiritual depression stalk Black America, and the price for survival often appears to be more than we are able to pay. On every side, in every area of our lives, the American institutions in which we have placed our trust are unable to cope with the crises they have created by their single-minded dedication to profits for some and white supremacy above all.

BEYOND THESE SHORES

And beyond these shores there is more of the same. For while we are pressed down under all the dying weight of a bloated, inwardly decaying white civilization, many of our brothers in Africa and the rest of the Third World have fallen prey to the same powers of exploitation and deceit. Wherever America faces the unorganized, politically powerless forces of the non-white world, its goal is domination by any means necessary—as if to hide from itself the crumbling of its own systems of life and work.

But Americans cannot hide. They can run to China and the moon and to the edges of consciousness, but they cannot hide. The crises we face as Black people are the crises of the entire society. They go deep, to the very bones and marrow, to the essential nature of America's economic, political, and cultural systems. They are the natural end-product of a society built on the twin foundations of white racism and white capitalism.

So, let it be clear to us now: The desperation of our people, the agonies of our cities, the desolation of our countryside, the pollution of the air and the water—these things will not be significantly affected by new faces in the old places in Washington D.C. This is the truth we must face here in Gary if we are to join our people everywhere in the movement forward toward liberation.

WHITE REALITIES, BLACK CHOICE

A Black political convention, indeed all truly Black politics must begin from this truth: The American system does not work for the masses of our people, and it cannot be made to work without radical fundamental change. (Indeed this system does not really work in favor of the humanity of anyone in America.)

In light of such realities, we come to Gary and are confronted with a choice. Will we believe the truth that history presses into our face—or will we, too, try to hide? Will the small favors some of us have received blind us to the larger sufferings of our people, or open our eyes to the testimony of our history in America?

For more than a century we have followed the path of political dependence on white men and their systems. From the Liberty Party in the decades before the Civil War to the Republican Party of Abraham Lincoln, we trusted in white men and white politics as our deliverers. Sixty years ago, W.E.B. DuBois said he would give the Democrats their "last chance" to prove their sincere commitment to equality for Black people—and he was given white riots and official segregation in peace and in war.

Nevertheless, some twenty years later we became Democrats in the name of Franklin Roosevelt, then supported his successor Harry Truman, and even tried a "non-partisan" Republican General of the Army named Eisenhower. We were wooed like many others by the superficial liberalism of John F. Kennedy and the make-believe populism of Lyndon Johnson. Let there be no more of that.

BOTH PARTIES HAVE BETRAYED US

Here at Gary, let us never forget that while the times and the names and the parties have continually changed, one truth has faced us insistently, never changing: Both parties have betrayed us whenever their interests conflicted with ours (which was most of the time), and whenever our forces were unorganized and dependent, quiescent and compliant. Nor should this be surprising, for by now we must know that the American political system, like all other white institutions in America, was designed to operate for the benefit of the white race: It was never meant to do anything else.

That is the truth that we must face at Gary. If white "liberalism" could have solved our problems, then Lincoln and Roosevelt and Kennedy would have done so. But they did not solve ours nor the rest of the nation's. If America's problems could have been solved by forceful, politically skilled and aggressive individuals, then Lyndon Johnson would have retained the presidency. If the true "American Way" of unbridled monopoly capitalism, combined with a ruthless military imperialism could do it, then Nixon would not be running around the world, or making speeches comparing his nation's decadence to that of Greece and Rome.

If we have never faced it before, let us face it at Gary. The profound crisis of Black people and the disaster of America are not simply caused by men nor will they be solved by men alone. These crises are the crises of basically flawed economics and politics, and of cultural degradation. None of the Democratic candidates and none of the Republican candidates—regardless of their vague promises to us or to their white constituencies—can solve our problems or the problems of this country without radically changing the systems by which it operates.

THE POLITICS OF SOCIAL TRANSFORMATION

So we come to Gary confronted with a choice. But it is not the old convention question of which candidate shall we support, the pointless question of who is to preside over a decaying and unsalvageable system. No, if we come to Gary out of the realities of the Black communities of this land, then the only real choice for us is whether or not we will live by the truth we know, whether we will move to organize independently, move to struggle for fundamental transformation, for the creation of new directions, towards a concern for the life and the meaning of Man. Social transformation or social destruction, those are our only real choices.

If we have come to Gary on behalf of our people in America, in the rest of this hemisphere, and in the Homeland—if we have come for our own best ambitions—then a new Black Politics must come to birth. If we are serious, the Black Politics of Gary must accept major responsibility for creating both the atmosphere and the program for fundamental, far-ranging change in America. Such responsibility is ours because it is our people who are most deeply hurt and ravaged by the present systems of society. That responsibility for leading the change is ours because we live in a society where few other men really believe in the responsibility of a truly human society for anyone anywhere.

WE ARE THE VANGUARD

The challenge is thrown to us here in Gary. It is the challenge to consolidate and organize our own Black role as the vanguard in the struggle for a new society. To accept that challenge is to move independent Black politics. There can be no equivocation on that issue. History leaves us no other choice. White politics has not and cannot bring the changes we need.

We come to Gary and are faced with a challenge. The challenge is to transform ourselves from favor-seeking vassals and loud-talking, "militant" pawns, and to take up the role that the organized masses of our people have attempted to play ever since we came to these shores. That of harbingers of true justice and humanity, leaders in the struggle for liberation.

A major part of the challenge we must accept is that of redefining the functions and operations of all levels of American government, for the existing governing structures—from Washington to the smallest county—are obsolescent. That is part of the reason why nothing works and why corruption rages throughout public life. For white politics seeks not to serve but to dominate and manipulate.

We will have joined the true movement of history if at Gary we grasp the opportunity to press Man forward as the first consideration of politics. Here at Gary we are faithful to the best hopes of our fathers and our people if we move for nothing less than a politics which places community before individualism, love before sexual exploitation, a living environment before profits, peace before war, justice before unjust "order," and morality before expediency.

This is the society we need, but we delude ourselves here at Gary if we think that change can be achieved without organizing the power, the determined national Black power, which is necessary to insist upon such change, to create such change, to seize change.

TOWARDS A BLACK AGENDA

So when we turn to a Black Agenda for the seventies, we move in the truth of history, in the reality of the moment. We move recognizing that no one else is going to represent our interests but ourselves. The society we seek cannot come unless Black people organize to advance its coming. We lift up a Black Agenda recognizing that white America moves towards the abyss created by its own racist arrogance, misplaced priorities, rampant materialism, and ethical bankruptcy. Therefore, we are certain that the Agenda we now press for in Gary is not only for the future of Black humanity, but is probably the only way the rest of America can save itself from the harvest of its criminal past.

So, Brothers and Sisters of our developing Black nation, we now stand at Gary as people whose time has come. From every corner of Black America, from all liberation movements of the Third World, from the graves of our fathers and the coming world of our children, we are faced with a challenge and a call: Though the moment is perilous we must not despair. We must seize the time, for the time is ours.

We begin here and now in Gary. We begin with an independent Black political movement, an independent Black Political Agenda, and an independent Black spirit. Nothing less will do. We must build for our people. We must build for our world. We stand on the edge of history. We cannot turn back.

APPENDIX VII

MODEL PLEDGE FOR BLACK CANDIDATES

As a candidate seeking the approval of the National Black Political Convention:

I pledge, that as I campaign, and if I am elected, I will conduct the daily affairs and decision making of my activity, and/or office, so as to reflect the actual, explicit desires and concerns of the Black Community beyond question. In this manner I will constantly act out my accountability to the manifest interests of the Black Community, as revealed, at present, through the National Black Political Convention and whatever instrument(s) this Convention will establish as a means of follow-through.

In regard to this pledge, I will do the following:

1. Without fear I will raise controversial issues, when the raising of such issues will serve the needs and interests of the Black Community.
2. I will constantly seek to expose the corrupt aspects of the system, as such exposure will raise the level of awareness in the Black Community.
3. I will take any steps necessary to increase power for the Black Community when such steps are not in conflict with the Convention's Agenda and the programs of its follow-up mechanisms.
4. I will support the right of the Black Community to control its own areas and the institutions thereof as this principle of control relates to Political Empowerment, Economic Empowerment, Human Development, International Policy and Black People, Communications, Rural Development, Environmental Protection, and Self-Determination for the District of Columbia.

I will make this pledge in dedication to a commitment to serve the Black Community, of which I am unquestionably a part, and I do so without reservation or intimidation.

Witness

Date

Signature

NOTES

INTRODUCTION

1. At times throughout the book I use the term "racial moderates" to broadly describe those who favored integration. This includes black elected officials, civil rights activists, and black integrationists. Manning Marable, *Race, Reform, and Rebellion: The Second Reconstruction in Black America, 1945–1990* (Jackson: University Press of Mississippi, 1991), 120; Peniel Joseph, *Waiting 'Til the Midnight Hour: A Narrative History of Black Power in America* (New York: Henry Holt, 2006), 5, 276; Stokely Carmichael and C. V. Hamilton, *Black Power: The Politics of Liberation* (New York: Vintage Books, 1967); Amiri Baraka, *The Autobiography of Leroi Jones* (Chicago: Lawrence Hill Books, 1997); Maulana Karenga, "US, Kawaida and the Black Liberation Movement in the 1960s: Culture, Knowledge and Struggle," in James Conyers, ed., *Engines of the Black Power Movement: Essays on the Influence of Civil Rights Actions, Arts, and Islam* (Jefferson, NC: McFarland, 2006, 95–133. Despite the importance of the National Black Political Convention, it has largely been ignored by historians. Komozi Woodard's *A Nation Within a Nation: Amiri Baraka (Leroi Jones) and Black Power Politics* (Chapel Hill: UNC Press, 1999) is the only meaningful in-depth account of the event. Robert Smith's excellent book, *We Have No Leaders: African Americans in the Post–Civil Rights Era* (Albany: SUNY Press, 1996), examines the NBPC from a political science perspective, as does Cedric Johnson's *Revolutionaries to Race Leaders: Black Power and the Making of African American Politics* (Minneapolis: University of Minnesota Press, 2007).

2. Bayard Rustin, "From Protest to Politics," *Harper's,* April 1965; Marable, *Race, Reform, and Rebellion*, 113, 119–20; Steven F. Lawson, *Running For Freedom: Civil Rights and Black Politics in America Since 1941* (New York: McGraw Hill, 1991), 143–45; Ronald Walters and Robert Smith, eds., *African American Leadership* (Albany: SUNY Press, 1999), 120. Steven F. Lawson's *In Pursuit of Power: Southern Blacks and Electoral Politics, 1965–1982* (New York: Columbia University Press, 1985) goes into great detail on the impact of the 1965 Voting Rights Act in the southern states. Surprisingly, scholars have not paid much attention to black political life in the 1970s. Three anthologies that predicted the political challenges of the 1970s are: Floyd Barbour, ed., *The Black 70's* (Boston: Porter Sargent, 1970); the National Urban League's *When the Marching Stopped: An Analysis of Black Issues in the 1970s* (New York: National Urban League, 1973); and Nathan Wright, ed., *What Black Politicians Are Saying* (New York: Hawthorn Books, 1972).

3. Julius Lester, *Look Out, Whitey! Black Power's Gon' Get Your Mama!* (New York: Grove Press, 1968), 97; Johnson, *Revolutionaries to Race Leaders*, 57–58; Harold Cruse, *The Crisis of the Negro Intellectual: From Its Origins to the Present* (New York: William Morrow, 1967); *New*

York Times, September 4, 1966; Wil Haygood, *King of the Cats* (Boston: Houghton Mifflin, 1993), 325; Chuck Stone, *Black Political Power in America* (New York: Dell, 1968), 20; Chuck Stone, "The National Conferences on Black Power," in Floyd Barbour, ed., *The Black Power Revolt: A Collection of Essays* (Boston: Porter Sargent, 1968), 189–90.

4. *Washington Post*, September 4, 1966; *New York Times*, September 7–8, 1966.

5. Komozi Woodard, *A Nation Within a Nation* (Chapel Hill: UNC Press, 1999), 84–85; Robert Allen, *Black Awakening in Capitalist America: An Analytic History* (New York: Anchor Books, 1970), 157–58; Stone, "The National Conferences on Black Power," 194.

6. Stone, "The National Conferences on Black Power," 191–97; Woodard, *A Nation Within a Nation*, 86–87; Dean Robinson, *Black Nationalism in American Politics and Thought* (Cambridge: Cambridge University Press, 2001), 96–97; Johnson, *Revolutionaries to Race Leaders*, 59–60.

7. Conference organizers attempted to internationalize the Black Power Conference in 1969 by holding the event in Bermuda. While this was admirable, it was a disaster. It was poorly attended largely because of the costs associated with getting to the remote island. Woodard, *A Nation Within A Nation*, 108–9; Allen, *Black Awakening in Capitalist America*, 163–65. For a more detailed look at the Black Power Conferences, see *Black Power Conference Reports* (New York: Afram Associates, 1970).

8. Marable, *Race, Reform, and Rebellion*, 97–99; Jerry Gafio Watts, *Amiri Baraka: The Politics and Art of a Black Intellectual* (New York: NYU Press, 2001), 404; Stokely Carmichael and Charles Hamilton, *Black Power: The Politics of Liberation in America* (New York: Vintage Books, 1967), 44–53; Stokely Carmichael, "Power and Racism," in *The Black Power Revolt*, 65. For the definitive work on Carmichael, see Peniel Joseph, *Stokely: A Life* (New York: Basic Civitas, 2014).

9. The literature on black nationalism has literally exploded over the past thirty years. William Van Deburg's *New Day in Babylon: The Black Power Movement and American Culture, 1965–1975* (Chicago: University of Chicago Press, 1992) provides an excellent overview of black nationalist ideologies. For more on Malcolm X and the Nation of Islam, see Malcolm X, *The Autobiography of Malcolm X* (New York: Ballantine Books, 1992); Manning Marable, *Malcolm X: A Life of Reinvention* (New York: Penguin Books, 2011); Claude Clegg, *An Original Man: The Life and Times of Elijah Muhammad* (New York: St. Martin's Press, 1997); Karl Evanzz, *The Rise and Fall of Elijah Muhammad* (New York: Vintage Books, 2011). For a local study on the Republic of New Afrika, see Donald Cunnigen, "The Republic of New Afrika in Mississippi," in Judson Jeffries, ed., *Black Power in the Belly of the Beast* (Urbana: University of Illinois Press, 2006), 93–115. The Black Panther Party has received the most attention from historians. For a representative sample, see Donna Murch, *Living for the City: Migration, Education, and the Rise of the Black Panther Party in Oakland, California* (Chapel Hill: UNC Press, 2010); Robyn Spencer, *The Revolution Has Come: Black Power, Gender, and the Black Panther Party in Oakland* (Durham, NC: Duke University Press, 2016); Joshua Bloom and Waldo E. Martin, Jr., *Black Against Empire: The History and Politics of the Black Panther Party* (Berkeley: University of California Press, 2016); Jama Lazerow and Yohuru Williams, *In Search of the Black Panther Party: New Perspectives on a Revolutionary Movement* (Durham, NC: Duke University Press, 2006); Judson Jeffries, *Comrades: A Local History of the Black Panther Party* (Bloomington: Indiana University Press, 2007). Jeffrey

Ogbar's groundbreaking book, *Black Power: Radical Politics and African American Identity* (Baltimore: Johns Hopkins University Press, 2004), looks at both the Nation of Islam and the Black Panther Party. The best study of RAM is Akbar Muhammad Ahmad, "RAM: The Revolutionary Action Movement," in *Black Power in the Belly of the Beast,* 252–80. For more on cultural nationalism, see Scot Brown, *Fighting for US: Maulana Karenga, the US Organization, and Black Cultural Nationalism* (New York: NYU Press, 2003); Keith Mayes, *Kwanzaa: Black Power and the Making of the African American Holiday Tradition* (New York: Routledge, 2009); Watts, *Amiri Baraka;* Maulana Karenga, "US, Kawaida and the Black Liberation Movement in the 1960s: Culture, Knowledge and Struggle," in James Conyers, ed., *Engines of the Black Power Movement: Essays on the Influence of Civil Rights Actions, Arts, and Islam* (London: McFarland, 2006), 95–133.

　　10. Robinson, *Black Nationalism in American Politics and Thought,* 75–76, 111; Floyd McKissick, "Programs for Black Power," in Barbour, ed., *The Black Power Revolt,* 179; Alex Poinsett, *Black Power Gary Style: The Making of Mayor Richard Gordon Hatcher* (Chicago: Johnson Publishing, 1970), 17–18. For a look at the political career of Carl Stokes, see Leonard Moore, *Carl B. Stokes and the Rise of Black Political Power* (Urbana: University of Illinois Press, 2002), and his autobiography, *Promises of Power: A Political Autobiography* (New York: Simon and Schuster, 1973).

　　11. Poinsett, *Black Power Gary Style,* 6–15; Tom Sugrue, *Sweet Land of Liberty: The Forgotten Struggle for Civil Rights in the North* (New York: Random House, 2008), 497–498; James Jennings, *The Politics of Black Empowerment: The Transformation of Black Activism in Urban America* (Detroit: Wayne State University Press, 1992), 30–32; Nathan Hare, "How White Power Whitewashes Black Power," in Barbour, ed., *The Black Power Revolt,* 187; Robert L. Scott and Wayne Brockriede, eds., *The Rhetoric of Black Power* (New York: Harper and Row, 1969).

CHAPTER ONE

　　1. James Meriwether, *Proudly We Can Be Africans: Black Americans and Africa, 1935–1961* (Chapel Hill: UNC Press, 2002), 160.

　　2. Robert Singh, *The Congressional Black Caucus: Racial Politics in the U.S. Congress* (New York: SAGE, 1996); Chuck Stone provides a good overview on the careers of Dawson and Powell in *Black Political Power in America,* 165–208.

　　3. Thomas Sugrue, *Sweet Land of Liberty: The Forgotten Struggle for Civil Rights in the North* (New York: Random House, 2008), 502.

　　4. Dean J. Kotlowski, *Nixon's Civil Rights: Politics, Principle, and Policy* (Cambridge, MA: Harvard University Press, 2002), 173–75; Steven Lawson, *Running for Freedom: Civil Rights and Black Politics in America Since 1941* (New York: McGraw Hill, 1991), 135–37; Joshua Farrington, *Black Republicans and the Transformation of the GOP* (Philadelphia: University of Pennsylvania Press, 2016), 179–81; Manning Marable, *Race, Reform, and Rebellion: The Second Reconstruction in Black America, 1945–1990* (Jackson: University Press of Mississippi, 1991), 126–27; Jerry Gafio Watts, *Amiri Baraka: The Politics and Art of a Black Intellectual* (New York: NYU Press, 2001), 402–3; Earl Ofari Hutchinson, *Betrayed: A History of Presidential Failure to Protect Black Lives* (Boulder, CO: Westview Press, 1996), 144–45; Leah Wright

Rigueur, *The Loneliness of the Black Republican* (Princeton, NJ: Princeton University Press, 2015).

5. Farrington, *Black Republicans*, 171–83; Rigueur, *The Loneliness of the Black Republican*, 137–38, 159–60; Earl Ofari, *The Myth of Black Capitalism* (New York: Monthly Review Press, 1970), 10, 71; Robert Allen, *Black Awakening in Capitalist America: An Analytic History* (New York: Anchor Books, 1970), 227–31. For the best overviews of black capitalism, see Robert Weems and Lewis Randolph, *Business in Black and White: American Presidents and Black Entrepreneurs in the Twentieth Century* (New York: NYU Press, 2009), and Laura Warren Hill and Julia Rabig, eds., *The Business of Black Power: Community Development, Capitalism, and Corporate Responsibility in Postwar America* (Rochester, NY: University of Rochester Press, 2012). McKissick would later use his relationship with Nixon for his ambitious Soul City project. See Devin Fergus, *Liberalism, Black Power, and the Making of American Politics, 1965–1980* (Athens: University of Georgia Press, 2009).

6. William Clay, *Just Permanent Interests: Black Americans in Congress, 1870–1991* (New York: Amistad Press, 1992), 117.

7. Ibid., 141.

8. John Conyers interview in *Eyes on the Prize Interviews Series II*, Washington University Libraries, Special Collections.

9. Norman Kelley, *The Head Negro In Charge Syndrome: The Dead End of Black Politics* (New York: Nation Books, 2004), 37.

10. "Congressional Black Caucus Outline for a Black Agenda," 1971, Box 35, Folder 2, Vincent Harding Papers, Emory University.

11. *Congressional Record,* 92nd Congress, First Session, Box 35, Folder 1, Harding Papers.

12. *Congressional Record,* March 25, 1971.

13. "Black Caucus Recommendations to President Nixon," Box 119, folder marked "Black Caucus Folder," Mervyn Dymally Papers, Special Collections, JFK Library, California State University–Los Angeles.

14. Ibid.

15. Ibid.

16. Clay, *Just Permanent Interests*. For a more detailed look at Nixon's black appointees, see Rigueur, *The Loneliness of the Black Republican*, 154–58, and Farrington, *Black Republicans and the Transformation of the GOP,* 192–94.

17. *New York Times,* March 26, March 27, 1971.

18. Clay, *Just Permanent Interests,* 150; Tanya Price, "'The Congressional Black Caucus: Black Power Realized," in James L. Conyers, Jr., ed., *Engines of the Black Power Movement: Essays on the Influence of Civil Rights Actions, Arts, and Islam* (Jefferson, NC: McFarland, 2006), 76–77. For good overviews on the Nixon administration and civil rights, see "Zigs and Zags: Richard Nixon and the New Politics of Race," in Kenneth Osgood and Derrick E. White, eds., *Winning While Losing: Civil Rights, The Conservative Movement and the Presidency from Nixon to Obama* (Gainesville: University of Florida Press, 2014), 26–54; Kenneth O'Reilly, *Nixon's Piano: Presidents and Racial Politics from Washington to Clinton* (New York: Free Press, 1995).

19. George Musgrove, *Rumor, Repression, and Racial Politics: How the Harassment of Black Elected Officials Shaped Post–Civil Rights America* (Athens: University of Georgia Press, 2012),

65–67. Musgrove writes that between 1965 and 1975, 76 percent of all black members of Congress were under some sort of surveillance.

20. *New York Times*, March 29, 1971.

21. Clay, *Permanent Interests*, 167; Louis Stokes/Congressional Black Caucus to Friends of the Congressional Black Caucus, October 21, 1971, Box 82, Folder 4, Julian Bond Papers, University of Virginia Special Collections; "Ossie Davis and Bill Cosby Address the Congressional Black Caucus," 1972, LP, Black Forum Label, public domain.

22. "Ossie Davis and Bill Cosby."

23. *New York Amsterdam News*, July 24, 1971.

24. Ibid.

25. Ibid.

26. Ibid.

27. Marable, *Race, Reform, and Rebellion*, 122; Hare, "How White Power Whitewashes Black Power," 188; Kelley, *The Head Negro in Charge Syndrome*, 37. The Congressional Black Caucus was also instrumental in the establishment of the Joint Center for Political and Economic Studies, a nonprofit think tank designed to provide research and technical assistance to black elected officials.

28. Richard Hatcher interview, *Eyes on the Prize Interviews Series II.*

29. Watts, *Amiri Baraka*, 381–86; Cedric Johnson, *Revolutionaries to Race Leaders: Black Power and the Making of African American Politics* (Minneapolis: University of Minnesota Press, 2007), 62, 69; Peniel Joseph, ed., *Waiting 'Til the Midnight Hour: A Narrative History of Black Power in America* (New York: Henry Holt, 2006), 254.

30. Komozi Woodard, *A Nation Within a Nation: Amiri Baraka and Black Power Politics* (Chapel Hill: UNC Press, 1996), 51–59.

31. Watts, *Amiri Baraka*, 141, 151–56; Woodard, *A Nation Within a Nation*, 59–74; Amiri Baraka, *The Autobiography of Leroi Jones* (Chicago: Lawrence Hill Books, 1997), 293–96, 339–46, 376. For a book-length study on Karenga and US, see Scot Brown, *Fighting for US: Maulana Karenga, the US Organization, and Black Cultural Nationalism* (New York: NYU Press, 2005).

32. Baraka, *The Autobiography of Leroi Jones*, 402–3.

33. Woodard, *A Nation Within A Nation*, 162–64; Robert C. Smith, *We Have No Leaders: African Americans in the Post–Civil Rights Era* (Albany: SUNY Press, 1996), 37–38; Komozi Woodard, "Amiri Baraka, The Congress of African People, and Black Power Politics from the 1961 Nations Protest to the 1972 Gary Convention," in Peniel Joseph, ed., *The Black Power Movement: Rethinking the Civil Rights–Black Power Era* (New York: Routledge, 2006), 62; Watts, *Amiri Baraka*, 382–83, 403–7; Baraka, *The Autobiography of Leroi Jones*, 405–7; Keith A. Mayes, *Kwanzaa: Black Power and the Making of the African American Holiday Tradition* (New York: Routledge, 2009), 112.

34. Baraka, *The Autobiography of Leroi Jones*, 406–7.

CHAPTER TWO

1. "Extension of a Strategy for 1971–1972," by Julian Bond, August 30, 1971, Box 82, Folder 4, Bond Papers.

2. Alex Poinsett, "Black Political Strategies," *Ebony,* March 1972; Shirley Chisholm, *The Good Fight* (New York: Harper and Row, 1973), 24.

3. Poinsett, "Black Political Strategies."

4. "Carl Stokes Statement," Container 64, Folder 1209, Carl B. Stokes Papers, Western Reserve Historical Society.

5. Poinsett, "Black Political Strategies."

6. Imamu Amiri Baraka, "The Pan-African Party and the Black Nation," *Black Scholar* 2, no. 7 (1971): 24–26; Dean E. Robinson, *Black Nationalism in American Politics and Thought,* (Cambridge: Cambridge University Press, 2001), 97–98; John T. McCartney, *Black Power Ideologies: An Essay in African American Political Thought* (Philadelphia: Temple University Press, 1992), 178; Amiri Baraka, "Gary and Miami—Before and After," *Black World* 21 (October 1972): 54–78.

7. *New York Times,* August 15, 1971.

8. *New York Times,* August 16, 1971; Julian Bond to John Cashin, July 13, 1971, and Julian Bond to Tally Hudson, July 29, 1971, Box 82, Folder 4, Bond Papers; "Resolutions Adopted by the Southern Black Caucus, Mobile, Alabama, August 13–15, 1971," Box 119, "Black Caucus Folder," Dymally Papers.

9. *New York Times,* August 16, 1971; "Resolutions Adopted by the Southern Black Caucus," Box 119, "Black Caucus Folder," Dymally Papers; Zelma Wyche of Tallulah, Louisiana, exemplified black political power at the local level, particularly in rural southern communities. See Adam Fairclough, *Race and Democracy: The Civil Rights Struggle in Louisiana, 1915–1972* (Athens: University of Georgia Press, 1999).

10. *New York Amsterdam News,* August 21, 1971.

11. *New York Amsterdam News,* August 21, September 11, 1971.

12. *New York Amsterdam News,* September 11, 1971.

13. *New York Times,* September 6, September 9, 1971; *New York Amsterdam News,* September 11, 1971.

14. *New York Times,* September 6, 1971.

15. Baraka, "Gary and Miami," 55; Amiri Baraka, *The Autobiography of Leroi Jones* (Chicago: Lawrence Hill Books, 1997), 407–8.

16. Julian Bond to Richard Hatcher, August 26, 1971, and "Draft re: 9/71 Chicago Conference," and "Agenda," and Willie Brown to Hatcher, September 3, 1971, all in Box 82, Folder 7, Bond Papers; Chisholm, *The Good Fight,* 28–29; Baraka, "Gary and Miami," 58.

17. "List of Potential Conferees and Invitees, 9/71 Chicago Conference," Box 82, Folder 7, Bond Papers; *Washington Post,* September 26, 1971; *New York Times,* September 27, 1971.

18. *New York Times,* September 20, 1971; Bond to Kelly, July 13, 1971, Box 82, Folder 4, Bond Papers; Julian Bond, "A Black Southern Strategy," in Nathan Wright, ed., *What Black Politicians are Saying* (New York: Hawthorn, 1972), 137–48; *New York Amsterdam News,* September 25, 1971; *New York Times,* September 20, 1971; Chisholm, *The Good Fight,* 29.

19. John Conyers, "A Black Political Strategy for 1972," 131–32, in Nathan Wright, ed., *What Black Politicians Are Saying;* Julian Bond to Black Political Activists in Georgia, December 1971, Box 82, Folder 5, Bond Papers; Chisholm, *The Good Fight,* 26.

20. John Conyers, "A Black Political Strategy for 1972," 134. For an in-depth observation of the Stokes and Hatcher mayoral campaigns, see William E. Nelson and Philip J. Meranto, *Electing Black Mayors: Political Action in the Black Community* (Columbus: Ohio State University Press, 1977).

21. *New York Amsterdam News*, September 25, October 9, 1971; "A Political Strategy for 1972," by John Conyers, Box 119, "Black Caucus Folder," Dymally Papers. For more on Stokes, see Leonard Moore, *Carl B. Stokes and the Rise of Black Political Power* (Urbana: University of Illinois Press, 2002).

22. Shirley Chisholm, *Unbought and Unbossed* (New York: Houghton Mifflin, 1970), 7–17; *Newsweek*, June 25, 1972.

23. Chisholm, *Unbought and Unbossed*, 18, 22, 34, 45–46; *Newsweek*, June 25, 1972.

24. *Newsweek*, June 25, 1972.

25. *Washington Post*, September 26, October 4, 1971; Chisholm to Hatcher, November 23, 1971, Box 119, "Black Caucus Folder," Dymally Papers.

26. *Race Relations Reporter*, January 1972, 11; Chisholm, *The Good Fight*, 30.

27. Chisholm, *The Good Fight*, 30; Kimberly Springer, *Living for the Revolution: Black Feminist Organizations, 1968–1980* (Durham, NC: Duke University Press, 2005), 26–29, 35–40.

28. Komozi Woodard, *A Nation Within a Nation: Amiri Baraka and Black Power Politics* (Chapel Hill: UNC Press, 1996), 193; Baraka, "Gary and Miami," 59.

29. Baraka, "Gary and Miami," 60.

30. Ibid.

31. Robert Smith, *We Have No Leaders: African Americans in the Post–Civil Rights Era* (Albany: SUNY Press, 1996), 41–42.

32. *Jet*, September 30, 1971.

33. *Jet*, September 23, September 30, 1971; *Freedomways* II, no. 4 (1971), 374–83; *Ebony*, December 1971, 64–68; Carl Stokes, "Black Political Action in 1972," September 30, 1971, Container 61, Folder 1149, Stokes Papers. Although the Black Expo was a success nationally, Jackson was forced to resign from his position within SCLC because of alleged improprieties. For more on this controversy, see Gordon K. Mantler, *Power to the People: Black-Brown Coalitions and the Fight for Economic Justice* (Chapel Hill: UNC Press, 2013), 237–38.

34. Stokes, "Black Political Action in 1972."

35. Ibid.

36. Ibid.

37. Ibid.

38. Ibid. For more on the political machine developed by the Stokes brothers in Cleveland, see William E. Nelson, "Cleveland: The Evolution of Black Political Power," in Michael Preston, Lenneal J. Henderson, and Paul L. Puryear, eds., *The New Black Politics* (New York: Longman, 1987), 172–99; and William E. Nelson, "Cleveland: The Rise and Fall of the New Black Politics," in Michael Preston, Lenneal J. Henderson, Jr., and Paul L. Puryear, eds., *The New Black Politics: The Search for Political Power* (New York: Longman, 1982), 187–208.

39. Stokes, "Black Political Action in 1972."

40. Ibid.

41. *New York Times,* October 1, 1971; *New York Amsterdam News,* October 2, 1971.

42. Chisholm, *The Good Fight,* 31–32.

43. Ibid.

44. Ibid.

45. Ibid.

46. Springer, *Living for the Revolution,* 21–23; Stephen Ward, "The Third World Women's Alliance: Black Feminist Radicalism and Black Power Politics," in Peniel Joseph, ed., *The Black Power Movement: Rethinking the Civil Rights–Black Power Era* (New York: Routledge, 2006), 124–25; Bettye Collier-Thomas and V. Franklin, "From Civil Rights to Black Power: African American Women and *Nationalism,*" in Bettye Collier-Thomas and V. P. Franklin, eds., *Sisters in the Struggle: African American Women in the Civil Rights Black Power Movement* (New York: NYU Press, 2001), 171–72; Cynthia Griggs Fleming, "Black Women and Black Power: The Case of Ruby Doris Smith and the Student Nonviolent Coordinating Committee," in Collier-Thomas and Franklin, eds., *Sisters in the Struggle,* 207–9. For an excellent overview of Chisholm's career, see the 2016 documentary, *Chisholm '72: Unbought and Unbossed,* directed by Shola Lynch. For the experiences of black women in politics, see Dayo Gore, Jeanne Theoharis and Komozi Woodard, eds., *Want To Start a Revolution: Radical Women in the Black Freedom Struggle* (New York: NYU Press, 2009); Linda Faye Williams, "The Civil Rights–Black Power Legacy: Black Women Elected Officials at the Local, State, and National Levels," in Collier-Thomas and Franklin, eds., *Sisters in the Struggle,* 306–31. For the broader experiences of black women during the Black Power movement, see Robyn Spencer, *The Revolution Has Come: Black Power, Gender, and the Black Panther Party in Oakland* (Durham, NC: Duke University Press, 2016); Elaine Brown, *A Taste of Power: A Black Woman's Story* (New York: Anchor Books, 1993); Assata Shakur, *Assata: An Autobiography* (Chicago: Lawrence Hill, 1987); Angela Davis, *An Autobiography* (New York: Random House, 1974); Paula Giddings, *When and Where I Enter* (New York: Morrow, 1994).

47. "Western Conference of Black Elected Officials Strategy Session," October 16, 1971, Box 119, "Black Caucus Folder," Dymally Papers.

48. Louis Stokes to Julian Bond, October 14, 1971, Box 82, Folder 4, Bond Papers; William Clay, *Just Permanent Interests: Black Americans in Congress, 1870–1991* (New York: Amistad Press, 1992), 193–94.

49. *Race Relations Reporter,* January 1972.

50. Clay, *Just Permanent Interests,* 195; *New York Times,* November 20, 1971; *Washington Post,* November 21, 1971.

51. Chisholm, *The Good Fight,* 50–51.

52. Clay, *Just Permanent Interests,* 196.

53. *New York Times,* June 25, 1972.

54. Chisholm, *The Good Fight,* 38; Joshua Guild, "To Make That Someday Come: Shirley Chisholm's Radical Politics of Possibility," in Gore, Theoharis, and Woodard, eds., *Want to Start a Revolution,* 262.

55. Clay, *Just Permanent Interests,* 197; Smith, *We Have No Leaders,* 43.

56. Woodard, *A Nation Within a Nation,* 195; Baraka, "Gary and Miami," 63–64; Clay, *Just Permanent Interests,* 197; *Race Relations Reporter,* January 1972, 10.

57. *Race Relations Reporter,* January 1972.

58. "A Call for A National Black Convention," from the Congressional Black Caucus, Box 35, Folder 1, Harding Papers; Clay, *Just Permanent Interests,* 202; *New York Times,* November 21, 1971; *Washington Post,* November 21, 1971.

59. "Statement of Political Strategy," Box 19, Folder 1, Robert S. Browne Papers, Schomburg Center for Research in Black Culture; Bond to Baraka, April 6, 1972, Box 82, Folder 5, Bond Papers; Baraka, "Gary and Miami," 63; Clay, *Just Permanent Interests,* 202.

CHAPTER THREE

1. "National Black Political Convention Press Conference," January 30, 1972, Box 119, "Black Caucus Folder," Dymally Papers; Richard Hatcher interview, *Eyes on the Prize Interviews Series II.*

2. "Black Political Power and Its Limits: Gary Mayor Richard G. Hatcher's Administration, 1968–1987," in David Colburn and Jeffrey Adler, eds., *African American Mayors: Race, Politics, and the American City* (Urbana: University of Illinois Press, 2001), 57–79.

3. Ibid.

4. Ibid.

5. Amiri Baraka, "Nationalist Overview," Folder 2, Institute of the Black World Papers, Schomburg Center for Research in Black Culture. Materials are in an unprocessed box marked "IBW-Strickland."

6. *Gary Info,* February 9, 1972; "NBPC Press Conference," January 30, 1972, Box 119, "Black Caucus Folder," Dymally Papers. For a good assessment of Gary, see Stephen O'Hara, *Gary, The Most American of All American Cities* (Bloomington: Indiana University Press, 2011).

7. Richard Hatcher interview, *Eyes on the Prize Interviews Series II.*

8. William Strickland, handwritten notes, Folder 2, Institute of the Black World Papers; "NBPC Press Conference," January 30, 1972, Box 119, "Black Caucus Folder," Dymally Papers.

9. "Formula for Determining Delegate Votes Per State," Container 64, Folder 1207, Stokes Papers; "Adjustment of Application of Baraka Formula," Container 64, Folder 1208, Stokes Papers; "NBPC Delegate Apportionment," Box 35, Folder 2, Harding Papers.

10. "Baraka Formula," Box 19, Folder 1, Browne Papers; "National Black Political Convention," Container 64, Folder 1207, Carl Stokes Papers.

11. "Platform Committee Staff Advisors," Box 19, Folder 1, Browne Papers; Convention Co-Chairs to State Conveners, February 19, 1972; "NBPC Minutes of Planning Conference," February 17, 1972, Box 119, "Black Caucus Folder," Dymally Papers.

12. "Committees," Container 64, Folder 1207, Stokes Papers; "National Support Committee," Box 35, Folder 2, Harding Papers; Baraka to Stokes, February 10, 1972, Container 64, Folder 1207; Stokes to Baraka, et al., Container 64, Folder 1207, February 28, 1972, Stokes Papers; Marguerite Ross Barnett, "Black Politics in a New Key: Gary and After," in *It's Nationtime: A Special Issue by the National Conference of Black Political Scientists,* 3–4.

13. National Black Political Convention to State Conveners, Box 35, Folder 2, Harding Papers; Walter Fauntroy to State Conveners, March 3, 1972, Box 19, Folder 6, Browne Papers.

14. *New York Amsterdam News,* February 19, 1972.

15. For more on the Black Power movement and its impact within New York City, see Stefan M. Bradley, *Harlem vs. Columbia University: Black Student Power in the Late 1960s* (Urbana: University of Illinois Press, 2009).

16. *New York Amsterdam News,* February 26, 1972.

17. *New York Amsterdam News,* March 4, 1972.

18. *New York Amsterdam News,* March 4, 1972.

19. Carl Stokes to Ohio Delegates, February 29, 1972, Container 64, Folder 1207, Stokes Papers; Ohio State Convention Report to the National Black Political Convention," Box 35, Folder 2, Harding Papers.

20. "Ohio Delegation Updated Recommendations to the Congressional Black Caucus Recommendations," March 7, 1972, Container 64, Folder 1207, Stokes Papers; Louis Stokes to Delegates, February 22, 1972, Container 64, Folder 1207, Stokes Papers.

21. "Ohio Delegates and Alternatives to the National Black Political Convention," Container 64, Folder 1207, Stokes Papers; "Press Release," March 6, 1972, Container 64, Folder 1207, Stokes Papers.

22. Carl Stokes to Hatcher, March 6, 1972, Container 64, Folder 1207, Stokes Papers; Carl Stokes to Baraka, et al., March 6, 1972, Container 64, Folder 1207, Stokes Papers; Ohio Delegation Press Release, March 6, 1972, Container 64, Folder 1207, Stokes Papers; *New York Times,* March 6, 1972.

23. *New York Times,* March 6, 1972. New Jersey had a robust state convention as well. See Box 19, Folder 1, Browne Papers. For other state conventions, see Box 19, Folder 2, Browne Papers.

24. "California Delegation Press Release," February 14, 1972, "California Black Caucus State Convention Agenda," February 26, 1972, Dymally to SFSU BSU," February 22, 1972, all in Box 119, "Black Caucus Folder," Dymally Papers.

25. "Update on State Conventions," National Black Political Convention, Box 119, "Black Caucus Folder," Dymally Papers.

26. "Budget—National Black Political Convention," March 11, 1972, Box 19, Folder 1, Browne Papers.

27. Richard Hatcher interview, *Eyes on the Prize Interviews Series II*; Gary Political Review, "Souvenir Edition," March 12, 1972, Box 35, Folder 1, Harding Papers.

28. *Gary Post-Tribune,* March 9, 1972; *Gary Info,* March 9, 1972; "Welcome Packet," Box 19, Folder 3, Browne Papers.

29. *Gary Post-Tribune,* March 11, 1972; Richard Hatcher interview, *Eyes on the Prize Interviews Series II;* "Minority Business Steering Committee to Delegates and Guests of the First National Black Political Convention," March 9, 1972, Box 35, Folder 2, Harding Papers; "Hotel Arrangements for the Convention," Box 119, "Black Caucus Folder," Dymally Papers.

30. *Gary Post-Tribune,* March 11, 1972; Richard Hatcher interview, *Eyes on the Prize Interviews Series II;* "Wisconsin Delegation Housing Memo," Box 82, Folder 5, Bond Papers.

31. *New York Times,* March 8, 1972; "NBPC Executive Committee Agenda," Box 82, Folder 5, Bond Papers.

32. *New York Times,* March 9, 1972; "Minutes of Planning Conference," February 17, 1972, Box 119, "Black Caucus Folder," Dymally Papers.

33. *Chicago Tribune*, March 8, 1972.

34. *Gary Post-Tribune*, March 4, 1972.

35. *Chicago Daily Defender*, March 11, 1972; Charles Eason, Acting Director, Eastern Region National Urban League to National Urban League Executive Directors, February 28, 1972, Box 119, "Black Caucus Folder," Dymally Papers.

36. Ibid., *Chicago Daily Defender*; "NBPC Press Release," Box 82, Folder 5, Bond Papers.

37. *Gary Info*, March 8, 1972; "NBPC Press Release," Box 82, Folder 5, Bond Papers.

38. *Gary Info*, March 8, 1972; *Chicago Daily Defender*, March 11, 1972.

39. "Tentative Schedule of the National Black Political Convention," Container 64, Folder 1207, Stokes Papers; *New York Times*, March 11, 1972; "Executive Committee Agenda— NBPC," February 25, 1972; Baraka to Diggs, Hatcher, et al., March 7, 1972, Box 119, "Black Caucus Folder," Dymally Papers; Devorah Heitner, *Black Power TV* (Durham, NC: Duke University Press, 2013).

40. Benjamin Chavis interview, *Eyes on the Prize Interviews Series II*.

CHAPTER FOUR

1. Richard Hatcher interview, *Eyes on the Prize Interviews Series II*.

2. *New York Times*, March 11, 1972; Joshua Farrington, *Black Republicans and the Transformation of the GOP* (Philadelphia: University of Pennsylvania Press, 2016), 208; Leah Wright Rigueur, *The Loneliness of the Black Republican* (Princeton, NJ: Princeton University Press, 2015), 185–86. For a contemporary view on black Republicans and their experience within the Republican Party, see Corey D. Fields, *Black Elephants in the Room: The Unexpected Politics of African American Republicans* (Oakland: University of California Press, 2016).

3. *Washington Post*, March 11, 1972; *Chicago Tribune*, March 11, 1972.

4. *New York Times*, March 11, March 13, 1972.

5. *New York Amsterdam News*, March 11, 1972.

6. William Clay, *Just Permanent Interests: Black Americans in Congress, 1870–1991* (New York: Amistad Press, 1992), 203; *Washington Post*, March 11, March 12, 1972; William E. Nelson, "Black Youth: An Untapped Resource," in *It's Nationtime!*, 11–12.

7. *Gary Post-Tribune*, March 12, 1972; *Chicago Tribune*, March 12, March 13, 1972; Fauntroy to Delegates of the National Black Political Convention, re: "Washington Agenda," March 9, 1972, Folder 1, IBW-Strickland Papers.

8. Gary Convention FBI File—File #157–5215. For more on the FBI's counterintelligence program targeting black activists, see Kenneth O'Reilly, *Racial Matters: The FBI's Secret War on Black America, 1960–1972* (New York: Free Press, 1991).

9. *Newsweek*, April 3, 1972; "Resolutions Committee," Folder 4, IBW-Strickland Papers. The following state delegations presented resolutions on that day of the Convention: Oklahoma, Nevada, Ohio, California, Illinois, Minnesota, New York, Florida, Washington, DC, and Michigan; "Rules for the Credentials Committee," March 9, 1972, Mervyn Dymally Papers.

10. *New York Amsterdam News*, March 18, 1972; *New York Times*, March 12, 1972; *Jet*, March 30, 1972; Joan Thornell to Fauntroy, March 9, 1972, Box 35, Folder 2, Harding Papers.

11. *New York Amsterdam News*, March 18, 1972.

12. Nelson, "Black Youth," 12. It appears that the NBPC did not capitalize on the energy of the black student movement. For more on black activism on campus, see Martha Biondi, *The Black Revolution on Campus* (Berkeley: University of California Press, 2012); Joy Ann Williamson, *Black Power on Campus: University of Illinois, 1965–1975* (Champaign: University of Illinois Press, 2003); and Stefan Bradley, *Harlem vs. Columbia University* (Urbana: University of Illinois Press, 2009).

13. "Resolution Adopted by the Gary Commission on the Status of Women Submits Eight Resolutions," Box 19, Folder 6, Browne Papers; "Resolutions—Suggested Committee Procedures," Box 35, Folder 2, Harding Papers; "Platform Committee Meeting," March 9, 1972, Box 35, Folder 2, Harding Papers; "Consolidation for Platform Committee Roles," March 9, 1972, Box 35, Folder 2, Harding Papers; "Resolution from Cairo, Illinois, and Wilmington, North Carolina," Folder 1, IBW-Strickland Papers.

14. *Gary Post-Tribune*, March 11, 1972; "Definitions of Work for the Two Committees," Box 35, Folder 1, Harding Papers; Vincent Harding notes, February 28, 1972, Box 35, Folder 1, Harding Papers; Barbara Jordan to State Conveners, re: "Resolutions from State Delegations," February 25, 1972, Box 119, "Black Caucus Folder," Dymally Papers.

15. Derrick White, *The Challenge of Blackness: The Institute of the Black World and Political Activism in the 1970s* (Gainesville: University of Florida Press, 2011), 101–20.

16. Frederick Harris discusses the phenomenon of black politicians leveraging their blackness to gain elective office, but then only to become race-neutral once they are in office. See Frederick C. Harris, *The Price of the Ticket: Barack Obama and the Rise and Decline of Black Politics* (New York: Oxford University Press, 2012).

17. Howard T. Robinson to Vincent Harding, February 26, 1972, Box 35, Folder 1, Harding Papers; "Tentative Items for Consideration—Platform/Black Agenda," Box 35, Folder 1, Harding Papers.

18. "Some Notes on the Platform Committee Meeting," February 16, 1972, Box 35, Folder 1, Harding Papers; National Black Political Convention—Platform Subject Areas," Box 35, Folder 1, Harding Papers; *Washington Post*, March 11, March 16, 1972; *Chicago Tribune*, March 11, 1972; "Outline for a Black Agenda/Platform," February 1972, Box 35, Folder 1, Harding Papers.

19. *Gary Post-Tribune*, March 11, 1972.

20. Harding to Carl Holman, March 1, 1972, Box 35, Folder 1, Harding Papers; "A Draft Document for the Platform Committee of the National Black Political Convention, Part 1: The Gary Declaration," February 1972, Box 35, Folder 1, Harding Papers; "Draft Preamble: Black Politics at the Crossroads," Box 35, Folder 1, Harding Papers.

21. "Draft Preamble."

22. Ibid.

23. Ibid.

24. Ibid.; David Holmes, "A Commentary on the National Black Political Agenda," Box 11, Folder 18, Coleman Young State Senate Papers, Detroit Public Library.

25. John A. Morsell to NAACP National Representatives at National Black Political Convention, March 10, 1972, Box 27, folder marked "National Black Political Convention," Roy Wilkins Papers, Library of Congress; *New York Times*, March 10, 1972; *Gary Post-Tribune*, March 11, 1972; *Washington Post*, March 11, 1972; *Chicago Tribune*, March 11, 1972.

26. Nelson, "The Ohio Delegation," in *It's Nationtime!*, 13–15.

27. *Chicago Daily News*, March 11, 1972; Baraka, "Gary and Miami," 66.

28. *Sacramento Bee*, February 12, 1972.

29. *Chicago Daily News*, March 11, March 12, 1972.

CHAPTER FIVE

1. See: *Chicago Tribune, Washington Post, Gary Post-Tribune,* and *New York Times;* Abby Kaighin, "How the Press Covered the National Black Political Convention," unpublished paper, University of Chicago, 1972. Percy Sutton spoke of the need for black people to control a system of mass communications "so that the lives of black people be portrayed accurately." See Percy Sutton, "Black Communications—Black Power: A New Strategy for Liberation," in Nathan Wright, ed., *What Black Politicians are Saying* (New York: Hawthorn Books, 1972), 144–64.

2. "Diggs Speech," Box 35, Folder 2, Harding Papers; *Gary Post-Tribune*, March 12, 1972.

3. "Richard Hatcher Address," March 11, 1972, Box 19, Folder 3, Browne Papers.

4. Ibid.

5. Ibid.

6. Ibid.

7. Ibid.

8. Ibid.

9. Ibid.

10. *Gary Post-Tribune*, March 12, 1972.

11. Jesse Jackson speech, in "Nationtime, Gary," a 1972 documentary film by William Greaves. Jackson is featured prominently in the documentary. Jesse borrowed the phrase from Baraka, who had written a poem called "It's Nation Time."

12. Ibid.

13. Ibid.; "Black America and the Democratic Party," February 1972, Box 35, Folder 1, Harding Papers.

14. Ibid. "Nationtime, Gary," documentary film by William Greave (1972).

15. Ron Walters, "New Black Political Culture," *Black World*, October 1972, 7–8; Jesse Jackson interview, *Eyes on the Prize Interviews Series II*.

16. *Gary Post-Tribune*, March 12, 1972.

17. *Chicago Tribune*, March 12, 1972; *Jet*, March 30, 1972; Benjamin Chavis interview, *Eyes on the Prize Interviews Series II*.

18. *Jet*, March 30, 1972.

19. Amiri Baraka interview, *Eyes on the Prize Interviews Series II*.

20. *Jet*, March 30, 1972; Amiri Baraka interview, *Eyes on the Prize Interviews Series II*.

21. Amiri Baraka interview, *Eyes on the Prize Interviews Series II*; Ron Walters, "The New Black Political Culture," 4–16.

22. *Jet*, March 30, 1972.

23. *Gary Post-Tribune*, March 12, 1972; *Chicago Sun-Times*, March 12, 1972; *The Black Panther*, March 18, 1972. Although black female luminaries such as Coretta Scott King,

Queen Mother Moore, Rosa Parks, Betty Shabazz, and Dorothy Height were in attendance at Gary and very visible, their presence was merely "symbolic." See Russell Rickford, *We Are An African People: Independent Education, Black Power, and the Radical Imagination* (Oxford: Oxford University Press, 2016), 137.

CHAPTER SIX

1. *Chicago Sun-Times,* March 12, 1972; *Gary Post-Tribune,* March 12, 1972; *Chicago Tribune,* March 12, 1972.

2. "What We Want," Black Agenda Notes, Box 35, Folder 1, Harding Papers; "Panel Members," Black Agenda, Box 35, Folder 2, Harding Papers; "National Black Political Agenda," March 11, 1972, Box 35, Folder 1, Harding Papers. Box 19, Folder 7 of the Browne Papers has the complete background research on each agenda topic.

3. "National Black Political Agenda"; "Preliminary Draft/Working Paper—Political Empowerment," Box 35, Folder 1, Harding Papers.

4. "Political Empowerment Committee," March 5, 1972, Box 35, Folder 2, Harding Papers.

5. "National Black Political Agenda."

6. Ibid.

7. C. Vernon Gray, "The Black Agenda and Political Empowerment," by C. Vernon Gray, in *It's Nationtime!,* 6–7. Economist Robert S. Browne drafted much of the economic portion of the Agenda. A strong proponent of self-help, he founded the Black Economic Research Center and its journal *The Review of Black Political Economy,* the Emergency Land Fund, and the 21st Century Foundation.

8. Ibid.; "Preliminary Draft/Working Paper—Economic Empowerment," Box 35, Folder 1, Harding Papers.

9. "National Black Agenda"; James Hefner, "Economic Empowerment in the National Black Political Agenda," in *It's Nationtime!,* 9–11.

10. "National Black Political Agenda"; "Recommendations from the Economic Empowerment Committee," March 5, 1972, Box 19, Folder 2, Browne Papers; Washington, D.C. Delegation to the National Black Political Convention re: economic ideas, March 9, 1972, Box 19, Folder 3, Browne Papers.

11. Strickland to Gouraige, May 17, 1972, Folder 2, IBW-Strickland Papers; "Black Political Convention in Gary: The Myth of Unity without Uniformity," March 17, 1972, Folder 2, IBW-Strickland Papers.

12. "Black Political Agenda"; "Preliminary Draft: Working Paper—Human Development," Box 35, Folder 3, Harding Papers; "Human Development Notes," Box 35, Folder 2, Harding Papers. For health care concerns during the period, see Alondra Nelson, *Body and Soul: The Black Panther Party and the Fight Against Medical Discrimination* (Minneapolis: University of Minnesota Press, 2011).

13. "Black Political Agenda"; Rural Development Committee to D.C. Delegates to the National Black Political Convention, March 9, 1972, Box 35, Folder 2, Harding Papers.

14. "Black Political Agenda."

15. Charles Diggs Speech, IBW-Strickland Papers. For book-length studies that look at the relationship between black activists and foreign policy, see Brenda Gayle Plummer, *Rising Wind: Black Americans and U.S. Foreign Affairs, 1935–1960* (Chapel Hill: UNC Press, 1996); Brenda Gayle Plummer, *In Search of Power: African Americans in the Era of Decolonization, 1956–1974* (Cambridge: Cambridge University Press, 2012); Carol Anderson, *The NAACP and the Struggle for Colonial Liberation, 1941–1960* (Cambridge: Cambridge University Press, 2014); Francis Njubi Nesbitt, *Race for Sanctions: African Americans Against Apartheid, 1946–1994* (Bloomington: Indiana University Press, 2004).

16. "Black Political Agenda"; Ron Walters, "Foreign Policy for Black People," in *It's Nationtime!*, 7–9.

17. "Black Political Agenda"; "Preliminary Draft—Working Paper Environmental Protection," Box 35, Folder 1, Harding Papers. The Agenda was prophetic in talking about environmental racism. Scholar Robert Bullard has devoted his life's work to this subject. See two of his books: *Dumping in Dixie: Race, Class, and Environmental Quality* (New York: Westview Press, 2008), and *Unequal Protection: Environmental Justice and Communities of Color* (New York: Random House, 1994).

18. "Black Political Agenda."

19. "Black Political Agenda"; "Preliminary Draft/Working Paper—Communications," Box 35, Folder 1, Harding Papers; "A Working Paper from the Communications Workshop," Box 35, Folder 1, Harding Papers.

20. "Nationtime, Gary." Documentary by William Greaves (1972).

21. "Press Release," March 12, 1972, Box 11, Folder 18, Coleman Young Papers; Coleman Young, *Hard Stuff: The Autobiography of Mayor Coleman Young* (New York: Viking, 1994), 189–90.

22. "Press Release," March 12, 1972, Box 11, Folder 18, Coleman Young Papers; "Hard Stuff"; Robert Smith, *We Have No Leaders: African Americans in the Post–Civil Rights Era* (Albany: SUNY Press, 1996), 49.

23. "Why Did Michigan Walk Out," March 18, 1972, Young Papers; *Michigan Chronicle*, March 25, 1972; Smith, *We Have No Leaders*, 49.

24. "Statement by the Michigan Delegation," March 12, 1972, Box 11, Folder 18, Coleman Young Papers.

25. "Minority Statement on the Michigan Walkout," March 12, 1972; *Gary Times*, March 13, 1972; Sherry Suttles to Moses Newson, March 15, 1972, Folder 1, IBW-Strickland Papers; "Gary—From My Perspective," by Sherry Suttles, Folder 2, IBW-Strickland Papers. For a more in-depth look at the relationship between Detroit's black activists and labor, see August Meier and Elliott Rudwick, *Black Detroit and the Rise of the UAW* (New York: Oxford University Press, 1979).

26. Coleman Young, *Hard Stuff: The Autobiography of Mayor Coleman Young* (New York: Viking, 1994), 190; Amiri Baraka interview, *Eyes on the Prize Interviews Series II*.

27. *New York Times*, March 13, 1972; *Gary Post-Tribune*, March 13, 1972; *Washington Post*, March 16, 1972; *New York Times Magazine*, March 12, 1972.

28. Clay, *Just Permanent Interests*, 225; Carl B. Stokes, *Promises of Power: A Political Autobiography* (New York: Simon and Schuster, 1973), 275–76.

29. Clay, *Just Permanent Interests*, 225; Richard Hatcher interview, *Eyes on the Prize Interviews Series II*.

30. Poinsett, "Black Political Strategies for '72," *Ebony* 72 (1972); Marion Humphrey, "The Convention and Shirley Chisholm," in *It's Nationtime!*, 15.

31. Amiri Baraka interview, *Eyes on the Prize Interviews Series II*.

32. Richard Hatcher interview, *Eyes on the Prize Interviews Series II*; *New York Times*, March 12, 1972.

33. *Chicago Tribune*, March 13, 1972.

34. *Indianapolis News*, March 13, 1972. The Indiana delegation appeared to be one of the more organized delegations at Gary. For details of the Indiana delegation, see National Black Political Convention Collection, 1972–1973, file at the Indiana Historical Society.

35. "Amiri Baraka Interview," in Henry Hampton and Steve Fayer, eds., *Voices of Freedom: An Oral History of the Civil Rights Movement from the 1950s Through the 1980s* (New York: Bantam Books, 1990), 576; *Gary Post-Tribune*, March 13, 1972; *New York Times*, March 13, 1972.

36. *New York Amsterdam News*, March 25, 1972; "Proposed Structure and Election Process of a National Black Political Structure to Continue Permanently After the National Black Political Convention," Box 11, Folder 18, Coleman Young Papers.

37. "Proposed Structure and Election Process"; *Gary Post-Tribune*, March 13, March 14, 1972; John Dean, "Black Political Assembly: Birth of a New Force," in *Focus* 2, no. 1 (November 1972).

38. *Gary Post-Tribune*, March 13, 1972; *Washington Post*, March 13, 1972.

39. Baraka, "Open Letter re: Status of National Black Political Assembly," May 1972, Box 27, folder marked "National Black Political Convention," Bond Papers; *New York Amsterdam News*, May 20, 1972.

40. *New York Amsterdam News*, March 18, 1972. Instead of busing, many activists demanded community control of public schools, while others established independent Pan-African schools. See Jane Anna Gordon, *Why They Can't Wait: A Critique of the Black-Jewish Conflict over Community Control in Ocean Hill-Brownsville, 1967–1971* (New York: Routledge, 2013), and Russell Rickford, *We Are An African People: Independent Education, Black Power, and the Radical Imagination* (New York: Oxford University Press, 2016).

41. "Initial Resolution on Education," March 12, 1972, Folder 3, IBW-Strickland Papers.

42. Ibid.

43. "Initial Resolution on Education"; *Gary Times*, March 13, 1972; Ronald Walters, *Black Presidential Politics In America: A Strategic Approach* (Albany: SUNY Press, 1988), 88–89.

44. *Chicago Tribune*, March 13, 1972; *Gary Post-Tribune*, March 13, 1972. The antibusing posture was part of CORE's proposed Community Self-Determination Act that President Nixon had agreed to support. See Joshua Farrington, *Black Republicans and the Transformation of the GOP* (Philadelphia: University of Pennsylvania Press, 2016), 184–85.

45. *Indianapolis Star*, March 13, 1972.

46. *New York Amsterdam News*, March 18, 1972; *New York Times*, March 16, 1972; *Sacramento Bee*, March 13, 1972.

47. Peniel Joseph, *Waiting 'Til the Midnight Hour: A Narrative History of the Black Power Movement* (New York: Henry Holt, 2006), 282; "Original Israeli Resolution," Folder 3, IBW-Strickland Papers.

48. Ronald Walters, *Black Presidential Politics In America: A Strategic Approach* (Albany: SUNY Press, 1988), 90–91; Cedric Johnson, *Revolutionaries to Race Leaders* (Minneapolis: University of Minnesota Press, 2007), 113–15.

CHAPTER SEVEN

1. *Gary Post-Tribune,* March 13, 1972.

2. *Gary Post-Tribune,* March 14, 1972; *Chicago Tribune,* March 14, 1972.

3. *New York Times,* March 16, March 19, 1972; *Chicago Daily Defender,* March 18, 1972.

4. *New York Amsterdam News,* March 18, 1972.

5. *New York Amsterdam News,* March 18, 1972; *Washington Post,* March 18, 1972.

6. *Michigan Chronicle,* March 25, 1972.

7. "Adoption to the Busing Resolution Passed at Gary, Indiana," March 24, 1972, Box 35, Folder 2, Vincent Harding Papers; "Resolution on Israel Adopted by Steering Committee, March 24, 1972, Folder 3, IBW Papers-Strickland; "Substitute Resolution on Israel Adopted by the Steering Committee," March 24, 1972, Folder 4, IBW Papers; *New York Times,* March 14, March 23, 1972; Ron Walters, "New Black Political Culture," 8.

8. "Reaffirmation of Unity-Steering Committee," March 28, 1972, Box 19, Folder 1, Browne Papers; Fauntroy and Barbara Jordan to Platform/Resolution Committee, April 19, 1972, Box 35, Folder 1, Harding Papers; "Joint Meeting of the Platform/Resolutions Committee, April 28, 1972, Box 35, Folder 3, Harding Papers; "Revisions to the National Black Political Agenda," April 27, 1972, Box 35, Folder 3, Harding Papers.

9. Baraka, "Gary and Miami"; "Resolutions Adopted at the Steering Committee Meeting," March 24, 1972, Folder 2, IBW Papers-Strickland; "Adoption to the Busing Resolution," March 24, 1972, Box 19, Folder 4, Robert S. Browne Papers; *New York Times,* May 19, 1972; "Appendix Material to be Discussed at Steering Committee Meeting," May 6, 1972, Folder 3, IBW Papers-Strickland; Wilkins to Baraka, June 7, 1972, Box 27, folder marked "National Black Political Convention," Roy Wilkins Papers. For more on the Jewish response to the Israel resolution, see Allison Schottenstein, "Dismantling Gary: Media Sensationalism, Black-Jewish Relations, and the National Black Political Convention—1972," unpublished seminar paper in possession of the author. For a broader discussion of Black-Jewish relations, see Cheryl Greenberg, *Troubling the Waters: Black-Jewish Relations in the American Century* (Princeton, NJ: Princeton University Press, 2010).

10. Roy Wilkins to Baraka, et al., May 6, 1972, Box 27, folder marked "National Black Political Convention," Roy Wilkins Papers; *New York Times,* May 15, May 20, 1972; *Washington Post,* May 18, May 20, 1972; *The Crisis,* August 1972, 229–30; "Black Agenda Ratification Resolution," not in folder, IBW Papers-Strickland; National Black Political Convention Press Release, May 19, 1972, Box 19, Folder 6, Browne Papers; National Black Political Agenda, May 19, 1972, Box 35, Folder 1, Harding Papers; "Editorial Changes and other Revisions to

the National Black Political Agenda," May 2, 1972, Box 19, Folder 2, Browne Papers; NBPC Co-Chairs to Steering Committee, "Memorandum of Clarification," May 2, 1972, Box 35, Folder 1, Harding Papers.

11. Baraka, "Gary to Miami," 68–69; Baraka to Wilkins, May 17, 1972, Roy Wilkins Papers; Wilkins to Baraka, June 7, 1972, Box 27, folder marked "National Black Political Convention," Roy Wilkins Papers; *New York Times,* May 20, 1972; *New York Amsterdam News,* May 20, 1972. As the entire NAACP-NBPC controversy grew, the NAACP published a pamphlet telling readers why they pulled out of the NBPC. See: "The NAACP and the National Black Political Convention," Box 27, folder marked "National Black Political Convention," Roy Wilkins Papers.

12. "Black Declaration of Independence," and "Black Bill of Rights," Box 82, Folder 4, Bond Papers; *New York Times,* May 19, June 16, 1972; *Washington Post,* June 2, 1972. Julian Bond predicted that tension between black elected officials and black nationalists would increase. Julian Bond to Richard Hatcher, April 6, 1972, Box 82, Folder 4, Bond Papers.

13. Baraka, "Gary and Miami," 71.

14. *Washington Post,* June 11, 1972.

15. Baraka, "Gary and Miami," 71–72.

16. Baraka, "Gary and Miami," 70–77.

17. Manning Marable, *Race, Reform, and Rebellion: The Second Reconstruction in Black America, 1945–1990* (Jackson: University Press of Mississippi, 1991), 136–37; Clarence Lang, *Grassroots at the Gateway: Class Politics and Class Struggle in St. Louis, 1936–1975* (Ann Arbor: University of Michigan Press, 2009), 238–39; Thomas Sugrue, *Sweet Land of Liberty: The Forgotten Struggle for Civil Rights in the North* (New York: Random House, 2009), 500–1.

EPILOGUE

1. Robert Smith, *We Have No Leaders: African Americans in the Post–Civil Rights Era* (Albany: SUNY Press, 1996), 60; David Chappell, *Waking from the Dream: The Struggle for Civil Rights in the Shadow of Martin Luther King, Jr.* (New York: Random House, 2014), 53.

2. *Washington Post,* March 23, 1974; Milton D. Morris, *The Politics of Black America* (New York: Harper and Row, 1975), 287.

3. Smith, *We Have No Leaders,* 63; *New York Times,* March 22, 1974.

4. *New York Times,* March 18, 1974; Chappell, *Waking from the Dream,* 55–56.

5. *New York Times,* March 18, 1974.

6. *New York Times,* March 23, 1974.

7. *Washington Post,* March 23, 1974; Ronald W. Walters and Robert C. Smith, eds., *African American Leadership* (Albany: SUNY Press, 1999), 120; George Derek Musgrove, *Rumor, Repression, and Racial Politics: How the Harassment of Black Elected Officials Shaped Post–Civil Rights America* (Athens: University of Georgia Press, 2012), 49; Steven F. Lawson, *Running for Freedom: Civil Rights and Black Politics in America Since 1941* (New York: McGraw Hill, 1991), 122.

8. Smith, *We Have No Leaders,* 64, 75; Jerry Gafio Watts, *Amiri Baraka: The Politics and Art of a Black Intellectual* (New York: NYU Press, 2001), 404; Norman Kelley, *The Head Negro*

in Charge Syndrome: The Dead End of Black Politics (New York: Nation Books, 2004), 110. Jane Rhodes, *Framing the Black Panthers: The Spectacular Rise of a Black Power Icon* (New York: The New Press, 2007), looks at the role of the media in crafting popular images of Black Power groups and celebrities.

9. Smith, *We Have No Leaders,* 75–77.

10. David Colburn and Richard Adler, *African American Mayors: Race, Politics, and the American City* (Urbana: University of Illinois Press, 2001); Richard Hatcher interview, *Eyes on the Prize Interviews Series II*; Peniel Joseph, *Dark Days, Bright Nights: From Black Power to Barack Obama* (New York: Basic Civitas Books, 2010), 200–1; Michael Eric Dyson, *The Black Presidency: Barack Obama and the Politics of Race in America* (New York: Houghton, Mifflin, Harcourt, 2016).

WORKS CITED

PRIMARY SOURCE MATERIAL

Manuscript Sources

California State University–Los Angeles, JFK Library, Special Collections
    Mervyn Dymally Papers

Detroit Public Library
    Coleman Young State Senate Papers

Emory University
    Vincent Harding Papers

Howard University, Moorland-Spingarn Research Center
    Ron Walters Papers

Indiana Historical Society
    National Black Political Convention Collection, 1972–1973
    Guy E. Russell Papers

Indiana University Northwest, Calumet Regional Archives
    Henry Coleman Papers
    National Black Political Convention, 1972 File

Library of Congress
    Roy Wilkins Papers

Schomburg Center for Research in Black Culture
    Black Economic Research Center Records
    Robert S. Browne Papers
    Institute of the Black World Papers
    Julian Mayfield Papers

Robert Sengstacke Papers
William Strickland Research Files

University of Virginia Special Collections
Julian Bond Papers

Washington University Libraries, Special Collections
Eyes on the Prize Interviews Series II

Western Reserve Historical Society
Carl B. Stokes Papers
Louis Stokes Papers

Microfilm
The Black Power Movement—Part 1: Amiri Baraka from Black Arts to
Black Radicalism
NAACP Papers Part 30

FILM

Nationtime: Gary

NEWSPAPERS AND PERIODICALS

Black Panther
Black World
Chicago Daily Defender
Chicago Sun-Times
Chicago Tribune
Cleveland Call and Post
Cleveland Plain Dealer
Cleveland Press
Congressional Record
Crisis
Ebony
Gary Info
Gary Political Review
Gary Post-Tribune
Gary Times
Indianapolis Star

It's Nationtime!
Jet
Los Angeles Herald Dispatch
Los Angeles Sentinel
Michigan Chronicle
Newsweek
New York Amsterdam News
New York Times
New York Times Magazine
Race Relations Reporter
Sacramento Bee
Washington Post

EYES ON THE PRIZE INTERVIEW ARCHIVE, WASHINGTON UNIVERSITY LIBRARIES

Amiri Baraka
Harry Belafonte
Ben Chavis
John Conyers
Charles Diggs
Willie Felder
Richard Hatcher
Mary Hightower
Jesse Jackson
Maynard Jackson

SELECTED BIBLIOGRAPHY

Adler, Jeffrey, and David Colburn, eds. *African American Mayors: Race, Politics, and the American City.* Urbana: University of Illinois Press, 2001.

Alexander, Michelle. *The New Jim Crow: Mass Incarceration in the Age of Color-blindness.* New York: The New Press, 2010.

Allen, Robert. *Black Awakening in Capitalist America: An Analytic History.* New York: Anchor Books, 1970.

Baraka, Amiri. *The Autobiography of Leroi Jones.* Chicago: Lawrence Hill Books, 1997.

———. "Gary and Miami—Before and After." *Black World* 21, no. 12 (1972): 54–78.

———. "The Pan-African Party and the Black Nation." *Black Scholar* 2, no. 7 (1971): 24–32.

Barbour, Floyd, ed. *The Black Power Revolt: A Collection of Essays*. Boston: Porter Sargent, 1968.

———, ed. *The Black 70's*. Boston: Porter Sargent, 1970.

Bass, Amy. *Not The Triumph But The Struggle: The 1968 Olympics and the Making of the Black Athlete*. Minneapolis: University of Minnesota Press, 2002.

Bennett, Lerone. "A Black Agenda for the Seventies." In *Race Relations Reporter* (1972).

Biondi, Martha. *The Black Revolution on Campus*. Berkeley: University of California Press, 2012.

Black Power Conference Reports. New York: Afram Associates, 1970.

The Black Revolution: An Ebony Special Issue. Chicago: Johnson Publishing, 1970.

Bradley, Stefan M. *Harlem vs. Columbia University: Black Student Power in the Late 1960s*. Urbana: University of Illinois Press, 2009.

Brown, Scot. *Fighting For US: Maulana Karenga, the US Organization, and Black Cultural Nationalism*. New York: NYU Press, 2003.

Carmichael, Stokely, and Charles V. Hamilton. *Black Power: The Politics of Liberation in America*. New York: Vintage Books, 1967.

Chappell, David. *Waking From The Dream: The Struggle for Civil Rights in the Shadow of Martin Luther King, Jr*. New York: Random House, 2014.

Chisholm, Shirley. *The Good Fight*. New York: Harper and Row, 1973.

———. *Unbought and Unbossed*. New York: Houghton Mifflin, 1970.

Clay, William. *Just Permanent Interests: Black Americans in Congress, 1870–1991*. New York: Amistad Press, 1992.

Clegg, Claude. *An Original Man: The Life and Times of Elijah Muhammad*. New York: St. Martin's Press, 1997.

Collier-Thomas, Bettye, and V. P. Franklin, eds. *Sisters in the Struggle: African American Women in the Civil Rights–Black Power Movement*. New York: NYU Press, 2001.

Conyers, James L., Jr. ed. *Engines of the Black Power Movement: Essays on the Influence of Civil Rights Actions, Arts, and Islam*. Jefferson, NC: McFarland, 2006.

Cruse, Harold. *The Crisis of the Negro Intellectual: From Its Origins to the Present*. New York: William Morrow, 1967.

Dyson, Michael Eric. *The Black Presidency: Barack Obama and the Politics of Race in America*. New York: Houghton, Mifflin, Harcourt, 2016.

Evanzz, Karl. *The Rise and Fall of Elijah Muhammad*. New York: Vintage Books, 2011.

Farrington, Joshua. *Black Republicans and the Transformation of the GOP*. Philadelphia: University of Pennsylvania Press, 2016.

Fergus, Devin. *Liberalism, Black Power, and the Making of American Politics, 1965–1980*. Athens: University of Georgia Press, 2009.

Fields, Corey. *Black Elephants in the Room: The Unexpected Politics of African American Republicans.* Oakland: University of California Press, 2016.

Gore, Dayo, Jeanne Theoharis, and Komozi Woodard, eds. *Want To Start A Revolution: Radical Women in the Black Freedom Struggle.* New York: NYU Press, 2009.

Haines, Herbert. *Black Radicals and the Civil Rights Mainstream, 1954–1970.* Knoxville: University of Tennessee Press, 1988.

Hamilton, Charles V. *Adam Clayton Powell, Jr.: The Political Biography of an American Dilemma.* New York: Atheneum, 1991.

Hamilton, Charles V., and Dona Cooper Hamilton. *The Dual Agenda: Race and Social Welfare Policies of Civil Rights Organizations.* New York: Columbia University Press, 1997.

Hampton, Henry, and Steve Fayer, eds. *Voices of Freedom: An Oral History of the Civil Rights Movement from the 1950s to the 1980s.* New York: Bantam Books, 1990.

Harris, Frederick C. *The Price of the Ticket: Barack Obama and the Rise and Decline of Black Politics.* Oxford: Oxford University Press, 2012.

Haygood, Wil. *King of the Cats: The Life and Times of Adam Clayton Powell, Jr.* Boston: Houghton Mifflin, 1993.

Heitner, Devorah. *Black Power TV.* Durham, NC: Duke University Press, 2013.

Hill, Lauren Warren, and Julia Rabig, eds. *The Business of Black Power: Community Development, Capitalism, and Corporate Responsibility in Postwar America.* Rochester, NY: University of Rochester Press, 2012.

Hutchinson, Earl Ofari. *Betrayed: A History of Presidential Failure to Protect Black Lives.* Boulder, CO: Westview Press, 1996.

Jeffries, Hassan. *Bloody Lowndes: Civil Rights and Black Power in Alabama's Black Belt.* New York: NYU Press, 2009.

Jeffries, Judson, ed. *Black Power in the Belly of the Beast.* Urbana: University of Illinois Press, 2006.

Jennings, James. *The Politics of Black Empowerment: The Transformation of Black Activism in Urban America.* Detroit: Wayne State University Press, 1992.

Johnson, Cedric. *Revolutionaries to Race Leaders: Black Power and the Making of African American Politics.* Minneapolis: University of Minnesota Press, 2007.

Johnson, Ollie III, and Karen L. Stanford, eds. *Black Political Organizations in the Post–Civil Rights Era.* New Brunswick, NJ: Rutgers University Press, 2002.

Joseph, Peniel, ed. *The Black Power Movement: Rethinking the Civil Rights–Black Power Era.* New York: Routledge, 2006.

———. *Dark Days, Bright Nights: From Black Power to Barack Obama.* New York: Basic Books, 2010.

———. *Stokely: A Life*. New York: Basic Civitas, 2014.

———. *Waiting 'Til the Midnight Hour: A Narrative History of Black Power in America*. New York: Henry Holt, 2006.

Kelley, Norman. *The Head Negro In Charge Syndrome: The Dead End of Black Politics*. New York: Nation Books, 2004.

Killian, Lewis. *How Capitalism Underdeveloped Black America*. Boston: South End Press, 1983.

———. *The Impossible Revolution: Black Power and the American Dream*. New York: Random House, 1968.

Kotlowski, Dean J. *Nixon's Civil Rights: Politics, Principle, and Policy*. Cambridge, MA: Harvard University Press, 2002.

Lang, Clarence. *Grassroots at the Gateway: Class Politics and Black Freedom Struggle in St. Louis, 1936–1975*. Ann Arbor: University of Michigan Press, 2009.

Lawson, Steven F. *In Pursuit of Power: Southern Blacks and Electoral Politics, 1965–1982*. New York: Columbia University Press, 1985.

———. *Running For Freedom: Civil Rights and Black Politics in America Since 1941*. New York: McGraw Hill, 1991.

Lester, Julius. *Look Out, Whitey! Black Power's Gon' Get Your Mama!* New York: Grove Press, 1968.

Lomax, Louis. *The Negro Revolt*. New York: Signet, 1962.

Malcolm X. *The Autobiography of Malcolm X*. New York: Ballantine Books, 1992.

Mantler, Gordon K. *Power to the People: Black-Brown Coalitions and the Fight For Economic Justice*. Chapel Hill: UNC Press, 2013.

Marable, Manning. *Black American Politics: From the Washington Marches to Jesse Jackson*. London: Verso, 1985.

———. *Malcolm X: A Life of Reinvention*. New York: Penguin Books, 2011.

———. *Race, Reform, and Rebellion: The Second Reconstruction in Black America, 1945–1990*. Jackson: University Press of Mississippi, 1991.

Mayes, Keith A. *Kwanzaa: Black Power and the Making of the African American Holiday Tradition*. New York: Routledge, 2009.

McAdam, Doug. *Political Process and the Development of Black Insurgency, 1930–1970*. Chicago: University of Chicago Press, 1982.

McCartney, John T. *Black Power Ideologies: An Essay in African American Political Thought*. Philadelphia: Temple University Press, 1992.

McKissick, Floyd. "The Way to a Black Ideology." *Black Scholar* 1, no. 2 (1969).

Meriwether, James. *Proudly We Can Be Africans: Black Americans and Africa, 1935–1961*. Chapel Hill: UNC Press, 2002.

Moore, Leonard. *Carl B. Stokes and the Rise of Black Political Power*. Urbana: University of Illinois Press, 2002.

Morris, Milton. *The Politics of Black America.* New York: Harper and Row, 1975.

Murch, Donna. *Living for the City: Migration, Education, and the Rise of the Black Panther Party in Oakland, California.* Chapel Hill: UNC Press, 2010.

Musgrove, George Derek. *Rumor, Repression, and Racial Politics: How the Harassment of Black Elected Officials Shaped Post–Civil Rights America.* Athens: University of Georgia Press, 2012.

National Conference of Black Political Scientists. *It's Nation-Time.* 1972.

National Urban League. *When The Marching Stopped: An Analysis of Black Issues in the 1970s.* New York: National Urban League, 1973.

Nelson, Alondra. *Body and Soul: The Black Panther Party and the Fight Against Medical Discrimination.* Minneapolis: University of Minnesota Press, 2011.

Nelson, William E., and Philip J. Meranto. *Electing Black Mayors: Political Action in the Black Community.* Columbus: Ohio State University Press, 1977.

Nordin, Dennis. *From Edward Brooke to Barack Obama: African American Political Success, 1966–2008.* Columbia: University of Missouri Press, 2012.

Ofari, Earl. *The Myth of Black Capitalism.* New York: Monthly Review Press, 1970.

Ogbar, Jeffey O. G. *Black Power: Radical Politics and African American Identity.* Baltimore: Johns Hopkins University Press, 2004.

O'Hara, Stephen P. *Gary: The Most American of All American Cities.* Bloomington: University of Indiana Press, 2011.

O'Reilly, Kenneth. *Nixon's Piano: Presidents and Racial Politics from Washington to Clinton.* New York: Free Press, 1995.

Plummer, Brenda. *In Search of Power: African Americans in the Era of Decolonization, 1956–1974.* Cambridge: Cambridge University Press, 2012.

———. *Rising Wind: Black Americans and U.S. Foreign Affairs, 1935–1960.* Chapel Hill: UNC Press, 1996.

Poinsett, Alex. "Black Political Strategies for '72." *Ebony* 72 (1972): 66–74.

———. *Black Power Gary Style: The Making of Mayor Richard Gordon Hatcher.* Chicago: Johnson Publishing, 1970.

Preston, Michael, Lenneal J. Henderson, and Paul Puryear, eds. *The New Black Politics: The Search for Political Power.* New York: Longman, 1987.

Preston, Michael, Lenneal J. Henderson, Jr., and Paul Puryear, eds. *The New Black Politics: The Search for Political Power.* New York: Longman, 1982.

Ransby, Barbara. *Ella Baker and the Black Freedom Movement: A Radical Democratic Vision.* Chapel Hill: UNC Press, 2003.

Reed, Adolph. *The Jesse Jackson Phenomenon.* New Haven, CT: Yale University Press, 1986.

Rhodes, Jane. *Framing the Black Panthers: The Spectacular Rise of a Black Power Icon.* New York: The New Press, 2007.

Rickford, Russell. *We Are An African People: Independent Education, Black Power, and the Radical Imagination*. Oxford: Oxford University Press, 2016.

Rigueur, Leah Wright. *The Loneliness of the Black Republican*. Princeton, NJ: Princeton University Press, 2015.

Robinson, Dean E. *Black Nationalism in American Politics and Thought*. Cambridge: Cambridge University Press, 2001.

Rojas, Fabio. *From Black Power to Black Studies: How a Radical Social Movement Became an Academic Discipline*. Baltimore: Johns Hopkins University Press, 2007.

Scott, Robert, and Wayne Brockriede, eds. *The Rhetoric of Black Power*. New York: Harper and Row, 1969.

Shakur, Assata. *Assata: An Autobiography*. Chicago: Lawrence Hill Books, 1987.

Shank, Alan, ed. *Political Power and the Urban Crisis*. Boston: Holbrook Press, 1969.

Simanga, Michael. *Amiri Baraka and the Congress of African People*. New York: Palgrave Macmillan, 2015.

Singh, Robert. *The Congressional Black Caucus: Racial Politics in the U.S. Congress*. New York: Sage, 1996.

Smethurst, James Edward. *The Black Arts Movement: Literary Nationalism in the 1960s and 1970s*. Chapel Hill: UNC Press, 2005.

Smith, Robert. *We Have No Leaders: African Americans in the Post–Civil Rights Era*. Albany: SUNY Press, 1996.

Spencer, Robyn C. *The Revolution Has Come: Black Power, Gender, and the Black Panther Party in Oakland*. Durham, NC: Duke University Press, 2016.

Springer, Kimberly. *Living for the Revolution: Black Feminist Organizations, 1968–1980*. Durham, NC: Duke University Press, 2005.

Stokes, Carl. *Promises of Power: A Political Autobiography*. New York: Simon and Schuster, 1973.

Stone, Chuck. *Black Political Power in America*. New York: Dell, 1968.

Strickland, William. "The Gary Convention and the Crisis of American Politics." *Black World* 21, no. 12 (1972): 18–26.

Sugrue, Thomas. *Sweet Land of Liberty: The Forgotten Struggle for Civil Rights in the North*. New York: Random House, 2008.

Theoharis, Jeanne, and Komozi Woodard, eds. *Groundwork: Local Black Freedom Movements in America*. New York: NYU Press, 2005.

Thompson, Heather Ann. *Blood in the Water: The Attica Prison Uprising of 1971 and Its Legacy*. New York: Pantheon Books, 2016.

Van Deburg, William, ed. *Modern Black Nationalism: From Marcus Garvey to Louis Farrakhan*. New York: NYU Press, 1997.

———. *New Day in Babylon: The Black Power Movement and American Culture, 1965–1975*. Chicago: University of Chicago Press, 1992.

Walters, Ronald W. *Black Presidential Politics in America: A Strategic Approach.* Albany: SUNY Press, 1988.

————. "Foreign Policy for Black People." In *It's Nation Time,* 7–9.

————. "New Black Political Culture." *Black World* 21, no. 12 (October 1972): 4–16.

Walters, Ronald W., and Robert C. Smith, eds. *African American Leadership.* Albany: SUNY Press, 1999.

Walton, Hanes, Jr. *Black Politics: A Theoretical and Structural Analysis.* Philadelphia: J. B. Lippincott, 1972.

Washington, Harriet. *Medical Apartheid: The Dark History of Medical Experimentation on Black Americans from Colonial Times to the Present.* New York: Anchor Books, 2006.

Watts, Jerry Gafio. *Amiri Baraka: The Politics and Art of a Black Intellectual.* New York: NYU Press, 2001.

Weems, Robert, and Lewis Randolph. *Business in Black and White: American Presidents and Black Entrepreneurs in the Twentieth Century.* New York: NYU Press, 2009.

White, Derrick. *The Challenge of Blackness: The Institute of the Black World and Political Activism in the 1970s.* Gainesville: University of Florida Press, 2011.

Williams, Rhonda. *The Politics of Public Housing: Black Women's Struggles Against Urban Inequality.* Oxford: Oxford University Press, 2004.

Woodard, Komozi. *A Nation Within A Nation: Amiri Baraka (Leroi Jones) and Black Power Politics.* Chapel Hill: UNC Press, 1999.

Wright, Nathan, ed. *What Black Politicians Are Saying.* New York: Hawthorn Books, 1972.

Young, Coleman. *Hard Stuff: The Autobiography of Mayor Coleman Young.* New York: Viking, 1994.

Young, Richard P., ed. *Roots of Rebellion: The Evolution of Black Politics and Protest Since World War II.* New York: Harper and Row, 1970.

INDEX